Lafleur
The Legend

Steven Finn and **Pierre Gince**

Foreword by Wayne Gretzky

Translated by Pamela Murray

Published by Simon & Schuster

NEW YORK AMSTERDAM/ANTWERP LONDON
TORONTO SYDNEY/MELBOURNE NEW DELHI

A Division of Simon & Schuster, LLC
166 King Street East, Suite 300
Toronto, Ontario M5A 1J3

Published originally in French (Canada) under the title *Guy Lafleur et nous: 50 regards sur l'homme et l'athlète*

Published by arrangement with the original publisher, Les Éditions de l'Homme, an imprint of Groupe Sogides Inc.

This Simon & Schuster Canada edition October 2025

SIMON & SCHUSTER CANADA and colophon are trademarks of Simon & Schuster, LLC

Simon & Schuster strongly believes in freedom of expression and stands against censorship in all its forms. For more information, visit BooksBelong.com.

For information about special discounts for bulk purchases, please contact Simon & Schuster Special Sales at 1-800-268-3216 or CustomerService@simonandschuster.ca.

Book text design by Paul Dippolito

Manufactured in the United States of America

1 3 5 7 9 10 8 6 4 2

Online Computer Library Center number: 1492482340

ISBN 978-1-6682-0406-1
ISBN 978-1-6682-0441-2 (ebook)

Contents

Foreword

When I was a kid, like most Canadian boys my age, I played hockey—on the ice and in the street. And every Saturday night, my dad and I would religiously watch *Hockey Night in Canada*.

It wasn't long before I realized it takes more than talent to make it to the NHL. Which is why my favourite players were more than just "good"—they all had passion and drive.

They were great teammates; you could tell from the way they carried themselves on the bench. But it was also clear they were respected by their opponents and the referees.

Of all the superstars I admired, one stood out more than the others: Guy Lafleur, probably the most electrifying player ever to have worn the Montréal Canadiens jersey.

Beyond his athletic prowess—skating, shooting, reading the play—Guy Lafleur possessed a rare quality that gave him an edge throughout his career: his razor-sharp instinct. Even he could never quite explain, after the fact, what prompted his split-second decisions. Players like that like to improvise, and with Guy more often than not the puck would end up in the opposing net.

Instinct and anticipation are two important qualities I developed by paying close attention to Guy Lafleur. From a distance, at first.

Then, in 1981, I had the immense privilege of playing with him in the Canada Cup. I was twenty years old and blown away to find myself in a locker room with my idols. Guy went out of his way to welcome me to the team and, I'm proud to say, took me under his wing.

I learned so much from watching the man even I called the Flower. He taught me the importance of always bringing your A game, even when you're at the top of your sport. He also taught me how to act like a professional, showing up early and ready to work hard at practices and games, to give the fans a show they wouldn't soon forget.

You could tell that Guy was proud to represent his country, a team of hardworking guys, and no matter if he was wearing the Team Canada jersey or the Montreal Canadiens one, he had a healthy obsession for winning. He was a true champion.

Watching Guy, I also learned what it meant to be an idol to your fans—how to become one, how to act like one. You can't buy the fan love and admiration, you have to earn it. After that encounter in the locker room in 1981, my idol became my mentor. And he may have been a man of few words, but as far as mentors go, he was a shining example for a kid just starting out in his pro hockey career.

After the Canada Cup, he went back to the Canadiens and I returned to the Oilers. But that tournament had a lasting effect on me. You learn from being around the best in the business and like Guy in the '70s I wanted to win Cups!

The years flew by, and before I knew it, the Flower shocked the world of hockey by announcing his retirement. I thought to myself, *Wow that's way too young—we're all going to miss him!*

Then in 1988 Guy shocked the world of hockey again by announcing his comeback at thirty-seven years of age, only a few weeks after being inducted into the Hall of Fame. Only three players in the history of the game have done so: Gordie Howe, Guy, and Mario Lemieux.

On February 27, 1989, I was playing for the LA Kings, and we were at the famous Madison Square Garden, to face the Rangers and Guy Lafleur. I was excited to see him on the ice and you could tell that he was as passionate as ever and having fun. It was nice to see him make peace with hockey. The Rangers beat us 6–4. What was so remarkable is that Guy scored a hat trick that night. All competition aside, I was very proud for him.

After Guy's third goal the New York fans were ecstatic and on their feet, showing their love and respect for that remarkable athlete. Before the game was to resume, I took my time skating to the face-off circle. And once I was there, I asked the referee to take a little time, too, before dropping the puck—so that Guy and his fans could savour the moment.

I know it wasn't much, but those few moments of pure bliss were my humble way of saying "thank you" to Guy "the Flower" Lafleur, gone far too soon . . .

—*Wayne Gretzky*

Preface

Like the vast majority of boys my age, I played hockey in the street. I also got to play this wonderful sport on rinks in my neighbourhood of Pont-Viau, Laval, in countless arenas. We pictured ourselves as players for the Montreal Canadiens, especially its stars of the 1970s. Most of my friends were Guy Lafleur, powering their way towards the defenceman that I already was.

I often watched the Canadiens games on *Hockey Night in Canada*, always appreciating the flamboyant aspects of Guy Lafleur's game: his fluid skating, his stunning fakes, his devastating shot, and his unique ability to thwart his opponents. I was fascinated with the passion he brought to his sport—his intensity was absolutely undeniable.

Watching him play, I learned, unconsciously, what it meant to have a work ethic. Another lesson I learned early on would subsequently prove enormously useful for me, be it in the ranks of the minor leagues or wearing the colours of the Québec Nordiques, the Tampa Bay Lightning, or the LA Kings: It's possible to have a serious career in the NHL while still hanging on to the joy of "playing" a game.

Guy Lafleur and me

In 1984, the year Guy retired from hockey for the first time, I still hadn't made the leap to the NHL, and so I never met him while he was playing for the Canadiens. In my wildest dreams, I never could have imagined he would return to the game to play with the Rangers. And wilder still, that later on he and I would be teammates on the Nordiques for two years.

Throughout my career, from my days in the Quebec Major Junior Hockey League to the NHL, I had the privilege to play alongside many players who became legends, among them Mario Lemieux on the Laval Voisins and Wayne Gretzky on the LA Kings. But I played with only one teammate who was already a member of the Hockey Hall of Fame when he set foot in the Québec Nordiques dressing room—an athlete who granted us players our requests for autographs and to pose for photos: Flower!

I hold on to precious memories of this mentor, who led much more by example than anything he said. Even as he neared the end of his thirties, he still acted like a rambunctious kid on the ice during practices. Among the things I'll never forget: his humility and his generosity. Whether it was with his teammates or the fans, Guy had a gift for making us feel important. Not to mention his deadpan humour and his booming laugh!

Guy Lafleur and us

When Pierre Gince approached me to be the coauthor of this book, I was pleasantly surprised, and honoured, too. Pierre and I know each other from our previous professional lives and I was sure that our complementary strengths would make for an excellent partnership.

Just a few weeks after Guy Lafleur's passing, which had shaken up the entire hockey world, we threw ourselves headlong into this adventure, with an intensity taken from Flower's own playbook. Over the space of several months, we had the privilege of talking with forty-one different people, each sharing stories about "their" Guy Lafleur, very often with great emotion. Their words have been edited with a light touch to ensure a smooth reading experience, but the emotions remain fully intact. We thank every one of them for their candour and their trust.

As you probably know, and as you'll read in these pages, "the Flower" was the whole package: authentic, multifaceted, and as consistent as he was disruptive. So don't be surprised to see him described, time and again, as an intense athlete who was always the first player in the dressing room and on the ice for practices. From peewee level up to the NHL, his teammates speak of a player who was well respected and admired. And he was an inexhaustible source for journalists, who hung on his every word. Guy was equally recognized as someone with an unlimited availability for his fans and a citizen who made an outsized contribution to society.

Our contributors relate all these qualities in their own words, drawing from memory. For once, "what happens in the dressing room *doesn't* stay in the dressing room"—enjoy!

There will be some inconsistencies among the accounts from time to time, which is to be expected, since everyone's memories are different, and some of our contributors are looking back on events that happened several decades in the past. No matter—what ultimately counts is the authentic bond each one shared with Guy.

Guy Lafleur and . . . you

This book was conceived as a series of forty-one complementary profiles. They will enrich what you have observed from afar, or perhaps from up close—getting an autograph or a photo, or chatting with him. Collectively, these interviews allow us to get to know the real Guy in all his glory, both on the ice and off.

I truly hope that, as you read *Lafleur: The Legend*, you will be as delighted and moved as Pierre and I were in bringing this collection together.

—*Steven Finn*

Lafleur
The Legend

Pierrette Chartrand-Lafleur

Born in Fossmill, Ontario, in 1931, Pierrette Chartrand-Lafleur is Guy Lafleur's mother. Since 1939, she has lived in the city of Thurso, Quebec. While raising her five children, she held down different jobs in businesses and factories in the area and was an active volunteer at the local arena.

Note: Guy Lafleur's four sisters contributed to this interview granted by their mother.

Tell us about your son.

Guy was born in 1951, after Suzanne, and before Gisèle, Lise, and Lucie. He was sweet and shy as a child, although he did like to play pranks on his sisters!

He enjoyed going to Sainte-Famille school; he was in his element there. Réjean and I were firm with our children, telling them, "If you want to participate in extracurricular activities, your studies have to come first." So Guy was allowed to play hockey, since he was doing well at school.

It was no surprise that he loved hockey. When his grandfather Lafleur listened to Canadiens matches on the radio, silence was expected in the household. Whenever he could, my husband liked to relax in front of our black-and-white TV during the regular season and the playoffs. Guy would sit near him and watch, too. Sadly, his grandfather Lafleur died when Guy was a teenager, so he never got the chance to see the great heights his grandson achieved.

My husband made a big skating rink at the side of the house. He also built a slide, because the girls often preferred to play on that, using cardboard for sleds. As for Guy, he started skating by the time he was five. For Christmas we bought him a brown leather helmet, a Canadiens sweater, hockey pants, socks, pads, and skates. He learned to skate using a chair to push himself across the ice. It wasn't long before he began playing hockey in our yard, joined by cousins and friends in the area: Jacques Massie, Pierre Letang, Guy Laramée, Michel Paillé, Peter Simpson, and a few others. The Massies, whose house was behind ours, also had a rink.

On Saturday and Sunday mornings, Guy was awake very early. He must have been about seven when he started going by himself to the arena, which was very close to our house. Everyone else in the family was still asleep. Sometimes I had the impression that he went to bed wearing all of his gear. In the wintertime, he always had a smile on his face when he went outside.

Mr. Jean-Paul Meloche was the caretaker at the arena, and he lived there. He was not allowed to let kids come in outside of the official hours—however, he turned a blind eye with Guy, who knew an entrance where he could sneak inside. Even when it was still dark out, Guy would tirelessly practise his shots on the net and off the boards. The noise would wake up Mr. Meloche, but because he liked Guy and admired his perseverance, he let him continue. Mr. Meloche and Brother Léo Jacques were Guy's coaches at the mosquito level. They travelled with the team to Ottawa and also as far as Kingston, as well as the peewee tournament in Québec City.

When Guy started out in Mosquito, we didn't go to his games, since his father was working a lot of the time, and I had four other children to take care of at home. So we didn't realize just how talented he was. It was a man from the parish who said to my husband one day, "You've got to come and see your boy play—he's going to impress you, too!"

Even back then, Guy had a much harder shot than most players his age. Some of the goaltenders would scoot behind the net to avoid his shots!

Once, at a tournament in Rockland, a parent on the opposing team claimed Guy was too old to be playing Mosquito, because of all the goals he was scoring. A copy of his baptismal certificate in Hull had to be obtained to put the matter to rest.

Was the Quebec International Pee-Wee Hockey Tournament a big moment in Guy's life?

Oh yes! That tournament was very important for Guy—and for me, too!

For the first of the three years he played in the tournament, he was still Mosquito age. Thurso didn't have enough players to form a team, so Guy was recruited to play on a peewee team in Rockland, Ontario, since his reputation as a good player was well-known.

When Guy went to play in tournaments in Rockland, and also when he had to join his temporary team to go to Québec City, I went with him across the Outaouais River on cross-country skis. Picture it: the three of us—Jean-Marc Lalonde, Guy, and me—on skis carrying all of his baggage and equipment! The snow stuck to our skis and it was quite awkward.

At one point I was afraid I'd fall and slip under the ice. On the other riverbank, some parents were waiting to pick up Mr. Lalonde and Guy and drive them to the tournament in Québec City. It was snowing quite a lot—I seem to remember it took them ten hours to get to their destination. My husband and I and some other parents travelled there to see the finals. It felt quite strange to be cheering for Rockland.

How did he develop his talent as a hockey player?

He practised constantly! As an adolescent, Guy spent his summers working on building his strength. My husband made weights and dumbbells for him, and he did a lot of running. He went to work for a nearby farmer, Jean-Marc Perras. He also delivered cases of Labatt 50 beer to grocery stores and dépanneurs in the region. All of it helped make him get stronger.

It was when Guy was playing at the junior level that my husband and I started thinking he might make hockey his career. I have to say, not a day went by in Thurso without someone suggesting that to us. But I don't ever remember Guy saying in so many words "One day, I'm going to play in the NHL." As determined as he was, he was also reserved. He didn't say much.

Tell us about when Guy left home to live in Québec City.

He was still a few weeks shy of his fifteenth birthday when he left for Québec City. I was sad, for sure. I'd hear certain songs on the radio and tears would come to my eyes.

My husband fully encouraged Guy to do everything possible to realize his dream to have a career in hockey. For Réjean, there was no question that Guy should give up on this experience in Québec. Even though we didn't have a car, Réjean would leave his job at the mill in the middle of the afternoon to get a ride with Normand Chouinard, a teacher in Thurso. They drove to Québec, or to other arenas, just to see Guy play, arriving right as the games were starting. Then they would drive back home. My husband would sleep for an hour or two and then report for work at 7:00 a.m.

There were two things I was sure of: that Guy loved hockey enough to make great sacrifices but also that he really missed us. When he realized Friday was approaching, he would call me to say, "Come and see me on the weekend." My husband and I would go to Québec City with Normand, spend some time with Guy, go to his game, and return home on Sunday evening. We usually stayed in a motel, although there was one time, during the Carnaval, when everything was booked up and we had to sleep in Normand's car.

At first, Guy billeted with a family, along with two other teammates. He had to sleep on a couch with his feet hanging over the end. When he started making inquiries about another place to stay, someone told him, "Go over to the bowling alley in the Limoilou neighbourhood and ask for Madame Baribeau. She takes boarders." They got along very well right from the start, and she made up a very nice room for him. Guy was in such a rush to move that he went straight over with his suitcase and rang the doorbell. Madame Baribeau was taken by surprise—she hadn't been expecting him for two or three days!

Guy was allowed to eat for free at the Cendrillon restaurant, and to bring guests. Among those he invited was Madame Baribeau, to thank her for what she did for him. He also invited me and Réjean and our girls.

On a memorable day in 1971, Guy officially became part of the great Canadiens family. Tell us about that.

Guy was nervous on the morning he was drafted—more nervous than I'd ever seen him. And you could understand why!

He was driving the beautiful car that the Remparts had given him. We arrived in Montreal and I never understood how we managed to find ourselves in front of Saint Joseph's Oratory! Finally, we found our way to the Queen Elizabeth Hotel. We had just enough time to park before we entered the ballroom to hear Guy's name announced!

Now that we were there, my husband and I lost Guy in the haze. Between the Canadiens bosses and the press, they weren't letting him go! It was a new phase for him—and for us, too. It was a great source of pride for our family. Imagine: Just a few years before, Guy was watching Canadiens matches on TV with his father, and now he would be on the team. I can still see the tears in my husband's eyes.

When we returned to Thurso, a parade was held in Guy's honour!

What are your memories of his early days with the Canadiens?

He was working just as hard as he always had. Jean Béliveau had retired and the media were saying that Guy would take his place. They were big shoes to fill, but I don't think it bothered Guy.

When he first arrived in Montreal, Guy lived with the Béliveau family. He was proud of that, since Jean Béliveau was his first childhood idol. That's why Guy wore his number 4 in Québec City.

Réjean still didn't have a car, but very often Guy would give us tickets for his games at the Forum. My husband never had any problem finding someone who could give him a ride, take in a hockey game, and meet Guy afterwards.

After several years of dominating in the NHL, Guy slowed down. And things ended badly between him and the Canadiens. What do you know about that time?

Guy was hardly getting any playing time; he was unhappy. The Canadiens "dumped" him. It was very painful for me. Before he retired, he came to the house. He always sat at the end of the table, right where you're sitting. We were all there—my husband, my daughters, my sons-in-law, me. He said to us, "Soon, I'm going to have my own box at the Forum. Will you come?" We said yes, of course. Then he added, "Even if I'm not playing?" Someone replied, "You're not injured, so why wouldn't you be playing?" Guy didn't answer.

I always thought that he had come to Thurso to let us know that he was going to retire, but he hadn't been able to say it outright. In the end, we learned the news during a televised press conference.

Were you surprised when he came out of retirement?

Guy had felt rejected by the Canadiens organization. It was much too early for him to stop playing, and that's why he was bored, spinning his wheels. I remember him spending his time cleaning his car—with baby shampoo!

I was surprised when he came back to the NHL after several years away. My husband could tell he was unhappy and told him, "Why don't you come back and play for another team?" Finally, he tried and he succeeded. When he came to tell me he was going to New York, it was already in the papers—it all happened quite fast. But I was happy just to see the smile back on his face.

After that, for the next three years when he played for New York and Québec, we found it strange to be cheering for a team other than the Canadiens. But obviously, we cheered for Guy's team!

One evening, after a Rangers game at the Forum, my daughters and I were waiting outside the dressing room door. I turned around and saw that Céline Dion and René Angélil were there, too. I introduced myself and asked them which player they had come to see. Céline replied, “Well, come on—we’re here to see Guy!” Just as if it was as natural for them to be there as his family members.

When he took his retirement in Québec City, the time was right. I felt that he was at peace.

Did fame change him?

No. Probably because it was a gradual process. After playing in the peewee tournament, Guy wasn’t just a member of the family anymore. The public adopted him. Once he joined the Canadiens, he became the son of every parent in Quebec—everyone’s brother, everyone’s friend.

His first car was the one the Québec Remparts gave him. From then on, he always bought himself very nice cars. Whenever he came home—from the age of eighteen and right up until the end—people would see a car they thought might be his and would knock on our door to ask for an autograph and a photo. It never let up, at all hours, and often during mealtimes. He always said yes! Sometimes it would be people he’d known since his childhood in Thurso; other times, very often, they’d be strangers. It was all the same for Guy.

For a long time, he’d come by car to visit, but later, it would be by helicopter. Now *that* was impressive. We would go to his landing spot at the municipal garage, a five-minute walk from our house. Whenever a helicopter flew over Thurso, people knew that it was either the Sûreté du Québec or Guy! He would make passes over the house. People would come to the garage when they saw him coming in, and quite often he would go back up in the air with them because he liked them!

Which particularly memorable anecdotes could you share with us?

Oh my God, I have so many!

My husband was a welder at the Thurso pulp mill. When Guy was playing for the Canadiens, Réjean's boss would make him come to work just so that he couldn't go to the Forum. When Guy found out, he was shocked and he told reporters about it. The story went around the company, and it never happened again.

One evening, during a series against Boston, we were outside near the Forum with Guy, who was signing autographs. Nearby, there was a bus full of Bruins supporters—one of them opened a window and threw a beer on Guy. My husband felt the insult more than my son! Réjean got on the bus and asked, "*Qui a fait ça?*" [Who did that?] No one said a word. He could have gotten beaten up, but luckily, he came out of the situation safe and sound.

One summer, Guy came to the house and brought the Stanley Cup. He had given us advance notice and we'd told one person, who told another, and so on. So many people from Thurso and the surrounding area came to our yard. Guy washed the trophy with dish soap and cleaned it off with our garden hose! He made a special trip that day just so that "his people" in Thurso could share in his happiness.

What was your relationship like over the years?

He was my son. I loved him. That didn't stop me from giving him some straight talk sometimes.

Guy began smoking when he started playing in the NHL. I spent so much of my time saying to him and his father, "Stop smoking, for goodness' sake—you're going to get cancer!" They didn't listen to me. I made them smoke outside, whatever the season. They didn't like it but that was my rule. My husband died far too young, of lung cancer. And I said to Guy, "You have to stop smoking or you're going to end up like your father."

No matter how much time passed and how famous he got, he was "our Guy." We were family. Whenever he had a bit of time to himself or was having any problems, he'd call me in the morning and say, "I'm coming to Thurso." We'd simply spend time together—often, just the two of us. I would make him cabbage rolls, his favourite dish.

Guy also had a wonderful relationship with his father, which made me happy. Neither of them spoke very much, but they understood each other. When his father was dying, they shared some private moments, and I never found out what they spoke about. Which is as it should be.

I always found it difficult to learn news about Guy on TV or in the newspapers. Or to hear all sorts of things that weren't true.

I remember that I had been warned ahead of time about his big car accident. However, it was impossible to avoid seeing the endless stream of images on the television. As well, when [his son] Mark had difficulties, it was painful for me to see the televised images of the two of them, Mark and Guy, at the courthouse. One day, he came to visit me to talk about Mark. I can still see him sitting at his place at the kitchen table. I don't remember him saying a word—he was just crying.

What was his greatest quality?

Guy gave everything to everybody. He didn't hold anything back for himself. I even think it was his greatest failing.

I remember something that happened after he'd played in an NHL All-Star Game. At some point later, we went out to a restaurant as a family. He put his hand in his pocket and pulled out the ring that all of the players had received. He said, "Does anybody want it?" I quickly asked him for it, because I didn't want him to just give it away. After he died, I gave the ring to his son Martin, along with the one he received after winning the Stanley Cup.

What were your last moments with Guy?

My memories of his last year are very sad.

When my daughters and I went to visit him at his place, or at the end, at the palliative care home, he didn't talk much. But he paid close attention to us, and had tears in his eyes when we left.

It's still hard to look back on those days.

The last time I saw Guy, it was a Wednesday afternoon. That same night, when I went to bed, I said to my husband, up there, "That's enough. Come get your boy. He can't suffer anymore." And he heard me, because Guy died in the night between Thursday and Friday.

After Guy's death, how did you process the enormous wave of love from the public?

I was really overwhelmed, like any mother would be. And I was surprised by all the love the public still had for him. I knew he was very much loved, but never knew just how much.

The media featured countless photos of Guy giving autographs, and a huge number of people of all ages were wearing his number 10 sweater. Many people related how Guy had phoned them to cheer them up during an illness, or how they'd got to meet him at this or that place. It was a great comfort.

For days on end, the people in Thurso could speak about nothing but Guy. Here at the house, many brought flowers. They left them between the two doors, along with sympathy cards. Often, they were from people I knew, but complete strangers also left flowers and letters at my house and at my daughters'. Letters would arrive in the mail addressed to "The Lafleur Family,

Thurso, Quebec," full of stories of the beautiful moments they'd experienced because of Guy. We even received a letter from California! We were very touched.

I have a portion of Guy's ashes in a small urn. When it is my time to go, I would like for Guy to be buried by my side.

How would you like people to remember him?

I hope they will remember him as a really good guy, always available for his fans. He was genuine.

Jacques Massie

Born in Thurso, Quebec, in 1952, Jacques Massie was Guy's neighbour. Both of their fathers built and maintained backyard ice rinks where the boys in the area would pretend to be Maurice Richard, Jean Béliveau, and the other greats who played for the Canadiens. On two occasions, he was Guy's teammate at the Quebec International Pee-Wee Hockey Tournament.

What is your earliest memory of Guy Lafleur?

You could say we knew each other since birth. Guy was born September 20, 1951, and I came along the next year, on May 20. My parents' property backed onto the Lafleurs', and there was no fence. Our fathers both built ice rinks and we were always spending time at each other's houses.

In Thurso, our teachers were the Brothers of Christian Instruction at Sainte-Famille school. The brothers had two religions: Catholicism and hockey. They were extremely dedicated in taking care of the school's ice rink and showing us how to play.

From when he was very small—even before peewee—Guy was much better than anyone else on the ice. But never, absolutely never, did he say anything like "It's because of me that we're winning." He had a blast playing. It was like that for him his whole life, even in the NHL.

What was Guy's attitude towards school?

I wouldn't try to convince anyone that he liked school better than hockey. But Guy's parents were strict: If he wanted to play hockey as much as he wanted to at school or in our yards, he had to be serious about his studies.

When did you play peewee with him?

In 1963 and 1964, the two years when Thurso was able to send a team to the Québec tournament.

Going to Québec City from Thurso might as well have been the other end of the world. To get together a travel team took a lot of organizing—and money. We went door-to-door with our parents and volunteers. A huge thermometer, eight feet tall, was set up in front of the church to show our progress as we worked to achieve our ambitious goal of more than $1,000. And it was met! Our coaches, Jean-Paul Meloche and Brother Léo Jacques, were incredible. When we got to Québec City, local families welcomed us into their homes.

In 1964, it was Guy's third and final time to play in the tournament. The other teams were wary of him, and the fans were wild with joy to see him again. The Colisée de Québec had thousands more spectators than usual whenever Thurso was playing. We had trouble seeing each other on the ice with all the cigarette smoke in the air. For our semifinal game on the Saturday, we needed a police escort to enter and leave the Colisée, because there were so many people who wanted to get close to Guy.

That was the moment when the media in Québec and Outaouais and even in Montreal started to take notice of him.

When he was in peewee, Guy often played on bantam and midget teams in Thurso, and he did well. In minor hockey in Thurso—and in many places in Quebec—the two best players on any team wore the numbers 9 and 4 of Maurice Richard and Jean Béliveau. Guy wore 4 and I wore 9. He was already playing right wing and I was centre. For the forty-five minutes of a game, he could play up to forty-three!

After high school, Guy left for Québec City. Tell us about that.

Guy had both the talent and the determination to have a career in the NHL, so everyone in Thurso knew that Guy would need to move to a big city to play. His parents decided on Québec, first with the Aces, then with the Remparts. Guy already loved it there.

Mr. Lafleur worked as a welder in Thurso. He had five children and no car. During the school year, they had a boarder, Normand Chouinard, who was a teacher. He stayed in Guy's bedroom. Normand also had a car! He drove thousands upon thousands of kilometres in his Javelin so that he could take Mr. Lafleur to Guy's games in Québec City or other places the juniors played. They'd drive to the game and go straight back home, and both of them went off to work early the next day: one to the factory and the other to school.

Guy was quite young when he got his driver's licence but his father still didn't have a car. In the summers, when Guy was back from Québec, Normand would often lend him his. Guy was always grateful to his father and Normand for their unwavering support.

Normand also paid particular attention to Guy's studies. When Guy returned from Québec after the end of the season, Normand would quiz him on what he'd been learning. He wanted Guy to study for a few more weeks before starting his vacation in earnest. For two summers, in May and June, Normand gave me ten dollars a week to help Guy study certain subjects, especially

French and math. It was a lot of money back then. I took the responsibility seriously and Guy was fairly motivated, too. But in June, at the end of the school year, he'd had just about enough!

Tell us about the first time you saw him wearing the Canadiens uniform.

There are no words to describe how proud I was. It was Saturday, October 9, 1971, for a game at the Montreal Forum against the Rangers. That was the first time Guy played in the Canadiens uniform. In those days, the television broadcasts showed only the second half of the games. That was a drag, but it was better than nothing. The streets of Thurso were totally deserted—everyone was watching Guy! He didn't score any goals, and the game ended in a 4–4 tie.

What sort of career did you imagine he'd have?

Everyone from anywhere near Thurso was convinced Guy would become one of the best players in the NHL, along with Marcel Dionne, who we often played against in tournaments. The problem was that Guy barely got any ice time for his first three seasons. Once they gave him the chance, he became the Guy Lafleur the fans had been waiting for.

He had always been intensely focused on what he knew how to do better than anyone else: deftly and speedily moving the puck, and putting it in the net! The same went for how he played in the NHL.

During the playoff series in the 1970s, Pierre Bouchard told Guy, "You score, we'll take care of the rest." One year, John Wensink of the Bruins said to reporters, "Guy Lafleur better have eyes in the back of his head, because I'm going to cut his ears off." I wasn't able to follow the game live, but the next day as I drove to work, I tuned into the radio to find out what happened. Guy scored two goals and two assists and the Canadiens had won 4–2! I was so proud of my old buddy.

Were you surprised when he retired at the age of thirty-three?

No, because Jacques Lemaire was playing him for nine minutes a game! And with Guy, it was all or nothing: He couldn't imagine being stuck in a system where he wasn't able to give the game his all. He was no longer at the very top, but he wasn't getting ice time. So he left.

When he visited Thurso during his retirement, it was obvious he was bored. The fire of hockey was still burning inside of him. I wasn't surprised when he returned to the game, because he loved it. And he proved that he shouldn't have been pushed to retire at thirty-three.

I was very happy to see him play with the Rangers. During the time of the rivalry between the Canadiens and the Nordiques I hated Michel Bergeron. But I changed my opinion because he and Guy were happy together, and that continued in Québec the following year.

Did you gradually lose touch with each other?

I wouldn't say that. During the summers when Guy was in juniors, he spent just about all of his time in Thurso. The summer I was seventeen, he came over to my parents' house and said, "I spoke with Maurice Filion and you're coming to the Remparts training camp." I loved my experience there—all three days of it! Guy had been kind to get me the invitation.

Afterwards, during the time he was playing for the Canadiens, he made regular brief trips to Thurso to see his parents and his sisters. He and I would catch up every so often.

I remember one time in the 1970s, he came to stay overnight

at his parents'. The next day he saw my father outside. He walked over to chat with him and they went to have a beer together. Even though he'd become the best hockey player in the world, Guy stayed the little guy from Thurso, plain and simple.

In May 1978, he brought the Stanley Cup to Thurso, rolling around in his trunk! He just wanted to bring joy to the people who knew him. When he spotted me in the crowd, he motioned for me to step aside with my partner, Louise, and my daughter, Marie-Claude. We chatted for a bit and took photos, which our family still treasures.

The year 1986 marked Thurso's one hundredth anniversary. On November 8, Guy skated in the local arena for the first time since the 1960s. We brought together all of the players who'd represented our village at the Quebec International Pee-Wee Hockey Tournament, wearing a replica sweater for the occasion. That day we played against the NHL Legends team, and luckily, Guy was playing for Thurso, wearing number 4. I think we had even more fun than in 1963!

And, of course, he came to Thurso in 2013 for the unveiling of his bronze statue; Geoff Molson and Chris Nilan were also with him. Once again, when Guy saw me in the crowd, he went out of his way to come and talk with me. I sensed that he wanted to share his pride with me, as if it were the pride of all of Thurso.

Tell us about some unforgettable moments.

One day in the spring, when we were at the Saint-Michel high school in Buckingham, Guy showed up to class wearing Bermuda shorts, which were strictly forbidden. Even back then, Guy and other people's rules didn't get along—just like Guy and his coaches' game plans!

Guy always loved to drive fast. In Normand Chouinard's

Javelin, I remember him driving me to Buckingham to get my high school diploma, pedal to the metal, 160 kilometres an hour in the passing lane. Guy was reckless—but he was a very good driver.

The saddest moment I experienced relating to Guy was in February 2008. I was in Florida and had been playing golf with my brother-in-law. We were having a beer when the news came on the TV and we heard the anchor Pierre Bruneau say the words "arrest warrant for Guy Lafleur." We were very upset. In the end, matters were taken much too far. Guy defended his son Mark, like any good father would have done in his place.

What were your last moments with him?

During the last year of his life, Guy didn't visit Thurso nearly as often. Even though everyone in the province knew things were going less and less well for him, I found it upsetting to see him in a TV interview dressed in a bathrobe and without a single hair on his head.

When I heard about his death on TV, I was in shock. I'd just lost my brother. He was a model of success and pride. My childhood passed before my eyes like a sped-up movie, all the moments I shared with Guy. I cried like a child, probably more than when we *were* children. Then I went to play golf, as I'd planned—and I wore our peewee team's replica sweater.

Thanks to the television broadcast, I got to attend the funeral remotely. It did me good to hear his son Martin and other people talk about him. When the fans cried "Guy! Guy! Guy!" at the end, with hundreds wearing his sweater, it moved me to tears.

What is his legacy?

Just as impressive as anything Guy did on the ice was all that he did to please his fans and help people.

He showed us that it doesn't matter whether you're tired or not, you have to give your time to others. To our families, of course, but he was also very present for total strangers.

He was more than an ambassador for the Canadiens—he was one for hockey, all over the world. And definitely one for Thurso!

Marcel Dionne

Born in Drummondville, Quebec, in 1951, Marcel Dionne is one of the all-time highest scorers in the NHL. During the 1971 draft, Dionne, the highest scorer in the Ontario Hockey League, was drafted second in the first round by the Detroit Red Wings, immediately after Guy Lafleur. After Detroit, the centre would go on to play in Los Angeles and New York. In 1988–89, he and Guy Lafleur were teammates on the Rangers.

Marcel Dionne's name was never engraved on the Stanley Cup, but the Kings retired his number 16 and he was inducted into the Hockey Hall of Fame in 1992.

What is your earliest memory of Guy Lafleur?

I saw him play and played against him in peewee, bantam, midget, and junior levels. When he was still in peewee, he had the shooting ability of the best players in midget. Of course, goalie equipment was not as advanced back then as it is today. I saw goaltenders who were so fearful of Guy's shots that they'd prepare to face him by stuffing sections of phone books underneath their pads!

In the Junior A league, Guy played in Québec City and I was on the Drummondville Rangers. We were the same age, both born in 1951. We were aware of each other, but we weren't yet on speaking terms.

In 1969, after my first year with the St. Catharines Black Hawks, I wanted him to come play for us. Several junior teams in

Quebec and Ontario wanted him, including mine. I went to meet him at his parents' house in Thurso. I sang the praises of our organization and told him he could learn English quickly, like I had. But he chose Québec because he liked the city, and because the Remparts gave him $10,000—a real fortune at the time—and a car.

Our teams played against each other in the 1971 Memorial Cup. The Remparts won—that was a tough loss.

Year after year, in minor and then junior hockey, Guy just kept getting better. He was dominant on all of the teams he played for, but not necessarily from day one. With the Canadiens, he needed some time.

I couldn't have predicted when he came to juniors that he'd become one of the best players in the world. Just like I never could have imagined the career I would end up having.

Tell us about the 1971 draft.

Guy and I were the two first choices in the NHL draft that year: him for Montreal, me for Detroit.

Draft day wasn't like it is these days, with the stands full of family, friends, the players' agents, and media from all over North America. It was always held at the Queen Elizabeth Hotel in Montreal, and there weren't many people in attendance. My parents didn't come, and even I didn't want to be there! But I went, because the Red Wings management insisted.

Right up until the last minute, the Red Wings made every effort to exchange their second pick for the Canadiens' first choice, because they, too, wanted Lafleur. So when the NHL's president, Clarence Campbell, said into the microphone, "The first draft of the 1971 selection . . . ," the Canadiens' general manager, Sam Pollock, asked for a time-out. But the hockey men just laughed, knowing full well that Montreal wanted Guy no matter what.

Did you consider yourselves rivals?

Not at all, and for a simple reason: We were completely different players. We were proud to compete against each other, but I never sensed we had a rivalry. Quite the opposite—there was great respect between us.

On the ice we had nothing in common. First of all, he played right wing and I was centre. Guy had an extraordinary shot, while I really liked to handle the puck. We didn't have the same skating style, either. In the NHL, there was just one Guy Lafleur and just one Marcel Dionne. Setting aside comparisons, we both managed to have pretty decent success in our careers!

It wasn't Guy I compared myself to, but players more in my mould, such as Henri Richard, Yvan Cournoyer, Stan Mikita, and Dave Keon. I wanted to learn fast what they did to be able to have a lasting impact. As far as I could tell, it came down to one factor: the relentlessness of the work they put in, every time they hit the ice.

In your day, what was the relationship between professional hockey and money?

It was very different; there was no balance of power. The owners of the teams had the upper hand. One reason was that salaries weren't made public, as they are today.

With the arrival of the World Hockey Association in the early 1970s, the balance of power began to shift. Up until then, Gordie Howe had played twenty-five years in the NHL and hadn't made money. It was the same for Guy Lafleur and most of the other great players.

In 1975, my contract with Detroit ended. There were some NHL teams, including the Canadiens, who wanted me to sign with them, as well as the Oilers in the WHA. Making the most of the bidding war, I signed with the LA Kings at $300,000 a year.

The Canadiens, who were regularly winning Stanley Cups at the time, offered me peanuts. Sam Pollock said, "Take it or leave it." I left it—even though I would've loved to have played with Guy and the Canadiens. It's very prestigious to have your name on the Stanley Cup, but it doesn't put money in the bank for you during your career, and especially not afterwards.

Guy and I started discussing our contracts not long after we got to the NHL—what we liked and what we didn't. And he had some regrets. I was much more in tune with the business aspects of our careers than he was. And we also had quite different approaches. For example, in 1971 I insisted on signing a one-year contract so that my value would go up the following year, assuming everything would work out. As for Guy, he signed a three-year contract, and another one for ten years.

With that long contract, he earned $125,000 a year at the same time as I was making $300,000. It got so that Guy Lafleur, the best player in the league, had to threaten to go on strike—with the backing of his teammates—to get a better contract. But it was still far less than what other players and I made. He finally got more, but never as high as $600,000, $700,000, and $800,000 a year like some of us earned. The Canadiens trapped him and then they dumped him.

Guy served as the ambassador for his team and he was associated with all kinds of products. But it never allowed him to build up the sums that such an elite player should have received from the Canadiens.

Were you surprised by his retirement, and then by his return to the game?

I wasn't really surprised. Guy had said to me, "I don't like playing Lemaire's style of hockey." And that was understandable: Guy was intuitive and Jacques was cerebral. With Jacques, there was a precise game plan with a lot of back-and-forth between the offensive and defensive zones before going back on the attack. But Guy played the same way he had since he was in peewee: Give him the puck and he'd rush to the net. His exceptional instincts allowed him to skate fast, make passes, and shoot at the net.

During a game between the Canadiens and the Kings, not long before Guy decided he'd had enough, I remember him sitting at the end of the bench, an arm on the boards. He was discouraged because he'd barely had any playing time. I knew Lemaire and almost went over to ask him, "Why aren't you playing Flower?" Sooner or later, things were going to break down between those two.

You played together on Team Canada and on the Rangers. What was he like as a teammate?

It was really great to be in the same dressing room and on the ice with him.

We played together for the Canada Cup tournaments in 1976 and 1981, then on the Rangers. I enjoyed those occasions, even though his presence on the team did shorten my career in terms of ice time—on some nights, with the talent Michel Bergeron had at his disposal, he couldn't always use both of us.

What was his greatest quality?

Guy was the whole package. Passionate. He lived life at two hundred miles an hour!

I believe that Guy became as good a helicopter pilot as he was a hockey player. He took me flying with him. He was meticulous in respecting all the rules to follow. Just like in hockey.

One day, he called to say he was coming to my place by helicopter. I said, "Whoa, whoa, Guy, wait a minute!" But he had thought of everything. He had already figured out the location where he'd be able to land. He was like that—an idea came to him and he acted on it right away.

After his quadruple bypass operation, his pilot's licence was suspended. Boy, was he mad! Not being able to fly a helicopter was probably the thing he missed the most, along with not being able to eat out in restaurants as often, at the end of his life.

When I'm driving, I think of him. I tell myself he isn't dead, that he's just gone on a trip in his helicopter, and he's very happy.

At my place, I have a great many photographs taken throughout my career, and others come from the memorabilia store I used to own. Guy's image is everywhere.

He must have had some faults . . .

The biggest one he had was his stubbornness around smoking! I wish he'd have understood that cigarettes were deadly. Like everybody who smokes, he thought he was invincible. But illness does not discriminate. At the time when I was playing, smoking was the norm, but I never took it up.

I've read a lot about lung cancer. There are studies that say that the moment you start smoking it turns your body's clock ahead to fifty years old. However, it's a problem that can be overcome, even though Guy and Mike Bossy weren't able to.

What were your last moments with him?

We spoke on the phone and said some things that felt good to express, very moving—that I will keep to myself.

What is his legacy?

He did it his way.

I'm convinced that Guy Lafleur lived out all of his dreams. That's why he was—and remains—a huge inspiration for people from all walks of life.

Denis Potvin

Born in Ottawa in 1953, Denis Potvin, like Bobby Orr, was one of the most productive defencemen in the history of the NHL. Drafted first overall in 1973, he played fifteen seasons with the New York Islanders, including during four straight Stanley Cup wins. He was inducted into the Hockey Hall of Fame in 1991, and the Islanders retired his number 5 the following year.

Denis Potvin was a teammate of Guy Lafleur's during the Canada Cup, first in 1976 and again in 1981.

What is your oldest memory of Guy Lafleur as a player?

All the way back to peewee, in the early 1960s. My team from the Overbrook neighbourhood of Ottawa went to play in a tournament in Rockland, Ontario. Everyone was talking about a certain Guy Lafleur from Thurso, and we quickly found out why: When he fired his slap shots from centre ice, our goalie actually took cover behind his net!

Guy was older than I was by a couple of years. However, we did get to play each other that time in peewee, since I was playing up on Overbrook's scout team.

In the 1960s, during the Original Six era, there were a huge number of Canadiens fans in the Ottawa and Outaouais regions. In our family, there was only one thing you could be doing Wednesday and Saturday evenings: watching *La Soirée du hockey* with René Lecavalier. I found out later that Guy and his father were doing the same thing in Thurso.

After that encounter in peewee, we lost touch. Guy played as a junior in Québec City and I was with the Ottawa 67's in the OHL. We met again in the NHL in 1973 when I joined the New York Islanders.

Tell us about that first meeting.

It was on the ice of the Montreal Forum in 1973. I remember that game against the Canadiens very well. Henri Richard was playing centre, Guy right wing.

As much as you can try to mentally prepare for a big game like that, when any player from Quebec shows up to play the Canadiens in Montreal, those first few minutes are intimidating. And I knew very well that Guy, who'd been in the league since 1971, was a big threat to his opponents' defensive players. I was on my guard!

What type of player was he on the ice?

Intense, intense, intense! He was hard to slow down, harder still to control. Guy had a fearsome slap shot and, with his exceptional skating ability, you never knew where he was going to be. Like Gretzky's, Guy's play was cerebral. He analyzed each second of the action to anticipate what would happen next so he could decide where to go and what to do. He was always guided by his instinct, ever since his peewee days.

Back then, there was sixty feet between the two blue lines, which enabled an excellent skater like Guy Lafleur to take off from his own blue line and explode into the neutral zone while waiting to receive the puck at top speed. Defencemen had no option but to fall back, give up the blue line, and hope for a chance to counterattack.

Guy excelled at firing shots from the blue line to take goalies off guard—he had a gift for finding an opening in the net. But his game was much more varied than that. With his excellent line mates—Henri Richard, Pete Mahovlich, Steve Shutt, and Jacques Lemaire, among others—the puck moved very fast, and Guy even managed to be forgotten a little bit. And if you forgot about Guy for even a second, you were in trouble.

Opponents like Wayne Gretzky and Guy Lafleur were the ones who scared me the most—guys who scored goals when they were mad. If a player hit Guy with his stick, he didn't want to get even by fighting, but by scoring. He was a player who was both respectful of and respected by his opponents. He never would've hit anyone with his stick violently. And you sure didn't want to give him any motivation by going after him physically.

During a game in the early 1980s, Flower had crossed into the Islanders' zone and my hip check sent him flying head over heels. He was back on his feet pretty fast, though. Obviously, I had no intention of injuring him. There's a magnificent photo of that spectacular check.

When you played in the Canada Cup, you went from opponents to teammates. What was it like to play on the same team as Guy Lafleur?

Even though I really liked playing in Canada Cup 81—despite our defeat—I loved our first contest, in 1976. There was the gold medal, obviously, but also that was the occasion when I really got to know Guy Lafleur.

Canada Cup 76 was an extremely important event for me, since it was my very first international tournament. What an honour it was to find myself among the crème de la crème of the NHL! With the training camp and the tournament, we all spent a good month together, and I formed lasting bonds with Guy, Bobby Hull, and all the players.

After our first practice at the Forum, in August 1976, I went to the Hôtel Bonaventure. I opened the door to my room and—surprise—Guy was there. We were roommates! I don't remember saying much, because I was in awe. I was struck by his humility and how approachable he was.

At the time of Canada Cup 76, I had only three seasons' experience in the NHL. Being around my more experienced teammates, I was like a sponge, observing how they trained, how they behaved, etcetera. There were seven players from the Canadiens, and the coach was Scotty Bowman. I was the only player from the Islanders.

The Canadiens had just won the Stanley Cup, and I asked myself what the recipe was to triumph in the final series of the season and hoist the coveted trophy. It was while observing the Canadiens players during Canada Cup 76 that I noticed the importance Guy Lafleur had among the team's elite. And no one knew then that they'd go on to win three more Stanley Cups in a row in the 1970s. I am convinced that dynasty would not have been possible without Flower.

That was when I understood what a real winning culture was. For us on the Islanders, we were a young team with lots of talented players, but we didn't have a winning culture yet. We established one after losing twice in the playoffs to the Canadiens. We learned a lot by watching this team, which had such character. And then we won the Stanley Cup four years in a row!

Were you surprised by his retirement, and then by his return to the game?

I was more surprised by his return than by his retirement. Coming back to play with the Rangers like he did, it was truly unbelievable.

Unfortunately, I never played against him when he was with the Rangers and the Nordiques, because I had just taken my own retirement.

Tell us an unforgettable story.

It's a memory of something that lasted just a few seconds, but I'll never forget it because I still laugh about it.

It happened during Canada Cup 76 in a game against Czechoslovakia. I intercept a pass in our zone and I take off with the puck, fending off two opposing players. I get to the offensive zone. I look to my left and see Bobby Hull, an excellent scorer. I look to my right, and there's Guy Lafleur. I have a fraction of a second to decide what to do with the puck. I'm left-handed, so it's easier for me to pass right. Since we're in Montreal, I make the logical decision: pass the puck to Flower—who misses his shot! It was a rare thing to occur, but it happened then.

More than thirty years later, I was in Vancouver participating in a salmon-fishing tournament with NHL alumni. When I get to the hotel, they give me a key for room number 9. I open the door and Bobby Hull is there. Without even saying hello, he looks at me with a serious expression and says, "You should have passed me the puck." He remembered very well it was Flower I'd passed the puck to and not him in 1976.

What was Guy Lafleur's greatest quality?

He had many. I think one of them was being able to take on the responsibility of following in the footsteps of Jean Béliveau.

On the ice and in the hearts of the fans, and as an ambassador for the Canadiens, Jean Béliveau was in a class of his own. And there was immense pressure on Flower to continue his legacy. Guy did not become "another Jean Béliveau," but the one and only Guy Lafleur. He managed to attain, and even surpass, the popularity of Jean Béliveau. All over the world, both were recognized for their class, their sincerity, and their respect for the fans.

When Mr. Béliveau died, Guy went up to the casket and knelt. I've held on to this very touching photo, which illustrates so well the passing of the Canadiens' illustrious torch from one star to another.

How did your relationship evolve?

Sadly, we never saw each other again after we retired from the game. That's how it goes, most of the time—you lose touch, even with players you liked a lot, because you live in different cities and don't often participate in the same activities.

But I didn't hesitate for one second when the CHUM Foundation reached out and asked me to participate in a fundraising campaign for the Guy Lafleur Fund, supporting cancer research. The Club des 10 brought together ten hockey legends to chat on social media with hockey fans who had donated to the foundation.

It was the most natural thing in the world to do something to help Guy, and to pay it forward.

What is his legacy, the most beautiful memory that he left the world of hockey and all of society?

Guy Lafleur probably created as many memories as he had fans. I was and continue to be a fan of Flower's. But my best memories are probably not the same as those of my friends from Ottawa, or our Canada Cup teammates, or his opponents, or hockey fans worldwide. Everyone had their own relationship to Guy, their own story.

His legacy was to give us all wonderful moments to experience, both on the ice and off.

André Dupont

Born in Trois-Rivières, Quebec, in 1949, André Dupont is a defenceman who played thirteen seasons in the NHL, chiefly with the Philadelphia Flyers. In the 1970s, the man they called Moose was one of the Flyers' group of strongmen. Under coach Fred Shero, the team at that time embraced a rough, intimidating style of play, giving rise to the nickname the Broad Street Bullies. André was one opponent who had respect for Guy Lafleur.

What is your oldest memory of Guy Lafleur as a player?

That would be from the Quebec Junior A league in the mid-1960s, before the creation of the QMJHL [Quebec Major Junior Hockey League]. Guy was playing with the Québec Aces and I was on the Reds, and then the Trois-Rivières Maple Leafs. He was way ahead of everybody. Everyone was asking "Where did that kid come from?" Afterwards, I never saw him play with the Remparts, because I was with the Junior Canadiens in the OHL. But the media was always talking about him.

It was obvious he would continue to get better and stand out, and that he was headed for the NHL. The only idiots who didn't understand that were the Oakland Seals, who traded their first draft pick—and then the Canadiens got organized to jump on Guy!

What memory do you have of his early days with the Canadiens?

He didn't play much, because the Canadiens had a lot of depth. His momentum slowed down, and everywhere in the league we talked about it and couldn't understand it. He was still impressive right from the start. Any other rookie would have been happy to have his stats.

For spectators, he was a joy to watch, with his fluid skating, his hard shot, and his hair flowing in the wind. But for his opponents, he made us nervous: Guy was so fast and unpredictable that you had no idea what was going to happen—other than an explosion of power and a lightning-fast shot. But where? That was our main problem with him!

Guy gradually found his place on the Canadiens, surrounded by real warriors. I remember the first time I played against Henri Richard. I was surprised because he was not a big guy, but he would do everything to recover the puck and keep it—and to make you look bad while he was at it. He had a will to win that made him seem like a giant. Guy grew up with those role models: Jean Béliveau, Yvan Cournoyer, and many others. It explains why he was never happy scoring just one goal in a game. He wanted five!

Was there fierce competition between the Flyers and the Canadiens in the 1970s?

Looking back at the era, the Flyers were created in 1967 at the same time as the St. Louis Blues, the Minnesota North Stars, the Pittsburgh Penguins, the Los Angeles Kings, and the Oakland Seals.

The Blues played a rough game right from the start—I played with them for one and a half seasons in the early 1970s. Ed Snider, the Flyers' owner, said, "We're not going to be intimidated—not by St. Louis or anybody else!" And that's how the Broad Street Bullies were created. Fred Shero, who was the Flyers' head coach at the time, had been my coach in the Central Hockey League. He was the one who asked the Flyers to go and get me from St. Louis. He built a very tough team, specifically to face the Bruins.

In the years between 1970 and 1980, there were three dominant teams in the league: Boston, Montreal, and Philadelphia. The Bruins and the Flyers each won the Stanley Cup twice, and the Canadiens won it six times.

If you want to talk about fierce competition for the Flyers, that was with Boston. Not Montreal. The Canadiens were a very solid physical team but, first and foremost, extremely talented. We had to be very careful not to earn penalties, because they had a mighty power play with Lemaire, Shutt, Robinson, Lapointe, and especially Flower.

It's important to acknowledge that we were more than a bunch of brutes. The Flyers from my era were a very talented team, with Bill Barber, Reggie Leach, Rick MacLeish, Bobby Clarke, and Bernard Parent, among others. It would have been impossible to win the Stanley Cup if we were just brutes.

Another example of fierce competition that I had in the NHL was when I played for the Nordiques. In Quebec, it was war! The Nordiques hated the Canadiens, and the Canadiens hated the Nordiques. The fans of one team had absolutely nothing to do with the fans of the other. It caused divisions in families. The only player who was loved in both cities was Guy Lafleur. In Québec, he was applauded even while wearing his Habs sweater. And in Montreal, he was a god!

Did Fred Shero adjust his game plan when the Flyers played the Canadiens?

For sure! The plan was to smother Lafleur's game as he was leaving his end of the ice by gluing at least one player on Flower so he wouldn't receive the puck as he was picking up speed. We'd rather have Lemaire or Shutt get possession of the puck. They were very skilled, too, but less "dangerous" than Guy. In those days, we could stick close to our opponents and the referees wouldn't object.

You had to do anything you could to prevent Lafleur from getting the puck while he was moving in full stride—that was when he was at his best. When that happened, all I could do was pray to the good Lord!

How do you explain how he exploded after three years?

Simple: He finally got as much ice time as his talent warranted.

In 1974–1975 we saw a different Lafleur. It was that year he became a dominant player in the league. Compared to the previous year, he took a big step up. And the next season, he took another big step. Playing for the 1975–1976 Stanley Cup, when the Canadiens beat the Flyers in the final, I'd say that was when I started facing one of the greatest players in the world.

Try as we might to hit him in an effort to slow him down, it didn't work. A lot of fans called him "Ti-Guy" [Li'l Guy], but he was not little! He had legs like solid blocks and arms like Popeye's. He had paddles for hands. He dodged and deked, always moving a fraction of a second faster than the fastest players.

People often talk about his skating style and his shot. But Flower was an exceptional player because, first and foremost, he had exceptional instincts. When everyone was going right, he could decide he was going left—and the puck would just arrive there, on the blade of his stick. You can guess the rest . . .

What kind of opponent was he?

Tiring! There are no words to describe what it was like to play against Guy.

When we were playing the Canadiens, Shero used me a lot,

along with two excellent defencemen: Larry Goodenough in the five-on-five, and Joe Watson on the penalty kill. After spending sixty minutes trying to slow Flower down, our defence corps had more than earned a good long shower.

I have to say that, as tenacious as he was during every second of the game, he was always a very respectful opponent, even against the Broad Steet Bullies.

I remember one night at the Forum, Flower had received a soft pass from one of his defencemen in his own zone. He was vulnerable and I didn't hit him—I just took him out of play. In the same situation with a bigger player, I would have charged at him. Guy understood that I'd held back on the play. In the third period, with the Canadiens enjoying a comfortable lead, Lafleur and Lemaire skated into the neutral zone in a two-on-one. Guy passed the puck to Lemaire and then he took off for the Canadiens bench. It was his way of paying me back.

What do you know about the attempted kidnapping of Guy Lafleur during the 1976 playoffs between the Canadiens and the Flyers?

I didn't know anything about it at the time; no one talked about it in the dressing room. The management must have known, but not us. When we were in the playoffs during those years, there was a similar threat towards Bobby Clarke.

If gamblers really wanted to create a distraction so that Guy's performance would be affected, they missed their mark. He scored seven goals and the Canadiens won the Stanley Cup.

Were you surprised by his retirement, and then by his return to the game?

Completely surprised. I had taken my retirement, but of course I was still interested in what was going on in the NHL. Guy had slowed down—like we all do—but he was still making a decent contribution in goals and assists for the Canadiens. I quickly learned that the reason he took his retirement had to do with respect. He never should have left the Canadiens. Never. Because Guy Lafleur, he *was* the Canadiens. And the Canadiens were Guy Lafleur.

Probably the best present he ever received in his life was when the Rangers invited him to their training camp. It was like he'd picked up where he left off the day before—or almost—and with the same joy he had when he was a junior. Three and a half years later, he was still electrifying. He was a useful player for the Rangers and the Nordiques to have, as much in the dressing room as on the ice.

Was it really between his two NHL retirements that you got to know each other?

Yes, and afterwards as well. Up until then, I thought of him as the biggest star in Montreal, period—until I went to play with him on an NHL Legends tour outside of Quebec. In western Canada, in Ontario, in Russia, and other places, too, Guy Lafleur was a true living legend.

In western Canda, we were playing one afternoon game and another in the evening. There would be up to thirty thousand spectators a day. The fans came to see Guy.

On the road with the Legends team, I got to know him as a person. Of the guys in our group, he was one of the most humble. When it was just us players, he was one of the boys. He was very funny, deadpan—which kept us on our toes. Proud, too—there was no way our team of old-timers was going to get beaten by a team stacked with young players!

Do you have a story that comes to mind?

Guy loved Oh Henry! chocolate bars. The first time we went on tour he would make the bus stop in front of a dépanneur just so he could buy one. On the next tour I bought him a box of them—and he got through it in a few days. Obviously, with his metabolism, he didn't put on weight.

What is his legacy, the most beautiful memory that he left the world of hockey and all of society?

Respect and patience. Guy had an enormous amount of respect for his teammates and his opponents. And remarkable patience with the fans. For him, the two qualities were intertwined.

From the junior level onwards, he taught patience to all of his teammates because he was the player who was in the most demand to sign autographs, which always delayed team trips.

I believe that the respect and patience Guy showed in the realm of hockey can be transferred to our day-to-day lives.

He was honoured with a majestic funeral because he was both a great athlete and a remarkable idol for the entire hockey world.

Michel Bergeron

Born in Montreal in 1946, Michel Bergeron was a career hockey coach. Nicknamed the Tiger when he helmed the Trois-Rivières Draveurs in the QMJHL, he displayed the same zeal behind the bench of two NHL teams: the Québec Nordiques and the New York Rangers. It was in that capacity that he coached Guy Lafleur during his sole season in New York and his first season in Quebec.

What is your earliest memory of Guy Lafleur as a player?

It was during the Remparts era at the end of the 1960s. I regularly made the trip to see their biggest star in action, especially to Saint-Jérôme, Laval, and Rosemont. Once a year I'd go to see a game in Québec City—the ten thousand seats of the Colisée were always full.

When I became the coach of the Nordiques, my boss was Maurice Filion, who had coached Guy on the Remparts. At any opportune moment I'd ask him all sorts of questions: What was it like to coach Guy Lafleur? How did he handle himself even when he had nothing left to prove? What was he like with his teammates? Maurice's eyes would light up when he talked about Guy. He had nothing but praise for the way the young man conducted himself in the dressing room, on the ice, and in public.

You were coaching the Nordiques when Guy was playing with the Canadiens. How did you prepare to compete against him?

Guy was always a tough opponent for the Nordiques to face. It was usually Alain Côté's job to follow him like a shadow. Alain could read the game well and quite often he'd be able to intercept passes meant for Guy. But he was always eager for his shifts to end because he was exhausted! Guy didn't stick to north-south on the ice—he was all over the place.

I have so many great memories of Guy when he was with the Canadiens. In 1982, the Nordiques were only in our third season in the NHL and yet we knocked the Canadiens out of the playoffs. Dale Hunter quickly scored in overtime and the Quebec hockey world was turned upside down. Guy wasn't even on the ice at the time, since their coach Bob Berry had started the period with a defensive line.

Then, in 1984, there was the infamous Good Friday Massacre [when the Canadiens beat the Nordiques at the Forum during the second-round playoffs and a multi-period brawl resulted in injuries, ejections, and 252 penalty minutes]. Guy didn't fight and no one dared jump on him. I can still see him in the middle of the ice, with my player Jean-François Sauvé. They were holding each other's jerseys and talking!

Tell us about the very first time you met him.

In 1988, my general manager, Phil Esposito, had planned on holding the Rangers' training camp in Plattsburgh, New York, but not for any particular reason. Since I'd coached the Draveurs for six years, I wanted to do something fun for the people in Trois-Rivières, so I reached out to some contacts and set the wheels in motion. It was quite a big deal to have an NHL training camp in a city.

Three or four weeks before the start of the camp, I was preparing for it in my office at Madison Square Garden when the phone rang. It was Yves Tremblay, a guy I didn't know very well, a journalist—but I also knew he was a close contact of Guy Lafleur's. He said, "Flower wants to make a return to hockey and he wants it to be with the Rangers." I was so surprised I said, "Wait, I'm going to get a coffee. . . . Okay, go on." Tremblay explained to me that he was talking to a couple of teams. I told him, "Let me make a call and I'll get back to you."

I called Phil Esposito to fill him in. He said to me, "Bring him to New York." I personally went to pick up Guy and Yves at the airport. Guy was tanned and looked like a twenty-five-year-old player in great shape. Phil and Flower knew each other, having been Canada Cup teammates. After the meeting, I took Guy and Yves for a walk in the neighbourhood where most of the Rangers lived. I told him that in New York, he'd have the ability—just like I did—to go to the grocery store without being recognized. He still very much had the hockey bug, and the idea of being able to walk around without being constantly recognized seemed to appeal to him. He also told me he wanted to play for me—I was touched by that. So he agreed to participate at the Rangers training camp, even without a contract.

How did it go at the training camp in Trois-Rivières?

We stayed at the Le Baron motel. The night before the camp started, Guy came to my suite and stayed till two or three in the morning, drinking coffee. He was excited and also somewhat nervous. We left at 7:00 a.m. Already at that hour, there was a line starting at the baseball stadium all the way to the Colisée. And the arena was packed to the rafters!

Serge Savard was pissed off with me because none of the

media in Quebec were covering the Canadiens' training camp—they were all in Trois-Rivières. There were even some journalists there from New York and other places. When I ran into the veteran sportswriter Francis Rosa from *The Boston Globe,* I asked him, "What are you doing in Trois-Rivières?" He said, "Flower is back!"

I wanted Guy to look good right from the start, so I had him play with our excellent rookie Tony Granato. The first time they hit the ice together, Tony sent a neat pass to Guy as he was coming up on the flank. He fired off a Lafleur-from-the-good-old-days shot and boom—he scored against Bob Froese. It felt like the roof blew off the Colisée! Esposito and I said to each other that we had to sign him right away.

It all got settled quickly, because Guy was just as keen as Phil and I were. The Penguins and the Kings were also interested in him, but he had a clear preference for the Rangers and New York City. He told me later that Pittsburgh had offered him more money than we did, but he wanted to come to New York. He often said to me that he never should have retired, and that he should have insisted on being traded to the Rangers.

What kind of player was he in the dressing room and on the ice?

Without a doubt one of the most easygoing of the players I've coached!

He was thirty-seven years old in New York, coming back to the game after nearly four years away. He played on our third line, sometimes on the fourth. I also used him on the power play. But there were some nights I didn't play him. I found that hard, but he never said anything. He knew I was acting solely in the interests of the team. And for him, the team came first.

There are times when players ask coaches who they will be

playing with. Not him—he wanted to play, full stop. He made a request only once, when he hadn't scored in four or five games. He asked me to let him play with Marcel Dionne. I believe that, together, they had 3,000 points in the NHL. I accepted, and it didn't take long: In the very next game, on the power play, Marcel made a perfect pass to Guy, who scored. It was an electrifying moment. But they were both thirty-eight years old at the time. My biggest regret is not to have coached them when they were in their prime.

In New York, with the help of my assistant coach, Charles Thiffault, we implemented a game system—Charles made sure it was solid. However, Guy was not the most attentive when we explained the system to the players. He said to me, "I don't understand anything about your 1-2-2 zone entries." I said, "Okay then, just have fun!" I believe the only hockey language Guy understood was his own instinct.

Even though Guy Lafleur was the best hockey player on the planet in the 1970s, I still don't believe the Canadiens made the most of his full potential. He played mostly for Scotty Bowman and Jacques Lemaire, two coaches who had a mainly defensive outlook. And so Guy never played twenty or twenty-two minutes a game, like Mario Lemieux and Wayne Gretzky did. What's more, it's important to say that he never defied his coaches during games—I saw both Mario with Pittsburgh and Wayne with the Oilers leaving the ice when they were tired, not when the coaches told them to. Guy didn't do that sort of thing.

Tell us about the first time he returned to the Forum wearing a Rangers uniform.

Guy arrived at the Forum at two in the afternoon. He was smoking, nervous. But the most nervous person at the Forum that night was Ronald Corey. After everything that went down during Guy's last years in Montreal, Ronald was quite flustered!

That night, the Canadiens won 7–5 and Guy scored two goals against Patrick Roy. The crowd wasn't behind the Canadiens, but 100 percent behind Guy.

How did your relationship with him evolve?

Our professional relationship transformed. We became friends.

The year Guy played in New York, a friend we had in common, Richard Morency, came to spend time with my family over the holidays. On New Year's Day, my wife and I also invited Guy, Lise, Martin, and Mark. Guy brought the champagne and we had a superb New York party—*en français*.

Over time, he brought up the subject of his retirement from the Canadiens. It was still a sore subject. The only reason he gave me was that it was about his ice time. Before he decided to leave, he was playing eight to ten minutes a game under Jacques Lemaire's defensive system. Imagine Guy having to deal with that.

His return to the game gave him all kinds of reasons to be happy. When we went out to a restaurant, he'd often pick up the tab, saying, "It's crazy the amount of money you allowed me to make for my three years with the Rangers and the Nordiques!" It must have been quite different from what the Canadiens had paid him.

Thanks to the rapport we developed in New York, it had felt natural for him to join me when I went over to the Nordiques.

How did the move to Québec come about?

Marcel Aubut phoned me and asked me to come back to Québec. Martin Madden was the general manager. We met, I took a look at the lineup—and let's just say it wasn't exactly promising. Peter Stastny and Michel Goulet wanted to leave. The outlook for the coming years looked extremely challenging. Marcel asked me if Guy could help us out, since he was having a terrible time selling season tickets. "Let's sign him—maybe he can play on a fourth line."

When I came home after the first day of the training camp, my wife noticed that my level of enthusiasm was pretty low. I said to her, "In New York, Guy was playing on my fourth line. This year, he's my best right winger." We were together for one year in Québec, and then I was fired.

The Québec fans experienced a love story with Guy in three parts: the first in the peewee tournament, the second with the Remparts, and the third with the Nordiques. And in between, they still loved him, even when he was wearing a blue, white, and red sweater!

Tell us an unforgettable story.

The Rangers were in Calgary during a road trip in western Canada. As usual, the bus was ready to leave, but we had to wait while Guy signed autographs.

A limousine arrived. Two guys got out and started chatting with him. Guy got on the bus and said to me, "Bergie, these guys have a swanky steak house and they invited me to dinner. Since we're not playing tomorrow, I said yes, but on one condition: that the whole team is invited. They agreed." I let the guys go have dinner together. The bus took them all to the restaurant while I and my assistant coaches, Charles Thiffault and Wayne Cashman, went back to the hotel—in the limousine!

What was his greatest quality?

His focus. Guy was a hockey player twenty-four hours a day. His nervousness came from knowing the weight the Canadiens put on his shoulders. But he was always in control. In Boston, when John Wensink threatened to tear his head off, Guy still played an excellent game. His ability to stay calm was always impressive.

Guy was also a mentor for younger players. A star. Joe Sakic was destined to become one as well. So I decided they would be roommates on the road. On the day of Guy's funeral, Joe flew in from Denver to Montreal during the playoffs to pay tribute to him. That says it all.

He must have had his faults . . .

Sometimes he was not terribly diplomatic about the Canadiens organization when he was talking to the media. The other side of the coin was that he was direct and to the point. Transparent. Real.

What is his legacy?

I will always remember how he fought without complaining. And he fought for others, too.

When he first started playing for the Canadiens, he didn't play much and he didn't complain—at least not in public. Later, he fought a battle for one of his sons, which he did with dignity, under the gaze of the media—no surprise. When he got cancer, you never heard him ask "Why me?" On the contrary, he transformed his personal situation into a challenge to society by bringing together specialists and hockey stars through the Guy Lafleur Fund.

Of the various sweaters he wore, they almost never sported a letter. With the Remparts he had the "C" and on the Nordiques, an "A." That's it. He didn't need that to have a tremendous influence on his teammates, his opponents, the referees, and the fans.

André Savard

Born in Temiscaming, Quebec, in 1953, the centre André Savard played twelve seasons in the NHL for the Boston Bruins, the Buffalo Sabres, and the Québec Nordiques.

For four seasons, he played on the Québec Remparts, including two unforgettable years with Guy Lafleur. After that, they would always be opponents on the ice.

What is your first memory of Guy Lafleur?

Guy and I both came to the Remparts in 1969–1970, at the beginning of the Quebec Maritimes Junior Hockey League. The next year, in 1971, we won the Memorial Cup. He came from the Aces, in the Junior A league, and I had been at Amos. Maurice Filion had me sign a contract as a free agent.

I didn't know Guy Lafleur or Jacques Richard or any of the other players. But very quickly, I could see that Guy was a cut above everyone else, both on our team and in the league. Since I was younger than Guy—I was sixteen and he was eighteen—I stayed for two more years in Québec City.

One of the strengths of our coach, Maurice Filion, was that he demanded a lot from his players in terms of work and discipline. That enabled him to build a team with character, and it delivered results: two President's Cups and a Memorial Cup. Réjean Giroux, Jacques Richard, Pierre Roy, Charles Constantin, and many others were our lead players, and above all, Guy!

What was he like as a teammate?

I would say he was really good at winning!

I sat next to him in the locker room and observed him. Neither of us talked very much. He was very disciplined for his age and worked harder than anybody. He dressed with a little more style than the rest of us—no doubt because he was confident and was already in demand on Québec's social scene.

Even though we were a strong team, it was Guy who made us stand out. For those first two years of the Remparts, his name was always in the headlines of the three city newspapers: *Le Soleil*, *Le Journal de Québec*, and *L'action catholique*. Having Guy Lafleur on our team made us very popular. Our fans came to games mostly just to see him play.

It was also Guy who drew all kinds of personalities to our dressing room after our games—whether it was Premier Bourassa, the mayor of Québec, the co-owners of the Remparts, and so on. After Guy left to play on the Canadiens and I was made captain, the traffic in the dressing room died down.

At the very first game in the history of the Remparts, Guy scored four goals and one assist, helping us beat Sorel 10–5. At the start of our first season, there were nearly three thousand spectators in the stands at the Colisée. Then, in the fall, the numbers started to go up. During the playoffs, there were thirteen thousand, with lots of people sitting on the stairs. It was wild, an extraordinary atmosphere. Even fifty years later, it's unforgettable.

Guy was aware of his immense appeal, but he remained down-to-earth.

Were you line mates?

Yes, during our second season, when we won the Memorial Cup. I was playing centre and Michel Brière was our left wing. The three of us had different styles but the same work ethic.

It was wonderful to play with Guy because he was very creative. But it wasn't easy. Michel and I—and certainly all the other line mates Guy had, from peewee to the NHL—had to be very focused on the game because Guy was a fraction of a second faster than everybody else.

Did you feel like you were in the shadow of Guy Lafleur?

That didn't bother me at all. In the game where I scored twelve points, Guy and I were on the same line. All the players on the Remparts benefited directly and indirectly from everything Guy brought to the team because he allowed us to share the spotlight.

Guy's passion for the game and his desire to win were exceptional. He just scored a goal? He'd want to score a second, a third, etcetera. It motivated all of us.

What type of player was he?

Whether it was as a junior or in the NHL, Guy always had as much determination to win on the road as at home. He didn't have nerves. It was in his nature to be calm and in control of the situation.

He was very strong and solid on his skates. And he was extremely assured. During his two years with the Remparts he didn't just score a ton of goals and pass the puck to his teammates. He dominated with 100 penalty minutes per season. Later, in the NHL, his teammates took it on themselves to protect him so he could do what he did best: rack up the points.

Afterwards, you played against him when you were with the Bruins, the Sabres, and the Nordiques, right?

Yes, he was quite the adversary!

Whenever we were preparing to play against the Canadiens—no matter which team I was on—our number one strategy was to find ways to reduce Guy Lafleur's room to manoeuvre. And we knew he didn't need a lot of room to slip away and score a goal.

Especially during the 1970s, the rivalry between the Bruins and the Canadiens was intense. And yet, Guy never seemed intimidated to play at Boston Garden. He showed up with the same drive and the same desire to win as when he played at the Forum.

Back then, what kind of career did you think he'd have?

I expected to see Guy dominating as soon as he started playing for the Canadiens—just like Gilbert Perreault did in Buffalo and Marcel Dionne in Detroit. But that wasn't what happened. The big difference was that he didn't have nearly the same amount of ice time as those two.

He wasn't the player I knew for those first three years. It's probably because he wasn't playing enough to be able to give it his all. It became a vicious circle: You're not scoring because you're not playing much, and you're not playing much because you're not scoring.

I should say that, at the time, the Canadiens had such a strong lineup that they didn't have to play their rookies as much. But today, with the salary cap, no team would do that—they don't hesitate to play their rookies!

I never doubted that he'd break out in the NHL, but let's just say, I was eager for him to have that happen.

Were you surprised when he first announced his retirement and, later, when he returned to the game?

Like everyone, I was surprised both times. But when you think about it, they were very much Guy Lafleur–style decisions!

To retire so young—whatever his reasons—was out of the ordinary. To come back after three and a half years in a league like the NHL, and still be able to contribute—that was also out of the ordinary. What enabled him to stage his comeback was that his skating was still NHL calibre. Even though his shooting ability was somewhat diminished, he managed to get where he wanted to be to score.

Tell us an unforgettable story.

When he was in juniors, Guy was already playing for the fans. Late in the season of his first year, he had already scored ninety-four goals. We had one home game and one away game left, I believe. Guy absolutely wanted to reach the one-hundred-goal mark in front of the home crowd. But to score six goals in one game, with such strong competition—who would be able to pull that off?

The answer: Guy alone. The fans raised the roof at the Colisée! And he didn't stop at one hundred either, but scored three more goals on the road to finish off his first season. The next season he picked up where he left off, scoring 130 goals.

What was his greatest quality?

I think it was his exceptional commitment to whatever he did. You don't become a folk hero from talent alone.

If he had been just a very talented player but not friendly with his teammates, if he hadn't had an exceptional work ethic, if he hadn't had such pride, or if he hadn't been so close to the fans, he would not have been Guy Lafleur. It's all of it.

Guy was always there for his teammates and he remained so. When my father died, in 1993, Guy came to North Bay, Ontario, in a little plane with Marcel Aubut. My family and I were very moved.

What were your last moments with him like?

In the autumn of 2021, when the QMJHL retired his number 4, almost all of the Remparts from our era were there. I was asked to speak, which I did with great pleasure. I brought up his six-goal game at the Colisée and other accomplishments. He had tears in his eyes.

We all knew that he was very sick, and that it must have taken a great effort for him to be there that day.

That evening, Guy was giving back to all of those who worshipped him—the fans—as well as to his teammates. He was so happy to see us again, teasing each of us in turn. He took the time to take photos with my son, my grandkids, and me. He did the same for the families of our other teammates. We hugged each other and I told him, "*Je t'aime, mon Guy.*" Sadly, we never saw each other again.

What is his legacy?

He was a great athlete with a big heart. Let's all remember Guy Lafleur as a man who gave everything his all, 150 percent, on and off the ice.

Gilbert Perreault

Born in Victoriaville, Quebec, in 1950, the centre Gilbert Perreault was the very first player drafted by the Buffalo Sabres when they joined the NHL in 1970. Before that, he called the shots while he was playing with the Junior Canadiens of the OHL. It was during the 1970 Memorial Cup series that he first played against Guy Lafleur. They also competed together for the Canada Cup.

Perreault made his mark wearing the Sabres uniform for seventeen seasons as he led the French Connection along with Richard Martin and René Robert. He was inducted into the Hockey Hall of Fame in 1990, and the Sabres retired his sweater.

What is your oldest memory of Guy Lafleur as a player?

Even playing peewee, Guy had a shot like lightning that he fired off from the red line. All the goalies were afraid! We saw each other again at the Quebec international tournament, but we didn't face each other there.

Then Guy was on the Remparts and I joined the Junior Canadiens, which was the only team from Quebec in the Ontario Hockey Association. The first time we played against each other was in the semifinal of the 1970 Memorial Cup. The Junior Canadiens beat the Remparts in three games. That was the first time we spoke to each other. Then I was drafted by the Sabres and he continued to dominate for one more year with the Remparts before being drafted by the Canadiens.

In those years, despite the popularity of the Canadiens, the

Junior Canadiens could still draw eighteen thousand fans to the Forum. There was a strong rivalry between Montreal and Québec.

Did you ever think you might become teammates on the Canadiens?

No. In 1970, the Buffalo Sabres and the Vancouver Canucks both made their debuts in the NHL. That was the year the Canadiens lost the right to pick the two top players from the province of Quebec. I knew I wouldn't be drafted by the Canadiens, who had the fifth pick.

But yes, we can only imagine—if this rule had not been abolished—what it would have been like for me and Guy to play on the same line for the Canadiens, who were already dominant in the NHL.

What are your memories of your early seasons?

Our early seasons in the NHL were very different.

The Canadiens had such a strong team that even a player like Guy Lafleur had to take his place on it gradually, while observing the veterans. Despite everything, he scored around thirty goals in his first year.

It was very different for me in Buffalo. It was a new team and they had to sell their product in a new market. I got a huge amount of ice time right from the start.

In time, Guy would become one of the league's best players. In the semifinals of 1974–1975, when we eliminated the Canadiens, Guy was very impressive with his feints and his shots that came from just about everywhere. Don Luce in centre, Craig Ramsay as left wing, and Danny Gare often played against Guy's line, and they had some busy nights!

Guy was an electrifying presence for hockey fans, as well as for his teammates and opponents. He was very athletic and had exceptional stamina. Every time he was on the ice, he never stopped skating.

For Guy, the team always came first. That's why, on top of scoring a lot of goals, he was also always passing the puck to his teammates. And whenever they faced some of the toughest teams in the NHL, such as Philadelphia and Boston, it was known all over the league that Guy would bring his A game every night.

Are there players whose personalities are more suited to particular markets?

Yes, for sure. These days, teams interview players before the draft, to get a sense of their personalities. That didn't happen in my day.

But no interviews with Guy were needed for the Canadiens to know his personality would suit the Montreal market very well. And on the ice, he was truly spectacular. His exploits with the Remparts and his "Blond Demon" appeal made him a custom fit for the Canadiens.

All over the league, Guy was the player people wanted to see in action. There were a lot of hockey fans from St. Catharines and from around Buffalo who came to Sabres games wearing number 10 Canadiens sweaters.

You were teammates on Team Canada in 1976 and 1981. What do you remember about that experience?

It was during the Canada Cup tournaments that Guy and I became friends.

In 1976 we were playing in a best-of-three final against Czechoslovakia. Our coach, Scotty Bowman, had me playing left wing with Guy a few times. I remember one pass he made to me—I never really understood how the puck could have landed on the blade of my stick—and I took off on a breakaway.

In 1981, I had the privilege of playing on the same line as Wayne Gretzky and Flower. I was the left winger. I still have unforgettable memories of that—we complemented each other very well. It was as if we'd been playing together forever. An ankle injury prevented me from finishing out the tournament.

Were you surprised by his retirement, and then by his return to the game?

I was equally surprised by his retirement and his return to the game. Those two decisions were typical of his character.

I don't think he could have easily evolved as a player with the Canadiens, given the defensive system they had at the time. But I never thought he'd give up the bleu-blanc-rouge sweater at the age of thirty-three. And yet, it happened.

And then he surprised the whole hockey world when he came back, and also with what he was capable of accomplishing after a long time away. It took a real athlete to be able to pull off such a feat.

How did your relationship with him develop after your NHL career?

I played with him for about a dozen years in the NHL Legends alumni tournament. I don't think it would have existed without Guy Lafleur. Guy behaved the same way he did when he was in the NHL: three hours early for the games and with his skates already on as his teammates were just arriving. He often brought coffee and doughnuts—back then, we didn't worry so much about our waistlines!

With the Legends, we played games all over Canada—not just in NHL markets but also in the Yukon, Newfoundland, and anywhere else we were invited. Flower was always the most popular guy; after a game he could spend two hours signing autographs.

It takes a special man to always be so available. The other players and I signed autographs, too, but the lines were often not as long!

Do you have any stories you'd like to share?

The arenas were sold out when the Legends came into town, since the games were big fundraisers for the charities that hosted us.

Even though we were playing no contact, the games were competitive. The local players were often among the best in their region, and we still had our pride. And Guy was the proudest of all on our team. There was no question in his mind that our players would give less than 100 percent and risk being beaten.

One day—it seems to me it was in Halifax—we were playing our fourth game in as many days, against a team that had won the university championship the previous year. So these were very fit guys, with no extra pounds on them! We were trailing in the first period and Guy gave us all a pep talk about how we had a perfect record and we had to protect it. We ended up narrowly winning, something like 3–2, and I think it was Guy who scored the winning goal.

Another time, in Rimouski, we were trailing by a few goals—5–2, I believe—and there was a lot of loud talk in the dressing room between periods. When we returned to the ice, Guy said to the player shadowing him, "You want to follow me? Perfect—you're going to skate!" And that's what happened. We won 7–5.

What was his greatest quality?

His simplicity. For the fans and even the players, we couldn't believe how approachable he was. He was a really good person.

In the last years of his life, we spoke on the phone a few times. One day, someone close to me received a cancer diagnosis. Guy called me and that friend happened to be at my house. I said to Flower, "I'm going to pass you to someone who could use some encouragement in his battle with cancer. I'm sure you'll know the right thing to say." I passed my cell phone over and Guy took the time to help cheer up my friend.

What is his legacy, the most beautiful memory that he left the world of hockey and all of society?

His generosity.

If someone as busy as Guy Lafleur could manage to give so much quality time to other people, how could we not give more of ourselves?

Pierre Bouchard

Born in Longueuil, Quebec, in 1948, the defenceman Pierre Bouchard wore a Canadiens uniform for eight seasons, five of which were capped with a Stanley Cup. He finished his career with the Washington Capitals. His nickname was "Baby Butch," a nod to his father, Émile "Butch" Bouchard, who was a prominent defenceman for the Canadiens.

Physically imposing, Pierre Bouchard ensured that his teammate and friend had all the room he needed to manoeuvre so that he could make the most of his talent.

What is your oldest memory of Guy Lafleur as a player?

I didn't see him play with the Remparts. We got to know each other after he arrived at the Canadiens training camp in 1971. I remember seeing him proudly behind the wheel of the Buick Riviera that the Remparts had given him as a present. He was always impeccably turned out in a suit and tie, even when he came to practices.

Once or twice a week after practice he would make a quick trip to Québec City to see his friends and also Madame Baribeau, whose house he'd lived in for a long time. He still felt at home in Québec—that's where he got his hair cut!—and hadn't yet got his bearings in Montreal. He fit in well with his new teammates, but he was shy.

Back then, what kind of career did you think he'd have?

There's no doubt he felt an enormous weight on his shoulders, as the presumed successor of Jean Béliveau.

On the ice it was obvious how talented he was, but it seemed like the brakes were on to a certain extent. The fact was, at that time, the Canadiens did not play their rookies very much. Every young player had to earn his spot, even if his name was Guy Lafleur. He didn't get the ice time he wanted, and he was not dominant in the league at the start.

Gradually, things fell into place for him. I watched him get better—it was like he was climbing a staircase one step at a time. But to be perfectly frank, in the early 1970s I could not have said he would become one of the best players in the history of the Canadiens, out of all the future Hall of Famers we had. Starting from his fourth season with the team he became one of the best players in the NHL—if not *the* best—and possibly, in the world.

What was he like as a teammate?

An original! He drank coffee before games and sometimes took a few puffs of a cigarette between periods with Mario Tremblay, among others. According to an urban legend, our trainer and equipment manager Eddy Palchak would light a cigarette for Guy and give it to him discreetly when he returned to the bench. But that's not true.

What made the Canadiens such a powerhouse in the 1970s was that we all had complementary roles. For Guy, his was scoring. My role, along with Gilles Lupien and Rick Chartraw, was to create space around Guy and our other top scorers. In other words, we were there to shove aside the big players from Boston and Philadelphia like John Wensink, Mike Milbury, and Dave Schultz. In the '70s and '80s, those guys were trying to slow down their best opponents but weren't looking to hurt them. Nobody wanted to be the numbskull who'd deliberately hurt Gordie Howe, Guy Lafleur, or Wayne Gretzky.

Besides, none of the opponents tasked with shadowing Guy managed to slow him down—he skated much faster than they did. And Guy took it as motivation that people wanted to slow him down and intimidate him. It just made him play even better.

For Flower, all his teammates were of equal importance. And even when he began to emerge as one of the greats, he still saw himself on the same level as everyone else. He was one of the boys, and never condescending.

Tell us about the player.

Guy was impulsive with the puck and liked to improvise. One day, his winger Steve Shutt asked him, "Where do you want me to be on the ice?" Flower replied, "Put yourself wherever you want, because even I don't know what I'm going to do. But I'll find you!"

For the first seasons he coached Guy, Scotty Bowman was strict with him. And then he let him play his game—Bowman realized that he would contribute to the team's success by playing "à la Guy Lafleur." Bowman also allowed Frank Mahovlich to play "à la Frank Mahovlich."

What kind of relationship did you and Guy Lafleur have?

We got along well right from the start. We both lived in Longueuil, not far from the Béliveaus. In those days, Guy and I were among the few bachelors on the team. And then, after he got married, he came to live across the street from me, in Verchères.

He lived in Verchères for three or four years in the mid-'70s. He and Lise had been living in an apartment on Nuns' Island, but they wanted to have more space as they were starting their family, and for their two dogs to be able to run around. Sadly, one of the dogs got killed by a car, just in front of their house.

In 1976, I was probably the last one to hear that Guy was dealing with threats of being kidnapped—even though an unmarked car was posted outside 24/7. He told me what was going on after I started asking him questions.

We were teammates for seven years on the Canadiens. And we spent time together year-round: in the winter on the ice, and during summer in parks, since the Canadiens had a softball team. We enjoyed a family-type ambiance in those days, and the bonds we forged with our teammates remained. And that's especially true regarding my friendship with Guy.

In a way, you were the one who triggered the salary demands that prompted Guy to threaten to strike. Tell us about that.

In 1978 we were in my car, driving home from a practice, after collecting our paycheques at the Forum.

At that time, we were paid every eighteen days and received ten paycheques a year. Guy opened his envelope and I saw a number: $7,500. I asked him, "What's that? A bonus?" He replied, "No, that's my pay." I was surprised to see that I was earning much more than he was, which was really not right at all.

There were two reasons for that. First, Guy was stuck in a ten-year contract, whereas I had taken advantage of the overbidding that arose from the creation of the World Hockey Association, and so was able to obtain a respectable salary. It must be said that I had someone to take after in regard to obtaining respectable contracts: My father, Émile "Butch" Bouchard, had fought for an NHL players' association. In fact, it was at his Montreal restaurant, during the All-Star break of 1957, that two sworn enemies—Ted Lindsay and Doug Harvey—met with

Dollard St.-Laurent to lay the foundation of our future players' association.

I always said that Sam Pollock had been a bad businessman with regard to Guy's contract. He knew full well he had a franchise player for a long time; there was no need to exploit him as he did. His attitude was, "If you signed, you signed," and he didn't care if Guy was unhappy. Pollock and the general managers of his era had learned how to manage during the economic crisis and they had not changed their views on contracts. But that doesn't take away from Pollock's talent for having found a very original way of securing the first draft pick of 1971!

Guy's first agent was Gerry Patterson, who had represented Jean Béliveau. Jean also advised Guy—while still part of the Canadiens organization—and he was accustomed to lower salaries. But when Guy hired a new agent, his situation improved: In Toronto, Jerry Petrie suggested Guy threaten to go on strike, and he signed a better contract.

Have you got some unforgettable stories?

Of course! Once in a while Guy would come over to my place to play poker. But he had no poker face whatsoever—with one glance, every other player at the table knew whether he had a good hand or not. One night, after one of our card games, we'd had a few Brazilian coffees. Leaving my place, he said he would come to my farm to go running the next day. Guy was not a regular runner, but he managed to cover quite a distance in just a few minutes. I followed him in my Jeep as I timed him, laughing. Even though I knew he was very athletic, I still couldn't believe it.

What's more, Guy's intensity was not limited to the ice rink—it was part of everything he did. When he moved to Verchères, he tapped into his Mr. Fixit side, buying all sorts of useful and questionable tools. One day, he had installed a very thick shag carpet on his upper floor and a door was sticking on it. He took some measurements and then removed half an inch off the door. The problem was, he'd sawn off the wrong end—so the door still stuck on the rug but now there was a nice gap at the top!

At the time when Guy announced his first retirement, you were no longer teammates. From a certain distance, how did you see that?

My impression is that in the years before he took the first retirement, his level of play was back to where it was at the beginning of his career. His instincts weren't quite the same. I was playing with the Washington Capitals at the time and I wasn't seeing him as much.

When you're a fraction of a second slower, it's not obvious to the fans in the stands. But on the ice, for the players, it's huge. It messes with your confidence and rattles you. I believe that's what happened with him.

Afterwards, I was surprised and disappointed that he'd taken such an early retirement. I think it was his impulsive side that led him to that decision.

At the time, I was cohosting a radio show on CKAC with Danielle Rainville, *Amateurs de sports*. I thought that at the age of thirty-three, with the talent he still possessed and being in great physical shape, it just didn't make sense. But his game had changed: He often found himself outside of the action, no longer in the mix.

During his first retirement, occasionally Danielle and I would invite Guy to appear on our show. He would comment on the Canadiens' performance with the directness he was known for. The fans loved it.

And then, I was surprised when he returned to the game. But if any player could succeed after such a long absence, it was him.

He was no longer the Guy Lafleur of the '70s, but the contribution he made to the Rangers was worth it. And as for him, he made his peace with hockey.

How did your relationship evolve?

I consider it a privilege to have experienced his best years with the Canadiens. When he was going through a dark time, both personally and professionally, I was in Washington. We reconnected a little during his first retirement, and especially after the final one.

I'm pretty much convinced that all of the former Canadiens players were happy that Ronald Corey and Réjean Houle brought Guy back into the family. I saw him from time to time at the Bell Centre at different events.

In August 2019, we went out for dinner with Yvon Lambert and a few friends—I have a great photo; Guy was beaming! Another time we had lunch with Réjean Houle and Ronald Corey. I was also at his seventieth birthday lunch. Each time, he seemed in pretty good shape. I never could have imagined he'd be gone so soon.

On February 20, 2022, a few weeks before he died, he was suffering enormously. Still, he took the trouble to send me a text message wishing me happy birthday. I've held on to that precious message, of course.

What was his greatest quality?

One quality? It's impossible to choose only one!

The first that comes to mind was how much he loved the fans. I used to call him "La Poune," after a popular Quebec comedienne and humourist who used to say "I love my fans and the fans love me!"

Guy granted respect to the people he met, no matter what they did in life.

I can't speak about Guy without highlighting his strong professionalism. On the ice and in the dressing room, he always showed up. He had a positive influence on his teammates, not so much through what he said, but through his actions.

Another quality: his commitment. Everything he did, he gave his all. I was touched that he continued to support the QMJHL, since my father had contributed to its creation. My father was proud that the Remparts—with Guy leading them—had won the Memorial Cup. He loved Guy for his talent and his passion.

Guy was also unabashedly true to himself. You had to take him as he was. I remember that he was the spokesman for General Motors. He would have been happy for them to loan him a Cadillac, but he was associated with the Monte Carlo brand. He didn't want to drive a Monte Carlo, though, so he loaned the car to one of the Canadiens' trainers, "Boom Boom" Meilleur.

And despite his contract, he continued to drive his black Ferrari.

I will keep myself to five qualities and end by mentioning his ability to focus. When he was talking with a teammate, that was the only person who mattered. When he signed an autograph, he asked for the person's name and paid attention. And when it was time to get some goals, he scored!

What is the most beautiful memory he left behind?

Guy left behind the memory of an ordinary superstar. Everywhere, in all kinds of circumstances, people encountered a superstar who related to them. It's why the public was so shaken in the days following the announcement that he'd died. He left us the memory of a man who was real.

Scotty Bowman

Born in Verdun, Quebec, in 1933, William "Scotty" Bowman became the head coach of the Montreal Canadiens in 1971–1972, the season Guy Lafleur started in the NHL. Bowman coached the team for eight seasons. Together, they won the Stanley Cup five times. In the history of the NHL, Scotty Bowman is the coach who has had the most wins in the regular season (1,244) and in the playoffs (233). As well, his name has been engraved on the Stanley Cup more times than any other: nine times as a coach, five times as an executive.

What is your oldest memory of Guy Lafleur?

I didn't see him play on the Quebec Remparts, since I was in St. Louis with the Blues. Claude Ruel and some other Canadiens scouts went to see him regularly. Claude told me a lot of good things about him when I came to the Canadiens, just ahead of the 1971 draft. It was a deep draft that year, with Marcel Dionne, who went to Detroit; Jocelyn Guèvremont to Vancouver; Gene Carr to St. Louis; Richard Martin to Buffalo, among others.

I remember on the day before the draft, Sam Pollock organized a meeting with "The Professor" Caron, Éric Martin, Claude Ruel, and a few other scouts. Al MacNeil was there, too—he'd been behind the bench for the Canadiens' previous season—and me, his successor. Their opinions were divided between Dionne and Lafleur.

In the end, Pollock put his trust in Claude Ruel's opinion. But he would have liked to have drafted Dionne, too, so he approached Ned Harkness, Detroit's general manager. Harkness considered a transaction that would have seen the second draft pick go to Montreal in exchange for an established defenceman like Jean-Claude Tremblay or Terry Harper, along with the forward Mickey Redmond. In Pollock's mind, bringing together Lafleur and Dionne would have created a new version of the Béliveau–Geoffrion duo that had brought so much success to the Canadiens. However, the Red Wings didn't fall into the trap.

The first time I saw Guy play was during the 1971 training camp. There was enormous attention from the media and the fans; he'd been the NHL's top draft pick and he came along just after Jean Béliveau took his retirement.

The fans imagined that he'd become a "new Béliveau" overnight—which was impossible in our situation. Also, they were comparing Guy's ice time and statistics to what Marcel was doing in Detroit. It didn't hold up. One was trying to break into a team that had just won the Stanley Cup, while the other was at the heart of a team doing a big rebuild.

Did he impress you right away? Did you have the sense that he would go on to have the kind of career he had?

There were two players I saw as teenagers who convinced me absolutely that they would be among the greatest in the world: Bobby Orr and Mario Lemieux.

With Guy Lafleur, his statistics with the Remparts made him, at the age of twenty, a high-quality prospect for the Canadiens. But it would take time for him to stand out when we had such depth in all of our positions.

I believe he was a centreman when he joined the Remparts.

Even though we already had Henri Richard, Pete Mahovlich, and Jacques Lemaire in centre, we tried Guy out in that position, which all NHL rookies find difficult. Back then, he had to go against experienced centremen like Phil Esposito for Boston, Bobby Clarke for Philadelphia, Jean Ratelle for New York, and Stan Mikita for Chicago, and try to win face-offs. It was tough. That's why I moved him to right wing.

I heard so much talk about his helmet. The fact that he didn't wear one set him apart for the fans. On top of how he played, his fans loved his unique look with his hair in the wind. The truth was, he started to have success when I made him play right wing. I didn't have time to worry about who was wearing a helmet and who wasn't.

Guy quickly felt comfortable as a winger because he had a special talent for rapidly building up speed. He could score goals and he could make plays. In his third or fourth season, I had him playing with Steve Shutt on left wing and with Pete Mahovlich—and later with Jacques Lemaire—in centre. The rest is history.

I don't think I did as much for Guy as he did for himself to become the exceptional player he was.

As the Canadiens' coach, did you feel pressure regarding how Guy Lafleur was performing?

In those days, and today, too, a head coach in the NHL has to manage the pressure for the whole team and win games. It's not his job to take on the pressure for any particular player—that's up to them—and that's even more true when it's a story the media have created.

Guy was a rookie who achieved very good results on a talented team. He was one element of the total amount of pressure that was on me. No more, no less.

Tell us about Guy as an athlete.

Guy always had the same intensity, as much in practices as in games. Playing hockey was his life, and he took an immense amount of pleasure in it. For the eight years I coached the Canadiens, I don't remember him taking a single day off. He'd often hit the ice a good twenty minutes ahead of his teammates.

One of my favourite moments during practices was to watch Guy—in the days when he was the best right winger in the NHL—playing against a defensive line with Bob Gainey, the best defensive forward in the league, playing left wing. Bob was Guy's shadow. I've had the privilege to coach a number of players with a great work ethic, and those two were among them.

I really liked that Guy always considered two options when he had the puck: shoot or pass. While the goals he scored dazzled the fans, it's easy to forget how good he was at making plays and how generous he was with the puck. If Steve Shutt enjoyed a great career, it's because Guy was always thinking of who had the best chance for the Canadiens to score. A lot of the time, it was him, but very often, it was Shutt or Lemaire.

On the day that Guy surpassed Bobby Clarke as the highest scorer in the league, I offered him my congratulations. He said to me that he didn't care about individual performances. It was true, and it explains why he was popular with his teammates. His leadership came naturally. He just performed.

He had a flair for the dramatic. He had a natural talent and he expressed it emotionally, both on the ice and off.

As a coach, you were known to be hard on your players. You coached some big stars, including Guy, with whom you won five Stanley Cups. What was your relationship like?

I considered it excellent—never mind what players thought about me or said—because I was coaching a group of athletes who had nothing on their minds but winning. And we did win.

With Guy, I didn't have to say anything in particular to motivate him. The source of his motivation came from the ice time I gave him and from the pleasure he got from playing.

At the beginning of his career, it wasn't a foregone conclusion that he'd find himself in the Hockey Hall of Fame and be called the best hockey player in the world in the 1970s. It happened gradually. I'm convinced that it came about thanks to his hard work and also because he didn't act like he was a star. He was one, but he didn't play that up. He was much shyer than people thought. His image was flashy, but he wasn't.

Did it surprise you when he retired the first time?

You have to take a moment to understand the events that led up to that retirement. The team had aged and many of its pillars—Dryden, Lemaire, Cournoyer, Savard, and others—had left. The run of Stanley Cup victories was over. Guy was no longer in his prime period, at the top. That's always very hard for athletes.

Were you surprised to see him don other sweaters besides the Canadiens'—that is, those of the Rangers and the Nordiques?

Yes, I was surprised when he returned to the game. And he did well for himself in New York and in Québec. But he almost wore the sweater of the Nordiques back in 1973.

It was during the playoff finals of 1972–1973, the Canadiens versus the Blackhawks, and Guy's contract was nearly up. Sam Pollock offered him a million dollars for ten years. His agent was Gerry Patterson. It was a lousy contract for Guy, especially in the later years. But he signed it under pressure. Pollock and Patterson would've insisted on the guarantee of payment of a contract from an NHL team rather than one from a league that was just starting up.

The next day, I believe, his father-in-law, Roger Barré—one of the Nordiques' shareholders—came by with a new offer from the team to play in the World Hockey Association. It was a much better offer, but Guy had already signed. He was pretty angry.

Tell us a story.

Before the Canada Cup was held in 1976, Guy had spent the summer partying in celebration of our win of the Stanley Cup a few months earlier. When he arrived at training camp, the medical team was getting all the players to do VO_2 max tests. Believe it or not, Guy had outstanding results. He spent the summer living it up—there was probably some champagne—and smoking. And on the first day of camp, he had the same VO_2 levels as a marathon runner! That guy was not normal.

How did your relationship with him evolve?

We didn't see each other often, but it was always a nice time when we did meet. I have a very beautiful photo that he signed for me and that has a place of pride on my desk.

In 2021, I returned to Verdun—where I grew up—because an arena there had been named in my honour. Guy sent me a text with his congratulations. I wish I could have seen him, but he was already having health problems, so it wasn't possible. We exchanged text messages a few weeks before he died, and those will be on my phone forever.

What is his legacy to the hockey world?

I'm certain that everywhere he played, people appreciated the excitement he created for the fans, and also for the Canadiens' opponents. He was an electrifying player.

As well, his work ethic was just as remarkable. Every player and coach who came into contact with him would say that.

Yvan Cournoyer

Born in Drummondville, Quebec, in 1943, Yvan Cournoyer is a right winger who spent his entire sixteen-season NHL career with the Montreal Canadiens. Nicknamed the Roadrunner, due to his great speed, he won the Stanley Cup ten times. In 1982 Yvan Cournoyer was inducted into the Hockey Hall of Fame, and in 2005 the Canadiens retired his number 12.

As captain of the Canadiens from 1975 until his retirement in 1979, he witnessed Guy Lafleur in his prime.

Tell us about the very first time you met Guy Lafleur.

It was at the Canadiens training camp in 1971. Jean Béliveau had just retired. He had told us that Guy Lafleur was excellent, but I'd never seen him play with the Remparts.

The first day of camp, as soon as he jumped onto the ice at the Verdun Auditorium, I said to my teammates, "That's going to be some hockey player!" And I wasn't wrong.

Our team had won the Stanley Cup the previous season. Even though he was the first draft pick, Guy had to earn his place with us because, back then, only one or two rookies managed to make the team.

How did he fit into your team, with its reputation of being very tight-knit?

It took a little time because he was shy. And also, coming from Québec, he still hadn't got his bearings in Montreal. For me, when I came up to the Canadiens, I'd been playing on the Junior Canadiens; our team practised at the Forum, and I got to rub elbows with the players. It was much easier.

At the beginning, I spent a lot of time with Guy. We would go out to eat—when he wasn't making quick day trips to Québec City. Afterwards, when he got married, he had a house built in Baie-D'Urfé, close to mine, and we went to practices and games together. We always got along well.

What kind of career did you think he'd have?

I knew he'd have a wonderful career, but success didn't happen overnight. It was quite a big step up from the Remparts to the Canadiens, and he didn't get nearly the same amount of ice time as in juniors.

Flower was under a lot of pressure because everyone said he was taking over from where Jean Béliveau left off—that's why he started at centre. But Guy was a right winger, and that's quite different. Our captain, Henri Richard, and I, in particular, were the ones to encourage him a lot during his first years. We helped him to be patient, since the team had some excellent right wingers who'd proved themselves. One day Henri and I told him to just do as he pleased and play the way he wanted. He was sure to help us win, and that would make Scotty happy!

Guy had all the ingredients of success: an athletic build, superb skating, a very good shot, true instinct, and a great work ethic. Finally, everything clicked in his fourth year. The Canadiens became his family and the Forum, his house. He was home.

Up until then, he'd play with his helmet sometimes, then take it off, then wear it again. When he finally decided not to wear it at all anymore, he felt more at ease, with his hair flowing in the wind. And the fans loved him even more because he was truly spectacular.

Tell us about him as a teammate.

Guy didn't talk much. He expressed himself by how he played and contributed to the team's success.

He never trained in the summertime. Of course, training wasn't customary in the NHL, the way it is today. Guy once told me he had a stationary bike—and he used it to hang clothing on!

And as a man, what was he like?

He always had to be in motion!

He almost always had a meeting scheduled after practices, often to do an ad or to support a cause.

When he *really* retired, he had restaurants and became a helicopter pilot. Then he launched his wine, gin, and vodka. He set big challenges for himself, which kept him stimulated.

For a guy as active as he was, it made no sense for him to stop playing at thirty-three. One day, I made a phone call to find out what was going on with the new retiree. He said, "Well, today I washed my car—three times!"

Guy liked to play hockey! He would have loved to play hockey twelve months a year and he never would have retired if that had been possible. He was very happy when he was on the ice. I knew very much where he was coming from: After I hung up my skates, it took me at least a year and a half until I was able to watch a Canadiens game. Before that, I'd cry—because I still wanted to be playing with my teammates.

Were you surprised the first time he retired?

No. Guy retired when Jacques Lemaire was the coach. He wasn't happy with his ice time or the new style of play. For an instinctive player like Guy, it wasn't working out. He was a player who had backbone, and he told the newspapers what he thought.

He didn't believe in half measures: It was "either play me a lot or I won't play anymore." And with the Canadiens, not with anybody else. I don't believe he wanted to be traded.

When I think about it again now, Guy felt alone in the months preceding his retirement. Surely he would have wanted his teammates or former teammates to help him out. His head wasn't in hockey. I don't think anyone intervened.

Maybe he never would have taken such serious action if the Canadiens' upper management had tried to hang on to him. Going through that was one of the saddest periods of his life.

Later, every time I saw Guy in a Rangers or Nordiques uniform, it made me very emotional. While it didn't seem possible that he could be wearing a sweater other than ours, at the same time I saw the very happy Guy I used to know.

And then afterwards, what was meant to happen did happen: He once again became a proud ambassador for the Canadiens to the very end of his life, because the CH logo was always tattooed on his heart.

In your view, was he the world's best hockey player in the 1970s?

No. And I don't say that to take anything away from Guy, who I adored as a player and as a man. For me, there's no such thing as "the best hockey player in the world." Maurice Richard, Jean Béliveau, Wayne Gretzky, Guy—none of them was the best in the world. My whole team was with me when I scored my goals. And it was the entire Canadiens team that regularly won the Stanley Cup, not just one player.

In our dressing room in the '70s, everyone was on the same level. We were a real family—it was incredible. It was like that before Guy played with us, and then he treated all of his teammates the same way, with the same respect. Of course, he was closer to some than others, but for him the Canadiens were a real family, where each person works to help the others.

It was a real love story between Guy and the fans. Tell us about it.

In the history of the Canadiens our fans were very important—both in Montreal and on the road. It was part of our attitude. We signed legible autographs and smiled while we did it. Guy signed more than all the rest of us because he was the most in demand. To the fans, he was the star!

How did your relationship evolve?

We were always very close friends. I don't know how many times I told him, "Flower, stop smoking." My words didn't do any good, unfortunately.

In all the time we were with the Canadiens, as players and as ambassadors, we never needed many words to communicate. Very often, we understood each other with just a look.

Do you think he was happy?

Oh yes, I have no doubt! Guy adored Lise, Martin, and Mark, and he always stayed strong, despite some difficult times. He loved playing for the Canadiens and being an ambassador for the team. And he knew what a privilege it was to be loved so much by the fans, everywhere. As well, he had many wonderful experiences piloting helicopters.

One of his disappointments in life concerned money. He remained bitter over not having been paid what a player of his talent deserved. I think that's why he did all kinds of ads and promotions. His restaurants and other activities were all about putting aside as much money as possible for his family.

How did you react during the time of his illness?

It's always so sad to see our loved ones suffer.

Throughout his career, Guy never had any major injuries the way I did, with my four back operations, the ones on my shoulders and knees, the broken nose, and so on. However, in the last years of Flower's life he was dealing with major problems from inside his body.

If I start to have pain somewhere, I call my doctor right away, without waiting. For Guy, it's obvious that in his last years, he had waited much too long. In fact, it was because he felt pain while he was flying a helicopter that he went to see his doctor, and then underwent emergency heart surgery.

Guy didn't take care of himself. If he had, he could have easily lived to the age of ninety. He probably thought he was invincible.

What were your last moments with him?

During the 2021–2022 playoffs, the Canadiens invited a few former players to attend games and be acknowledged by the crowd. Guy, Patrick Roy, and I were together on one of the nights. Guy left after the second period because his back was hurting him too much. It wasn't like him to leave during an event—especially a Canadiens game. He must have been suffering terribly for him to decide to leave.

It was also striking to see him at his seventieth birthday lunch in September 2021. You could tell he was not in his usual form. It was Guy—but it wasn't Guy.

For the next few months, and right up until the end, I kept up with his news by talking with his son Martin. The teammates who knew more also called me every so often.

When Guy's death was announced and during his funeral, you were quite upset. Can you describe what you were feeling?

It couldn't have been any other way; his family members were crying, his teammates and fans from all over the planet were crying. And I cried, too! I'm still sad because Guy was like a brother to me.

Ever since he left us, I sit down in the evening and smoke a cigar—without inhaling—and I think about him a lot of the time. He's still present in my life because we were close, and also because the media have kept his memory alive. For example, after he died, TVA reran an interview he did several years ago. He told Pierre Bruneau something like, "I've got a lot of things on the go, but when I'm seventy, I'm going to relax." Unfortunately, once he reached seventy, he didn't get to relax.

What is his legacy?

It's simple: Guy was real in everything he did. He made his teammates and his fans proud of his performances. I'm convinced that's why he will never be forgotten.

Élise Couture-Béliveau

Born in Québec City in 1932, Élise Couture-Béliveau is certainly the most well-known Canadiens spouse of all time. For decades, she supported her husband, Jean Béliveau, in his role as a Canadiens ambassador in aid of a large number of charitable causes. She is also known for attending innumerable Canadiens games with him and with their daughter and granddaughters.

When Guy Lafleur first started playing for the Canadiens, he boarded at the home of the Béliveau family.

Tell us about the first time you met Guy Lafleur.

It was the beginning of the fall in 1971. Jean had announced his retirement in June and the Canadiens had drafted Guy as the top pick a day or two after. My husband attended the start of training camp and came home with a proposition for me and our daughter, Hélène: that we take this young man in as our lodger, until he got to know his way around Montreal and find an apartment.

I can still see Jean saying with conviction, his finger waving in the air: "I just saw Guy Lafleur practising. Mark my words, he's going to be quite the player."

Guy had come from Québec covered in glory. But underneath was a shy young man from a good family from the little city of Thurso. Overnight, he was the NHL's top pick. There's no doubt he was aware of the pressure on him when he came to play for the Canadiens. And also, when he had played in Québec, he had chosen my husband's number. He knew very well that those were big skates to fill in the team dressing room.

So we gave him a warm welcome. He was twenty years old and Hélène was fourteen. Suddenly she had a big brother! They squabbled like a real brother and sister, which amused them both. When Guy moved out to his apartment, Hélène missed him very much, and so did I. The house felt empty. Happily, we always kept in close contact.

Our family had gotten bigger at our house for only three weeks. But in the hearts of all four of us, it was bigger for the rest of our lives. Our ties stayed very strong. Jean was always there for Guy. Hélène always considered him her brother. At the Forum and the Bell Centre, Guy would go out of his way to find me so he could give me a kiss!

After Guy's stay with us, I helped him find an apartment in a nearby building in Longueuil. Lise, who was from Québec, was a flight attendant working out of Dorval Airport. She would come to visit him.

Even though he was living on his own, he would still drop by. In the summer, several players and their families who lived in the area would come over to swim: Serge Savard, Jean-Claude Tremblay, Pierre Bouchard, and Guy, among others.

What was he like when he stayed with you?

At first he was timid, and then annoying! He was well brought up, very nice. The first few days, he made his bed and picked up after himself. Then he let things slide—like any young man would, I imagine.

I felt he was more at ease with me and Hélène than he was with Jean. I read somewhere that, after meeting my husband at the peewee tournament, he told his father that one day he wanted to be like Jean Béliveau. And there he was, living under the same roof as the idol of his youth.

Guy very quickly adopted the NHL lifestyle, but in a reassuring environment. I know his parents appreciated knowing he was with us at the beginning.

One morning at breakfast Jean said something to him like, “You'll see, a career goes by fast.” He was probably feeling nostalgic about his own career that had just come to an end. And Guy said something like, “I'm twenty years old—it won't go by that fast.” Once he took his first retirement, and then his second one, I'm sure he realized that his hockey-playing career had indeed gone by very fast.

What kind of relationship did Jean Béliveau and Guy Lafleur have?

Reserved, just like my husband!

When Jean was at home, he was truly present for me and Hélène. But he had an office. When the door was open, we could come in, but as soon as it was closed, we understood. That was where he made and received phone calls.

Jean told players he was their captain during the season, but also for the rest of the year. He listened to them and was always available to give them advice.

There was great mutual admiration between Jean and Guy. But as reserved as Jean was in public, Guy was talkative! There were times when he didn't do himself any favours.

As for me, if I wanted to know what was going on with the Canadiens, I read the newspapers. That's because, for his entire career as a player and later as vice president of the Canadiens, not one time did Jean ever say to me “Guess what happened today. . . .” Never.

So it was through the media that I learned about the times when Guy had put his foot in it with the Canadiens. I guessed that Jean had talked to Guy afterwards and he had listened. I imagine my husband would have reacted differently—but he never let anything slip.

Guy studied Jean, at our house and later on. He dressed stylishly every day, like my husband did. Even when he was going to practice.

Guy was also hugely present for and respectful towards his fans—my husband showed him that it started by saying "Bonjour!" and looking people in the eye, and taking the time to sign legible autographs.

Tell us about the player on the ice.

Oh my God! Guy was very talented. And it was electrifying the way he scored goals with his hair flowing in the wind. The fans in the Forum were crazy for him.

As soon as Guy joined the Canadiens he brought a great energy to the team for many years. All the players and their spouses talked about it after every game. He always gave 100 percent.

But Guy didn't have only happy times . . .

Oh no, unfortunately. And because he was a celebrity, the media were always revealing details about his private life.

When he had his big car accident—with the steel pole that almost impaled him—I was so upset, and all of Quebec was, too. Because he was more than just another athlete. He was "our" Guy.

When one of his sons had problems and Guy defended him, once again it deeply affected everyone in Quebec. We loved Guy the man just as much as Guy the hockey player.

What were your last moments with him?

Guy was a presence in our lives right up until the end. He took an interest in Jean, Hélène, and me. And as for us, Hélène stayed close to Guy and Martin. My daughter and Guy exchanged text messages right up to the end.

Until the end of his own life, my husband would receive up to three big bags of mail a week. Hélène would go to the Bell Centre to collect them and sort through them for him. There were hockey cards, photos, jerseys, and all kinds of objects to be autographed. The mail came from all over Quebec and beyond. There were also many requests for Jean to phone people who were ill, to cheer them up. He did that even when he himself was not doing well.

Guy did that, too. I imagine that Martin had even more mailbags to collect. I know that Guy also called a lot of people to cheer them up, even as the end was approaching. It says so much about the man he was. Everything he did to help the CHUM, it's incredible—especially since he knew that the research would not help him, but instead, the next generation. It's a great credit to him.

What is his legacy?

He was an exceptional athlete, always making himself available for the people who loved him, of course, but for pure strangers, too. I also think his legacy was his humility.

Réjean Houle

Born in Rouyn-Noranda, Quebec, in 1949, Réjean Houle was the top draft pick in 1969, chosen from among all eighteen-year-old French Canadians—a rule that used to favour the Canadiens team, and which no longer exists. Nicknamed Peanut, Réjean Houle played seven hundred games in the NHL and won the Stanley Cup five times.

He would sport the famous CH from 1969 onwards, except for the three seasons he wore the colours of the Québec Nordiques of the WHA. He was the general manager of the Montreal Canadiens from 1995 to 2000 and has been the president of the Canadiens Alumni from 1983 to 1995, and from 2000 to the present.

Réjean Houle was a close friend of Guy Lafleur's.

What is your oldest memory of Guy Lafleur as a teammate?

It was 1971, and Guy had just joined the Canadiens. Even though I was the top draft pick in 1969, for most of my first season I played with the Montreal Voyageurs, in the American Hockey League, before making it to the big team the next year. Guy, as we all know, came right away to our team.

In those days, players stayed two to a room on road trips. The Canadiens paired me with Flower—since we were both young, talented players with ambition, with our whole lives ahead of us. We hit it off right away.

I'll never forget the smiles we had on our faces the first time we set foot in San Francisco. At the time there were only fourteen teams in the NHL, two of them in California. The Canadiens were on a western road trip, and we were staying in the city before we played the Oakland Golden Seals. There we were, two young bucks of twenty and twenty-one, standing on the balcony of a magnificent hotel, looking out on San Francisco Bay and the Golden Gate Bridge. All we could say was, "Can you believe this? Here we are, in one of the most beautiful cities in America, playing for the Montreal Canadiens!"

What did you talk about when you were roommates?

There's a lot I can't tell you! But one thing is this: In his early years on the team, Guy wanted to get more ice time—he'd always had more than anybody else ever since he was in peewee. In those days, the Canadiens had a system of promoting their players in the NHL, gradually increasing the player's ice time little by little. And that's how it was even for the most talented players.

I heard him out. I said, "The team's going to win, no matter how many minutes anyone plays—you, me, all of our teammates. So we make the best of it and learn from what the veterans are doing. We need to be patient. You're going to get more ice time for sure, because the Canadiens know how talented you are." But no matter what I said, the situation grated on him. He felt he was being held back. And no surprise, he did get more ice time.

What kind of career did you imagine he'd have?

As soon as he came to the Canadiens, he was a cut above everyone else. On the ice, he could turn on a dime.

I was convinced he would have an exceptional career. Even during those early years when he wasn't playing much, he racked up around sixty points a season. Not all our players had results like that.

One element that was a big part of his success on the ice was his work ethic. He worked, worked, worked. He succeeded where others weren't able to, because of his outstanding perseverance and his professionalism. He always arrived on time. He was always the first one on the ice at practice and he often stayed afterwards on his own, so he could continue to perfect his shots on goal. On game days, most players arrived at 5:30 p.m. for our 8:00 games. Guy was often in the dressing room by 2:00 in the afternoon, and he spent a lot of that extra time on the ice.

I can still see him coming into the attacking zone during our games. Even he didn't know exactly what he was going to do and the next thing you knew, the puck would be in the net.

When the Canadiens were in the position of protecting a one- or two-goal lead, the other team would start to ramp up the pressure. Scotty Bowman said, "Flower, you take care of the point. Everyone else will take care of the rest. And when we get the puck, they're going to get it to you, and you do what you want with it!"

Tell us about Guy as an athlete.

He was nothing less than a true force of nature.

First of all, there were times when he smoked on the job. I remember vividly that Guy and Larry Robinson would go to the toilets between periods for a cigarette. From where I was sitting in the dressing room, I could see the smoke sneaking out of their little refuge.

Then, before the games, he'd ask our equipment manager, Eddy Palchak, to go and get him a couple of hot dogs. He'd put those away like they were a glass of water. And still he jumped out onto the ice like a rocket, night after night.

During practices when we were struggling a little, Scotty Bowman made us practise our five-on-five offensive. Then, four-on-four. Then, three-on-three. We all found that hard going, and we especially didn't want Guy to make us look bad in front of Scotty. So we'd push ourselves out of the action as much as possible so we didn't have to face him. If Guy were playing today, he'd be pulling off miracles in the three-on-three in overtime.

After the season ended, he didn't train, and he didn't play golf, either. Then he'd come to training camp and be all over the ice from day one.

Guy didn't need to wear a "C" on his sweater to be an inspiration for all of the Montreal Canadiens. I actually think it's a good thing that he was never our captain. It freed him of a great responsibility that would have put more pressure on him. Let's just say he didn't need that.

How was it that Guy became a legend, not just in Montreal but in the NHL and even in Europe?

Star power, charisma, magnetism—there's no explanation. You either have it or you don't. You don't have to look any further for proof than the fact that about ten Montreal Canadiens players in the 1970s were future Hall of Famers, but there was only one Guy Lafleur.

I believe that if Guy became so important in people's hearts—and for Quebecers in particular—it's because they saw themselves in him: At work he gave his all and he also knew how to enjoy life to the max. It was impossible to keep up with him, on the ice or at parties! Being exceptionally consistent and professional, he succeeded where others failed. Even if he'd been partying the night before, he always showed up on time for our practices—and none the worse for wear!

Did it surprise you when he returned to the game?

Yes and no. I found it bizarre to see him wearing a Rangers sweater—and it was probably the same for him. But being back playing in the NHL made him so happy. Michel Bergeron did him a great favour in making a place for him on his teams.

Playing one year with the Rangers and two with the Nordiques enabled Guy to be at peace. He could finally retire at the right time. And afterwards, he was warmly welcomed back into the Canadiens organization.

What kind of ambassador was he for the Canadiens?

He was always helping charitable foundations left and right. He also had a lot of brand associations. No matter where he went, he was seen as an ambassador for the Montreal Canadiens, even during the years when he wasn't officially associated with the club.

He was first named ambassador for the Canadiens in 1984, the year he hung up his blades for the first time. It lasted for about a year. I had taken my retirement in 1983 and was working at the Molson Brewery, so I wasn't following the team's activities on a daily basis. But I remember how shocked the public was when it all ended for Guy.

When I became the general manager of the Canadiens in 1996, I took a few months to familiarize myself with my new role. A few months later, I said to the president, Ronald Corey: "We have to bring Guy back into the fold. He's a Canadien for life." He said yes right away.

Another former player Mr. Corey brought back was Maurice Richard, who'd had his own differences with the Canadiens for a number of years. Jean Béliveau, Maurice and Henri Richard, Yvan Cournoyer, Guy, and I became a team of ambassadors, and we were well received by the fans. It was satisfying to see some other former players take over in the role in 2022: Vincent Damphousse, Guy Carbonneau, Chris Nilan, and Patrice Brisebois.

In the role of ambassador, Guy did everything he could to help the Canadiens, right up until a few weeks before he died.

What was his greatest quality?

His generosity, without a doubt. Whenever a few of us players got together in public, he always made everyone go in front of him so people would see us before they noticed him. Fans would ask for his autograph in a notebook, but then he'd pass it around so we could all sign it. For him, the team always came first, and he wanted the fans to know that.

For Guy, it did him good to do good for others.

People often gave him gifts when he left the ice after a game. He'd come into the dressing room and distribute the items among the trainers: Eddy Palchak, Gaétan Lefebvre, Pierre Gervais, and others. In restaurants or at parties, I cannot remember a single time when Guy did not pick up the tab.

He must have had his faults . . .

He was incapable of saying no. If a stranger spoke to him about a child who was ill, he agreed to place a call or even make a hospital visit.

When he arrived at the Forum, he was always dressed to the nines: a suit, a beautiful shirt, and cuff links. It was important to him. And right after our practices he had all sorts of commitments with charities and companies. His schedule was always way too full.

What were your last moments with him?

Very sad.

He'd have a little less energy from one visit to the next. He had never had breathing problems, but at the end, it was difficult for him. His voice was no longer the same. He was tired of suffering; he decided to go.

We loved him very much, our Flower.

What is his legacy, the most beautiful memory he left behind for the hockey world and for society?

The way he conducted himself on and off the ice.

Not everyone plays professional hockey, but all of us are responsible for how we conduct ourselves. Despite his flaws, Guy was a role model.

For the Canadiens, passing the torch to new generations was always important. I remember public outings where Guy Carbonneau, Vincent Damphousse, Patrice Brisebois, and others found themselves in Guy Lafleur's presence. They took note of the way he interacted with the fans. Flower must have had a positive influence on them, because today it's those former players who have taken over as the team's ambassadors.

Guy Lapointe

Born in Montreal in 1948, Guy Lapointe left an indelible impression on the Canadiens' blue line as a member of the Big Three, with Larry Robinson and Serge Savard. Nicknamed Pointu—in English, "pointy"—he played for fourteen seasons in Montreal before being traded to St. Louis and then to Boston. A creative player, he was also known as an inveterate prankster. A member of the Hockey Hall of Fame since 1993, he had his sweater retired in 2014. His name has been engraved on the Stanley Cup six times.

Guy Lapointe was close to Guy Lafleur up until the very end.

What is your oldest memory of Guy Lafleur?

It was the autumn of 1971, when he arrived at the Canadiens' training camp. I'd started my career with the team the year before, and I hadn't seen him play in juniors. But I'd heard about how talented Guy and Marcel Dionne were. Since Sam Pollock had negotiated to get the first draft pick from the Oakland Seals, it was obvious that one of those two would be joining the team to take over for Jean Béliveau at centre.

Tell us about the first time you met him.

When he first arrived at training camp, Guy was wearing a round helmet with three holes on the top—it looked like a bowling ball. It took us only a few minutes to see that this was no bowler, but a very special hockey player, who represented the future of the Canadiens.

Guy was already serious, in his element. His work ethic was NHL-level. Even though he was shy, he fit in very well with our family of players.

What kind of career did you imagine he would have back then?

Honestly, I did not imagine at first that he would become the best hockey player on the planet during the 1970s and early '80s. A superior player? Yes, but not beyond that.

The thinking in Montreal was that rookies had to start at the bottom of the ladder. And almost all of the Canadiens players of my era had played in the minor leagues—they used to call them farm teams—before coming up to the big team. Guy came to the Canadiens right away, but he didn't get to play as much as he wanted since, despite Jean Béliveau's having left, the team had a lot of offensive depth. Still, he scored twenty-nine goals in his first season. For his first three seasons, he accumulated 64, 55, and 56 points. And then in his fourth year, he exploded, more than doubling his production. And he continued to improve on his record.

Often, talented young players don't put in more work than they have to. And there are others who have less talent, but who work like a dog in practices and games. If Flower had an exceptional career, it was because he did whatever he wanted to do on the ice—truly anything he wanted!—and he was a machine in our practices and games.

There's one thing I'm convinced of: Flower contributed to the success of the Canadiens as a team, and also to propel the careers of the players, coaches, and staff of the team. And I benefited just as much as anyone. Going on the attack from the blue line works out pretty well when you are part of Guy Lafleur's team for eleven years!

What was he like on the ice?

In my day, players hardly trained at all off the hockey rink. In the summer we played softball. The team would mail us a printout with a few recommended exercises. It's a complete contrast to the super well-equipped gyms we have today and the players who stay in top form twelve months a year.

And so, when we arrived at training camp, we had to get back into shape in four or five tough weeks. We had all put on seven or eight pounds, sometimes more. At every camp, there was one player who'd done nothing all summer—except a little waterskiing—but who jumped into his skates and gave the impression that the last season had never ended: And that was Flower! Just one practice and he was ready to start the season.

At training camp and practices the players were divided into two groups to scrimmage: the reds and the whites. Guy was continuously pushing to get possession of the puck. With his intensity level, he might as well have been in game seven of the Stanley Cup playoffs.

Physically and mentally, Guy Lafleur was out of the ordinary. He had to be, to be able to come back to the game at the age of thirty-seven, after a nearly four-year absence from the NHL, and to get forty-odd points, despite injuries.

What was he like as a teammate?

Guy was motivated for every game. It didn't matter whatever bad thing might have happened in his life that day, he'd be the first one in the dressing room, where he would relax and get focused.

He was a simple guy. Humble. Friendly. And very generous. One of the boys. He always gave his all to the team, so we could win. Whenever a trophy was given out for an individual performance—the Conn Smythe, for example, given to the most valuable player during the Stanley Cup playoffs—he always said it was an award for the whole team. Because without the team, he couldn't have won it.

He wasn't our captain, but he was a leader who inspired our entire team. He valued every player. And even though he was always very busy with all sorts of activities off the ice, he was available to lend a hand to his teammates, whether it was to do with hockey or their personal lives.

In the 1970s, your games in Boston and Philadelphia weren't exactly a walk in the park. Tell us about that.

It was our job to go and win games. Everywhere. Simple as that. Win, win, win—that was in the Canadiens' DNA. In 1976–1977, we had 60 wins, 8 losses, and 12 tie games for 132 points. And yet, after each loss, you could have heard a pin drop in our dressing room.

Whether it was in Philadelphia, Boston, or anywhere else, no one could intimidate Flower because the whole team was there to protect him. It was clear in his mind that, above all, he was there to score, and not only with his stick—it was also by dominating our opponents psychologically.

In the Stanley Cup Final against Boston in 1977, John Wensink and Mike Milbury were the Bruins' two most intimidating players. They threatened to rip Guy's head off in Boston Garden. His first reply was a death stare, which he followed up with two goals and two assists. And then we won the Cup!

Tell us about how he was with the fans.

I've never seen an athlete give as much time to his fans, in Montreal or anywhere else.

On road trips, there was always a bus to take players and staff from the hotel to the arena, and from the arena to the airport.

I can't remember a single time the bus was able to leave right away, because we always had to wait for Flower.

When we were playing at the Forum in Montreal, the players had to park their cars on the other side of Sainte-Catherine, at the Alexis Nihon Plaza, and then walk across the street. For Guy, it could take him forty-five minutes to cross the street!

One reason it took him so long was that Jean Béliveau taught us how important it was to respect the fans. One of the ways to show that was by taking the time to sign autographs that were legible. On a day when the veteran player was with me, I was tired and had quickly scribbled my autograph for a fan. Seeing that, Monsieur Béliveau put his hand on mine and said, "Take your time. They deserve for you to take time to write your name so they will feel proud looking at it." I never forgot that. I'm sure that Guy, who was very heavily influenced by him, learned that life lesson in the same way.

Everywhere we went, Flower was the big star people wanted to meet. The fans often wore Canadiens caps or had brought a pennant to be signed—this was back when fans weren't able to buy NHL team jerseys like they can today. The fans were very proud to meet Guy, and he was happy to meet them as well. Taking a photo wasn't the simple affair that it is with today's cell phones. Sometimes, the fans would have a Polaroid camera or a little apparatus with a flash cube. A simple autograph on a scrap of paper would make them happy.

When it came to the fans, for Guy the word "no" did not exist. It seemed he needed his daily dose of interacting with them.

Tell us some unforgettable stories.

I always loved to play pranks on people. And I even liked to play them on Guy.

He was meticulous in everything he did, and in particular

when it came to his ritual of taping his sticks. It was something he did in the afternoon of game days, having arrived early in the dressing room. But as soon as his back was turned, I'd steal the tape. When he would realize it was gone, it was always the same suspect he called out. "Come on, Big Nose—I know it was you!" I would play innocent, but he didn't believe me.

Guy was a unifier, and there was a very particular thing he would do. Right before leaving the dressing room for a game, players usually have their heads down, visualizing how things are going to go. Before certain important games, Flower would get up quietly and, with all his might, bring his stick down on the table in the middle of the room, making all the players jump. And then he'd say, "Let's go, we're gonna go out there and win it!"

Whenever I wanted a little boost before a game, I'd leap out onto the ice behind Flower. As our fans screamed "Guy! Guy! Guy!," I pretended they were shouting for me. It gave me the momentum I needed!

What was his greatest quality?

Only one? It's not an easy choice, but let's go with his kindness. Everywhere we went, whether it was any of the NHL cities or at home in Montreal, I would hear people saying, "He's so nice and so approachable!" In Edmonton, Calgary, and Vancouver, he was more popular than their local stars. Wherever we went, we'd see fans wearing Canadiens jerseys with the number 10.

What were your last moments with him?

A few years ago, when I learned that I had cancer, Guy quickly found out and he phoned me. He regularly reached out to get my updates and give me encouragement.

And then, a few months later, it was his turn to receive a

cancer diagnosis. We became even closer; we each knew what the other was going through.

What is his legacy, the most beautiful memory he left behind for the hockey world and for society?

Before we knew each other, Guy and I shared the same dream: to play for the Canadiens. And we both had the same idol, Jean Béliveau. We dreamed, and we dreamed some more—and we played with Monsieur Béliveau and the Canadiens.

The right to dream is one of Flower's legacies. Through his perfect performances on the ice, he passed the dream on to the entire population of Quebec and all over the world. He also passed the dream on to boys and girls everywhere to keep pushing their limits, to take on all kinds of great challenges.

Guy Lafleur left us the possibility of dreaming to always do better. And he showed us that even the wildest dreams can become a reality.

Peter Mahovlich

Born in Timmins, Ontario, in 1946, Peter Mahovlich is a centre who played for sixteen seasons in the NHL, nine of them with the Canadiens. Nicknamed Little M, he won the Stanley Cup four times with the Canadiens, including two times with his brother, Frank, a.k.a. Big M.

The 1974–1975 season was a defining one for the veteran, when he was paired with two line mates who both took some time to make their presence felt: Steve Shutt and Guy Lafleur. That season, Shutt scored 30 goals and Lafleur scored 53. Mahovlich was no slouch himself, with 35 goals and a remarkable 82 assists—a team record that he holds to this day.

What is your first memory of Guy Lafleur as a player?

My oldest and most beautiful memories of Flower didn't happen during games.

Guy came to Montreal in 1971 at an interesting time: Our captain Jean Béliveau had just taken his retirement, the Canadiens had won the Stanley Cup a few months earlier, and Scotty Bowman was our new coach. Even though he was shy, Flower had to fit into our very close-knit group.

When I think of him, I can still hear the beautiful sound of his skates on the fresh ice. There was nothing Guy loved better than to be the first one out there. Before practices and games, long strides fed the kick of his skates and powered his first shots onto the boards. Even when he was very young, he set the pace, and everyone else had to catch up to him.

I've known some very good hockey players who considered it "going to work." Guy Lafleur didn't make hockey his "work"—neither did I, for that matter. He was a real hockey player. And a player plays. His enthusiasm was a product of the pleasure he took from playing, from having fun, despite all the serious work he put in to become a cut above the rest.

Tell us about his beginnings with the Canadiens and how he developed as a player.

He started with us as a centre. But Henri Richard, Jacques Lemaire, and I already played that position, so Scotty had him play right wing. And then one day, he brought us together: Steve Shutt on left wing, Flower on the right, and me at centre. The three of us had chemistry right away. That was the beginning of his breakout.

It was great how our three very different personalities complemented each other, just like our playing styles. I was certainly the most extroverted. The oldest, the biggest, the toughest, and also the one who had the most experience in the NHL. There were times I could calm both of them down with just a comment or a look.

For me, as a centre, I had great options: pass the puck to Shutty, who was an impressive goal scorer, or to Guy, who skated like a dream, and who loved to throw the other team's defence off-balance. Our trio stayed intact for a good three years.

Starting in 1975–1976, Scotty had Jacques Lemaire as the centre with Flower and Shutty. He had me playing between Yvon Lambert and Murray Wilson because he wanted a centre with my style of play to balance out his lines.

In 1976, Shutty, Flower, and I had another terrific adventure when we all played together at the Canada Cup.

What was he like as a player?

In day-to-day life, Flower was an introvert—that is, a reserved guy with a deadpan sense of humour, like my brother, Frank. But on the ice, no one was more extroverted than he was.

He worked very hard, and he was strong. His legs and arms gave him the explosive force behind all the plays he made: his skating, his strides, and his powerful shots.

I would often begin an attack in our zone by passing the puck over to Flower, and he'd go on a breakaway to score. It helped my stats, even though I hardly had time to go past the red line.

Flower was more than just an exceptional scorer. He was also excellent at making plays and passed very quickly and accurately. Look at his NHL statistics—he has far more assists than goals, and actually holds the career record for assists with the Canadiens.

In his mind, Scotty's game plan was . . . for other people! He played the Guy Lafleur way—that is, mostly by trusting his instincts. During a game he might give the impression he was improvising but, in reality, he was reproducing shots from impossible angles that he had perfected during practices when he hit the ice forty-five minutes or an hour before the rest of us.

What was he like as a teammate?

An excellent teammate, committed to the team and respectful to each one of us. The kind of teammate anyone involved in team sports would want. Guy influenced us all by having the attitude of a winner and a warrior.

For big guys like me, it was demanding to go against the Bruins and Flyers on their home turf, at the Boston Garden or the Philadelphia Spectrum, because they had very rugged teams. I always thought it had to be worse for the guys who weren't so big. There was one thing you could count on: There were at least two Canadiens that our adversaries targeted to try to slow them down: Shutty and Flower. Neither was at all intimidated by the size of their opponents. In fact, it drove them to perform.

You talk a lot about Scotty Bowman. What was it like to play under him?

It was an intense and unforgettable experience playing for Montreal in the 1970s. We were a war machine, designed for winning, with Bowman on top. He gave us a hard time, and he infuriated us because he was so demanding, during both practices and games. I think all the players at some point believed that Bowman hated them personally.

Several years after I'd retired, I realized two important things. First, Scotty wasn't heading up the Canadiens so he could win a popularity contest, but instead, to win the Stanley Cup. And second, I understood that he loved me. He loved Flower. He loved his players. All he wanted was victory.

I had the privilege of winning the Stanley Cup my very first year with the Canadiens, in 1971. Then Scotty and Guy came on board and together, we won it in 1973, 1976, and 1977. I participated in so many victory parades on Sainte-Catherine Street, sitting in convertibles, that I knew the signs of the stores, restaurants, and bars by heart.

Tell us about the athlete with the fans.

Flower was the most generous with his time of any athlete I've ever known. And I'm convinced that no other person since him has had such patience. He picked that up by being around three of the greats: Maurice "Rocket" Richard, Jean Béliveau, and Henri Richard.

It was amazing to see how much the fans worshipped him, even though he was a very humble guy.

What was his greatest quality?

Everything he said came from the heart. I couldn't tell you how many times he made things uncomfortable for team management with his statements—but he took responsibility for what he said. And he spoke out on behalf of the team, not for his own personal gain.

It was a good thing for him that he wasn't captain. It would have put an extra weight on his shoulders, and he already had enough to deal with.

He must have had his faults . . .

His greatest fault was smoking. Him and his damned cigarette! Flower smoked probably two packs a day. It was obviously the cause of his lung cancer and all of the other health problems he had.

What were your last moments with him?

In the last years when he still was healthy, one of the times we'd regularly see each other was the annual golf tournament that Serge Savard organized at the Mirage Golf Club. It was really good to see Guy in great form, always with his dry sense of humour.

Later, I heard what was going on with him, and I cried. I couldn't believe Flower had such serious health issues.

Our last moments didn't go the way I would have wanted at all. During the last six months of his life, I went to Montreal three times. But each time, we weren't able to see each other, either due to COVID-19 or because of his state of health during my visit. We had to say goodbye at a distance, which is a terrible thing to do when you are close to someone.

How did you react when you heard he'd died?

I was at home in Florida. Since I'm an early riser, I found out the news via the media—so before I had any calls or texts from former teammates. It destroyed me. I went back to bed, not wanting to face the day.

In the hours and days that followed, I talked to many former players who were also very upset. And then I jumped on a plane to attend his funeral.

What is his legacy, the most beautiful memory he left behind for the hockey world and for society?

He was Guy Lafleur. Nothing less. That's what he left us.

Larry Robinson

Born in Winchester, Ontario, in 1951, Larry Robinson played for seventeen seasons on the blue line for the Canadiens, including as part of the Big Three with Guy Lapointe and Serge Savard. The name of the man they called Big Bird is engraved six times on the Stanley Cup, along with those of his Canadiens teammates. He is the holder of a mind-blowing record with the Montreal team, playing in 203 playoff games.

Larry Robinson was a mentor for Guy Lafleur and his confidant when he announced his retirement.

What is your oldest memory of Guy Lafleur?

We knew each other in peewee. Our teams from Thurso, in Quebec, and Russell, in Ontario, used to play each other in regional tournaments once in a while. To go from one small city to another, we would cross the frozen Outaouais River.

After that, we lost touch. Guy played at the junior level in Québec City, and I was in Brockville and Kitchener. Fortunately, the Canadiens drafted us both in 1971: him first, me twentieth. That year the Canadiens had six out of the top twenty-six draft picks, including Murray Wilson.

The Canadiens were spoiled for choice between Marcel Dionne and Guy Lafleur as the successor to Jean Béliveau. But the shoes of the great Jean were not easy for his successor to step into. It didn't take long for Guy to feel the pressure.

Tell us about your early days on the team with Guy.

It was sensational. The team had just won the Stanley Cup. It was obvious from the first day of training camp that Guy would stay with the team. We were all impressed by his skating and his devastating shot.

As for me, I went to the farm team, the Nova Scotia Voyageurs, for one and a half seasons before the Canadiens called me up. I was paired defensively with Jacques Laperrière for about two years, and then was part of another duo for seven unforgettable years with Serge Savard.

Guy and I quickly developed a strong relationship, even though our personalities were very different. As a player he was very intense, a bundle of nerves. Sometimes he smoked between periods, along with Chris Nilan, Mario Tremblay, and others. And even though I didn't like the taste of cigarettes, occasionally I went and took a few drags with those guys to calm myself.

We liked having Guy as a teammate: He had both a remarkable work ethic and was also friendly and funny. For all of my years as a player and a coach, I kept company with some exceptional athletes—particularly Wayne Gretzky and Mario Lemieux. Every era has its superstars. If it were up to me to choose an athlete of the 1970s to build a team around, it would be Flower.

Tell us about the player on the ice.

That's easy—he was always on the ice!

When we had our practices, he'd jump onto the rink twenty or thirty minutes ahead of the rest of the team. He had time to take a hundred, maybe two hundred shots. He was recording in his mind the trajectory of the puck if he did this or that movement, from this or that point on the ice.

During the games, from all sorts of angles, he put into action what he had practised—but this time, under pressure. Mike Bossy, Wayne Gretzky, and Flower managed to put almost all of their shots into the net. If they didn't score on the first try, it was much easier for them or their teammates to recover the puck and finish the play.

It didn't take long for the whole team to understand that Guy would not play according to an established game plan. Following steps A, B, and C was not his style. And when you wanted to pass the puck to this particular right winger, you couldn't presume that he'd be on the right wing. You always had to keep your eye on Guy because he had figured out how the play would evolve. And he could sniff out an opening—a breach in the opponent's defence—before anyone else.

One wonderful ability Guy had was receiving the puck a teammate passed to him—not just on the blade of the stick, but just about anywhere around his body and his skates. He'd pick it up in a fraction of a second, in all sorts of ways—with two hands on his stick, or just one; at his side or behind him—and then off he went, like a rocket, his hair flowing behind him.

What kind of athlete was he?

He was a talented athlete, like each of the members of the Canadiens family. Because that's what we were: a family.

Guy probably stopped growing while he was in juniors. Then he put on muscle mass with the Canadiens by running outside, by skating, and practising shooting. His arms, legs, and cardio were all solid.

Flower's role was to score goals, and to help his line mates score, too. You never had to say, "You protect Flower and I'll take Shutty." It was a given that the big guys among us—Rick Chartraw, Gilles Lupien, Pierre Bouchard, myself, and later, Chris

Nilan—would make ourselves known to any opponents who imagined they were going to intimidate our best scorers.

I remember an afternoon game we played at the Forum in the '70s against the Flyers. A bench-clearing brawl had broken out on the ice just as I was headed to the infirmary because I had something in my eye. My teammates yelled, "Larry! Larry!" I quickly went back out on the ice, took a look around, and saw that only two players weren't part of the brawl: Guy and the tough guy Dave Schultz. So I headed straight for Schultz and we started fighting. I wanted to make sure he didn't go after Flower.

Guy was very much in demand off the ice—were you aware of it?

Yes, very much so. Guy's love for his fans was as immense as the love they had for him. Wherever we were, whether it was in Montreal or on the road, fans of all ages were waiting for him. He had enormous patience with them. And it helped us, his teammates, to work on our own patience—because we were always having to wait for him. He couldn't go anywhere without being recognized.

Guy was also in high demand by businesses who wanted to be associated with his image, whether they were brands of cars, clothing, or food. While his teammates were getting their rest, Flower would be at an ad shoot, doing promos, and so on.

Tell us what was going on behind the scenes when he left the Canadiens.

The situation had changed: Scotty and certain key players had left, Jacques Lemaire became our coach, and the players who remained—like me and Guy—were no longer the workhorses we once were. We were still good players who could still help our team, but we were getting less and less ice time.

Jacques and Guy were my friends. I knew them well and I understood where each was coming from: One wanted to establish a structured game system and the other wanted to play as freely as he always had. There was a huge gulf between the two of them. But even though Flower wasn't happy, he trained as seriously as ever.

I believe that Guy consulted Jean Béliveau before taking his retirement. Obviously, I was surprised when it happened. After a game we played at the Forum, he took me aside to tell me he probably wasn't going to be on the plane with the team for our next game.

Since you went from being a player to becoming the coach of the Los Angeles Kings, it might be easier for you to put yourself in Jacques Lemaire's shoes.

Yes. Hindsight helps, too. With the Kings, first I was Wayne Gretzky's teammate, and then his coach. When I was named coach, he and I had a discussion about his style of play and about the game system I wanted to set up. Wayne had to realize that both he and I wanted the team to succeed, but he wasn't surrounded by the same players as before.

A similar thing happened between Lafleur and Lemaire. In both instances, there was a coach who wanted to make a change to realign the team and a star who wanted to keep on playing the same way he always had.

Were you surprised by his return to the game in 1988?

Yes and no. Yes, mostly because you need to be in very good physical shape to allow yourself to even consider the possibility, and then to pull off a return to the NHL after such a long absence. No, because this was Guy Lafleur—and hockey was still coursing through his veins.

After wearing a Canadiens uniform for seventeen years, I played for three seasons with the Kings. I remember the precise moment when I first put on the new uniform. It was truly bizarre. I also remember the first time I came to the Forum with the Kings. The fans were incredible.

I imagine that Guy had the same kind of feeling the first time he wore the Blueshirt. And he never forgot how the Montreal fans reacted after he scored two goals against the Rangers when he came back home. And that night he even scored one of those goals against me.

For both Flower and for me, to enter the Forum by a different door than usual and to sit on the visitors' bench was . . . strange. I had to remind myself to focus so I wouldn't head to the Canadiens' bench during shift changes. But in my case, I'd been happy to go to Los Angeles to end my career; for Guy, his departure had been a bitter one. And he was already in the Hockey Hall of Fame! He must have had some very mixed feelings.

Were you and Guy very close?

Oh yes. Ever since we both came to the Canadiens. We had shared values, which helped to bring us closer.

We also both had the same way of analyzing the business side of professional hockey. That was why we decided one day to join forces. At the end of the 1970s, the government of Canada changed its tax deferral program for professional athletes. Before then, it had allowed athletes to spread their salaries over several years in order to be taxed on a smaller amount earned during a season, and to receive the balance upon retirement, when income would be lower.

Before the start of the 1981–1982 season, Guy and I wanted to review our contracts so the Canadiens' organization would take into account this new rule that was penalizing us. He came over to my place to discuss the details with Norm Kaplan, a lawyer, and we worked on our arguments until late that night. Our agents communicated our request to the Canadiens' management, but there was no follow-up from them.

Guy and I remained close, even though we didn't talk on a regular basis. In the last years when he still had his health, we participated in a few promotional activities together, including one for the Montreal Playground Poker Club in Kahnawake.

One time, Guy and I had been invited to an NHL activity, and he came to pick me up in a helicopter, along with his friend Rob MacDuff. What struck me—but didn't surprise me—was that Flower was just as perfectionistic and impressive at the controls of a helicopter as he was during a Canadiens game. I had complete confidence in him.

Tell us an unforgettable story.

In the middle of NHL dressing rooms there was a big table where there'd be orange juice, towels, pucks, etcetera. In the final minutes before the start of a game, the room would go quiet, with each player in his own bubble. Once in a while, Guy would get up slowly, take his stick, and bang it down on the table with all his might, startling us all. He would yell out a battle cry, and the room would be jumping again.

He wasn't our captain and yet it was one of the ways he displayed his leadership. Usually he'd yell, "Come on, guys. Let's go!" and say something like, "We didn't feel like going to school? Well, then, we better go play hockey!"

What was his greatest quality?

His big heart. Guy was generous, both in terms of how he spent his money and also the way he gave quality time to the people around him. He devoted himself to the fans, his team, the NHL,

Canada, and numerous causes in the community. His main fault was not knowing the definition of the word "no"!

Tell us about your last moments together.

We spoke on the phone about a week before he was admitted to a palliative care home. He tried to act as if he was in great shape, but I knew that he was going downhill. And he knew it, too, I'm sure. I preferred to say goodbye over the phone and to keep my memory of the strong, muscular athlete I'd played 918 games with. For his own sense of pride, it was better that way, too.

Ever since he died, I've felt a huge void, similar to what I've experienced since the death of my brother fifteen years ago. I want to wake up from the bad dream, but I can't. The people we're close to always leave us too soon.

The Canadiens let me have the privilege of paying tribute to him at his funeral. It felt natural to speak both in French and English since, for the seventeen years that my family lived in Montreal, my wife and kids and I were influenced by the francophone culture. At the end, I added a touch of humour, which Guy would've loved. I said that heaven had just added Guy Lafleur and Mike Bossy to its hockey team, and that it was my hope and my prayer that they weren't looking for a big defenceman just yet.

What do you believe is Guy Lafleur's legacy?

Flower was someone who inspired people of all ages and well beyond his performances on the ice. Everyone felt good around him because he was a real person.

Serge Savard

Born in Montreal in 1946, Serge Savard grew up in Abitibi. He made his debut on the Canadiens' blue line in 1966 and had a consistent impact there until 1981, notably as part of the Big Three with Guy Lapointe and Larry Robinson. Savard, nicknamed the Senator, ended his playing days with the Winnipeg Jets.

It was under Savard's leadership, as general manager of the Canadiens, that his former teammate Guy Lafleur announced his retirement in 1984. Even though there were hard feelings at the time, they ultimately reconciled.

Serge Savard won the Stanley Cup ten times with the Canadiens—eight times as a player and twice as GM, in 1986 and 1993. He was inducted into the Hockey Hall of Fame in 1986. In 2006 his number 18 was retired and raised to the rafters of the Bell Centre.

What is your oldest memory of Guy Lafleur as a player?

I was playing for the Canadiens when Guy was drafted. In those days players weren't chosen from the age of eighteen the way they are now. They had to have finished their time in juniors.

He was already being talked about in the media. He was the best junior player in Canada, maybe in the world. It was known that he'd be joining the Canadiens, and naturally, the whole team was thrilled. It was a new chapter, with Jean Béliveau retiring and Guy Lafleur joining the team. Jean even took Guy under his wing and had him staying with his family for a little while in Longueuil.

There was talk that Guy would take Jean's number 4, since that was what he'd been wearing with the Remparts. I don't remember that Jean was bothered by the idea. But he did tell Guy, "It's not the number that gives you your identity. It's you who makes the number you wear come alive." In those days, everyone's number was below 30, which was reserved for goaltenders. At the beginning of the 1971–1972 training camp, Guy had several numbers to choose from. He took 10, which had been worn by Ted Harris.

Tell us about Guy Lafleur's beginnings with the Canadiens.

He connected with everyone on the team very quickly. We were a close-knit bunch and we always wanted our rookies to integrate well with the group.

Guy was nice but quite reserved. I didn't realize that he was making day trips to Québec City to see his sweetheart, Lise, and his friends—we learned about that from the newspapers. When he drove, it was pedal to the metal—the way he lived his life!—and there weren't too many police officers on Highway 20 to stop him.

In time, he felt more at ease and he loosened up, and then there was no filter. He said some things that he really shouldn't have, but he stood by his words and didn't have regrets. His stature allowed him to make dramatic statements. Journalists would write, "Only Guy Lafleur can say that." And that just encouraged him!

What kind of athlete was he?

Without his rather exceptional work ethic, Guy never would have had such an impact on the NHL. He was a thoroughbred—he never showed up at a game without giving 100 percent.

Even though he hadn't trained at all during the summer, he

would arrive at training camp in great shape. And right up until the last day of the playoffs he was constantly working to improve his shots, whether at practices or during games.

While my teammates and I would arrive for games at the Forum or at arenas on the road at 5:00 p.m., in advance of an 8:00 game, Flower would be on the ice by the middle of the afternoon, and he'd already worked up a good sweat by 5:00. At noon he'd put away up to a dozen eggs and he'd head to the arena with the equipment managers. He didn't take naps. He practised his shots, he tried out dozens of sticks, etcetera. Guy ate, slept, and breathed hockey.

Obviously, every athlete dreams of playing with the best players for many years. Every hockey player dreams of winning the Stanley Cup. Over half of the members of the team Guy was part of are in the Hockey Hall of Fame. But there's a price to pay for that: You can't play all the time.

I find it funny when people say Scotty Bowman didn't play Guy. Just about as soon as he came to the Canadiens he was on the second power play. But in a hierarchical system, Guy had Jacques Lemaire and Peter Mahovlich ahead of him at centre. On right wing, where he was moved to, Yvan Cournoyer and other talented players were already there. It was in that context that Guy had to make a place for himself on the team.

Bowman wanted both to win with the exceptional team he had on his hands and to "build" Lafleur in the same way you'd construct a building: first the foundation, then the beams. When Guy exploded in his fourth year, it was because Scotty had done what he had to do beforehand, in a gradual way.

In those days there was no video analysis of edited sequences of game play. Coaches had videocassettes of entire games, and that was it. As for Guy Lafleur, he used his great sense of observation and his exceptional memory to analyze opposing players and to visualize what he would have to do to fully dominate them.

You were teammates for nine years on the Canadiens. What was he like?

For many years, Guy carried the Canadiens. It isn't necessary to wear a letter on your sweater to command respect. In fact, I don't remember why it was he didn't have an "A." For Guy, the team was sacred. He didn't see himself as the number one player on the team, and in his eyes, there wasn't a number twenty. Everyone was equally important.

In my day, captains were elected by the players. I never understood why management ended this tradition to decide for themselves who the captain would be. Bob Gainey was chosen. Guy probably would have been elected—but there wasn't a vote. When I became the general manager, I decided to give back the choice of captain to the players. Guy Carbonneau and Chris Chelios were elected in a tie.

Would you say the 1970s were particularly hard in the NHL?

Oh yes. The NHL was hard and our division was hard!

We played Boston and Philadelphia a few times a year, and on top of that, the Canadiens also arranged for some exhibition games against them. We hated the Big Bad Bruins. And when we played the Broad Street Bullies in Philadelphia, the benches were cleared every time! The Canadiens had several players who were bigger and stronger than the other teams, including Larry Robinson, Guy Lapointe, Pierre Bouchard, Bill Nyrop, and me. Our game was physical, but not violent.

During our 1976 training camp we went to Philadelphia for an exhibition game. The Canadiens leaned on the farm team, bringing up players like [Brendan] Shanahan, Chartraw, and whatever other muscle the organization had. And we crushed them. That was the end of the Flyers' ability to intimidate us: We didn't lose a single game to them in four years.

In the midst of the rough play, our most talented players had trouble expressing themselves since the rules were barely applied. Tiger Williams, who played for Toronto and Vancouver, could glue himself to Guy along the two hundred feet of the rink and not be penalized.

Even though he didn't fight, Guy wasn't afraid of anybody. He was protected by Pierre Bouchard and others. In his own way, Flower helped change things, making hockey more spectacular and less violent.

What are your thoughts on his career with the Canadiens?

Guy's career had three stages: There were the first three years, the next seven, and the final three.

At the start, his stats were twenty-nine, twenty-eight, and twenty-one goals a season, and a lot of assists. That's very good for a new player. But Guy always wanted more ice time, and he said it to journalists and in the dressing room. I think he'd have played sixty minutes a game if the coaches had let him have his way.

In the dressing room, we asked ourselves the same question that the newspapers kept repeating: Would Lafleur break out, or remain a talented player and nothing more? We all got our answer in his fourth season. From that moment on, he dominated the NHL for roughly seven seasons. He was so dominant you could have awarded him all the individual trophies he'd receive before the season even started.

We had an excellent team, but Guy made all of us better players. More than half of the Canadiens' players from that era would become Hall of Famers. You can put them in two categories: Guy Lafleur, and the rest. Maurice Richard, Jean Béliveau, and Guy Lafleur are the iconic trio of the Montreal Canadiens. It goes without saying. But Maurice and Jean did not dominate the league with their statistics the way Guy did.

Later, he was disappointed with his last three seasons in the NHL, just as he'd been with the first three. He wanted to play more, but he started to perform less well.

When a professional athlete starts to decline, it's because the speed and agility of the hands diminishes. It's a question of mechanics. Hockey is similar to golf in this way: Athletes can still be in the same physical shape, but their hands don't perform the way they used to. Guy had the same skating ability, the same strength, the same energy. But what had changed was his hands—a key element in scoring.

The tying goal Guy scored in the 1979 Stanley Cup Final was an absolutely incredible shot, perfectly placed! But a few years later he wasn't able to shoot with the same precision. When there's a decline, it naturally affects the morale for any player, especially playing at an elite level. That's what happened with Guy.

You were able to see Guy Lafleur's decline and retirement up close.

When I became the general manager of the team in 1983, Bob Berry had just been fired. I would have liked to have given the position of coach to the former player Dickie Moore, with Jacques Lemaire as assistant for one year. Then Jacques would have taken over. But both of them refused to consider that plan. I asked Bob to come back, and he accepted. Then he lost control of his dressing room, and when I fired him, he let out a huge sigh of relief. It was what he'd been hoping would happen.

I had to work very hard to persuade Jacques Lemaire, who had had success as a coach in Switzerland and in Longueuil in the QMJHL, to accept the job as the Canadiens' coach. He knew what kind of pressure came with the territory. When Jacques came onboard, the Canadiens were playing under .500, and he quickly straightened the team out with his game system.

Guy didn't decide to take his retirement on a whim. He came to see me in my office—I seem to remember it was the day before a game at the Forum against Detroit. He was unhappy with the game system that Jacques was putting into place. I remember saying to him, "I'm taking off my general manager's hat and putting on my teammate's hat. What do you want? I've never intervened with a coach but if you want me to, I'll talk to Jacques."

These were Guy's exact words: "If I take my retirement, will you pay out the rest of my contract?" He had two years left. I said to him, "The Canadiens usually pay one additional year of salary at retirement after ten years on the team. But two years would be okay." That tradition ended not long afterwards. Guy replied, "Let me have the weekend to think about it."

After the game against Detroit, Guy decided not to come to Boston with the team. He asked to speak to me and took me by surprise. We agreed to tell journalists that he had a groin injury—we weren't going to say Guy was thinking about retiring.

It was Guy who made the announcement in the Monday *Gazette* before he'd confirmed his decision with me. It was Guy or someone in his entourage, but not me. Guy being Guy, he thrived on big headlines. Obviously, media all over Quebec and beyond seized on the news and the Canadiens held a press conference on the Monday afternoon. There were three of us: Ronald Corey, Guy, and me.

It was his decision, but he wasn't ready to take his retirement. And he regretted it. The mood was heavy; it was a sad ending to a very beautiful era.

He didn't leave empty-handed: I gave him the two years'

salary he'd wanted and Ronald Corey also paid him for his work as an ambassador.

At that time in his life and career, he was tired. In his later years with the Canadiens, he wasn't eating Pablum in the morning, and he wasn't going to bed at 9:00 in the evening. It caught up with him. He wasn't able to accept that even the best athletes in the world slow down eventually.

If you could turn back time, would you have acted the same way regarding the conflict between Lemaire and Lafleur?

With some distance—and it's true for all sorts of situations—it's easy to say, "I could have done this or that." It's like taking an exam with the answer key in your hands. But that's not how life works.

I don't know of any coaches who make decisions so they'll lose. All coaches in amateur and professional sports want to make only the best decisions. But it's impossible. Jacques Lemaire was an excellent coach who made an enormous number of good decisions.

Why did Lafleur leave the organization so quickly after his retirement?

During the press conference, Ronald Corey said Guy would be with the Canadiens "for life." He was named an ambassador, but he had no training for that role. He learned on the job with Claude Mouton, who handled communications and marketing. Guy also participated in a lot of activities with Frank Léveillé and Molson Brewery. One day, Guy told Ronald he had two jobs, and so he wanted two salaries. If that had come to pass, he might have been making more than the club president.

But what really lit the fuse was when he talked to the papers, claiming he was underpaid. He also said he wanted to be the president of the Canadiens within two years. Try to imagine being in Ronald's shoes.

Opportunities in management were pretty rare, and I know Guy would have liked to have been involved in that side of the business. But there was only one coach, not five the way it is today. Video to support hockey management didn't exist, scouts were often part-time volunteers, etcetera.

I regretted not having integrated him into my hockey department. But would he have enjoyed that? Would he have wanted to go watch games in Boston or in Chicoutimi?

What happened next?

After losing his job in public relations with the Canadiens, he came to see me to ask me to trade him.

I told him, "We won't trade a Guy Lafleur just like we wouldn't trade a Jean Béliveau." But he was insistent and gave me a list of six teams that he was interested in. I contacted all of them, and none was interested. I gave the contact information of the six general managers to Georges Guilbault, who took care of Guy's business affairs, telling him he could verify with them. I never heard anything more about it.

Finally, when Guy wanted to return to the game to play for the Rangers, Phil Esposito called me to release the rights for Guy, which the Canadiens still held. Naturally, I agreed.

What were your last moments with him?

In more recent years we spoke on the phone, and right up till the end, we exchanged some heartfelt text messages.

I was invited to a meal to celebrate his seventieth birthday. There were a dozen or so of us former teammates, along with Geoff Molson, France Margaret Bélanger, Martin, and Mark.

I remember a roller coaster of emotions: We laughed as we recalled magical moments we shared, and then Guy talked about his cancer treatments. His tears were flowing, and so were ours. And then someone would tell a story to change the mood and we'd be laughing again. And it went on like that.

Since Guy Lapointe was there, it was fitting that he played a couple of pranks just like in the good old days. So he asked Mario Tremblay, who was more flexible than he was, to crawl under the table and put ketchup on the shoes of a few of the guests. Not on Guy's—and Mario also avoided the suede footwear of Geoff Molson!

What is his legacy?

He made a difference in the lives of a great many people. And in the lives of an entire nation. Guy always gave back—that is his greatest legacy.

In the last year of his life, he founded the Guy Lafleur Fund, which raised millions of dollars for the CHUM Foundation, bringing together personalities from the world of hockey. Even when he was dying, he was phoning donors to thank them. His son Martin is carrying on with the work.

Guy was truly extraordinary, right up until the end. He said, "These new advances in cancer research won't benefit me, but I'm in it to help others." He fought until the end with the same determination he always had on the ice—even morphine was not effective to treat the pains he had in his back. He wanted to keep on living.

Darryl Sittler

Born in Kitchener, Ontario, in 1950, Darryl Sittler was a centre who played for fifteen seasons in the NHL, most of them with the Toronto Maple Leafs, where he was captain. A first-round draft pick in 1970, he has been a member of the Hockey Hall of Fame since 1989.

Darryl Sittler and Guy Lafleur were fierce rivals, but were also teammates during the 1976 Canada Cup.

What is your oldest memory of Guy Lafleur?

We started to play against each other when he came to the Canadiens in 1971. By then I'd been with the Maple Leafs for a year. His talent was undeniable from the moment he arrived in the NHL. He had great intelligence, supported by different skills: his skating and his craftiness, his powerful shot, and his agility. Guy also had an extraordinary passion for hockey, similar to Bobby Orr's.

When he arrived with the Canadiens, he shouldn't have tried to become a second Jean Béliveau. There were already comparisons between the two players, who had been standouts with their junior hockey teams in Quebec. What's more, Guy had worn the number of his idol. It was a heavy burden to carry, since Mr. Béliveau had become an institution in the NHL. Flower had to make his mark in his own way to become Guy Lafleur in the eyes and the hearts of the public. And he succeeded quite well at that.

Tell us about your first encounters with him.

In our day, players rarely met up with their opponents, whether it was during the season or in the summer. And it wasn't uncommon for a player to spend his whole career on one team. They were very tight-knit clans. It explains why the rivalry between Toronto and Montreal, for example, was particularly intense. Even though the NHL welcomed new teams for the first time in 1967, the competition among the Original Six—Toronto, Montreal, Boston, Detroit, Chicago, and New York—was strong.

Guy and I rubbed shoulders during All-Star games and in international competitions like the Canada Cup in 1976. He always played clean hockey, and that was part of what his opponents respected so much. He had been a star in juniors and it didn't take him long to be one in the NHL. Still, he was very humble. One of the boys.

Did you grow up in a family of hockey lovers?

Oh yeah! There were eight of us kids in my family. There was a big hockey atmosphere growing up, always playing it and watching games on *Hockey Night in Canada* in our pyjamas. Even though we lived in Kitchener, my father was a big Canadiens fan. It was no accident that when I was five or six, there was a Jean Béliveau sweater for me under the Christmas tree.

Mr. Béliveau was an idol for Guy, for me, and for a huge number of hockey lovers because he stood out both on and off the ice. I experienced three remarkable moments connected to Jean Béliveau. The first was that magnificent number 4 sweater underneath the tree. I wore it everywhere: to school, at home, and at the rink. I became the "Jean Béliveau of Kitchener." And then, at the age of twenty, I found myself looking into his eyes at centre ice at the Montreal Forum, for the first face-off of a game. At forty, he was very calm—but at twenty, I sure wasn't! And finally, in October 2001, I received a call from Mr. Béliveau after my wife had died, offering his condolences. He managed to find my number so he could provide some support. I was extremely touched.

I often crossed paths with Mr. Béliveau during official activities in the NHL, but that was it. Guy had the privilege of being around him to draw inspiration from his idol's day-to-day life. I still feel envious.

What kind of player was Guy Lafleur?

The trio he formed with Jacques Lemaire and Steve Shutt was one of the most difficult I had to confront in all my career. The dynamic they had, and Guy with his hair streaming behind him—it was a constant threat. Guy, Bobby Hull, and Lanny McDonald, in particular, were able to enter the attacking zone along the boards, fire off a precise shot, and beat the goalie. It was a predictable play, and yet they pulled it off all the time.

I remember, for example, the playoffs of 1977–1978 and 1978–1979. We played against the Canadiens, and both times they beat us before going on to win the Stanley Cup. Guy was a big part of those victories, scoring huge goals against us in those games.

What memories do you have of playing with him in the 1976 Canada Cup?

What an experience! Team Canada training camp was held in Montreal. There were thirty-five players to start with, and twenty-four were chosen to be part of the team.

We were the cream of the crop, but not everyone had the same attitude in the dressing room. For example, the coach,

Scotty Bowman, had me playing on the wing with Bob Gainey on a checking line, even though I was an offensive centreman. I didn't care—because I was part of Team Canada and we were on a mission to win and make our country proud. It was the same for Guy: He would've played any position or worn any number—he was also there to win. And to have fun! But some of the players had more trouble accepting the roles Scotty assigned them, since it meant they might get less ice time than they were used to having on their respective teams.

I always liked to arrive early before games to relax in the dressing room. But during the Canada Cup, I was never the first one there—Flower was there before me.

Tell us an unforgettable story.

In the 1970s, during an intense game—like they all were against the Canadiens—I hit Flower with my stick and broke one of his fingers. I have to say, gloves didn't do a very good job of protecting hands back then. Flower didn't blame me; he knew it had been an accident. And it didn't really slow him down—he came back to the game quickly.

Were you surprised by his retirement? And by his return to the game?

Yes, I was surprised. I retired in 1984–85, just like Guy. The difference is that I didn't change my mind later on! He was frustrated by what he was going through in Montreal.

I know, having lived through it, that retiring is difficult for an athlete. Overnight, everything stops: the discipline to do the work, giving it your all on the ice, the collaboration with twenty guys you appreciate, both in your home city and out on the road. I had prepared myself for that loss; I chose my moment. It was different for Guy.

I was impressed when he came back to play for the Rangers and the Nordiques. I was happy to see him so happy. He was still in excellent physical shape, even though he was a smoker.

How did your relationship evolve?

Starting when he first retired, we played together and against each other in all sorts of games reuniting NHL alumni, all over Canada. He had the same passion and the same work ethic as when he was playing "for real" in the NHL. Guy was at home on the ice and in the dressing room, and he loved to tease his teammates.

Even when he was playing with the Legends, he was still an idol in the eyes of hockey lovers. It was crazy how much time he took to sign autographs and pose for photos with fans. It didn't matter if it was Edmonton and Calgary, where there'd be eighteen thousand people, or in smaller arenas. I don't remember a single place we played where the fans hadn't shouted "Guy! Guy! Guy!" It was automatic, the second he jumped on the ice.

After he retired for good, we played together again with the Legends for several years, and we also ran into each other at various activities organized by the NHL.

I believe the last time we saw each other was in 2016. Canada Post had launched a series of stamps featuring Canadian hockey players. Guy and I had the honour of each being represented on one of the series. We were very proud to attend the unveiling ceremony at the Hockey Hall of Fame.

Afterwards, I heard that he was in failing health. I wasn't a close friend, but I sent him some words of encouragement a few times. Speaking with former players who he'd been close with, they let me know what was going on with him, even when the news was bad.

What was his greatest quality?

Guy was a very responsible man. From the start of his career, he understood that the fans adored him, that the players respected him, and that the media would always want to get his opinion. He was also sought out by everyone in the community. All of that takes time, and his time is what he gave. He carried himself like the idol he became. With humility.

What is his legacy?

Guy Lafleur received the famous torch of the Canadiens dressing room from Jean Béliveau, who had received it from Maurice Richard. That torch is a symbol of a very great organization in the game of hockey, but also very much in the community as well. Guy understood the importance of that great responsibility, and he knew how to carry it to the end of his life.

Ronald Corey

Born in Montreal in 1938, Ronald Corey is a businessman who made his career in marketing before becoming president of the Canadiens from 1982 to 1999. It was during that time that Guy Lafleur had two ruptures with the club: first as a player, then as an ambassador. The Canadiens won two Stanley Cups during Corey's tenure, in 1986 and 1993.

What is your earliest memory of Guy Lafleur?

The first time I saw him play he was with the Remparts. Their coach was Maurice Filion, who I knew fairly well. He became the general manager of the Nordiques a few years later.

And then I remember meeting him, along with the other Canadiens players, in the early 1970s. I was the director of public relations for Molson, and I'd created the Molson Cup to generate visibility for the brand. Players earned points based on the stars they received at the end of games, and whichever player had the most points in a month was awarded the cup. Obviously, Guy earned it several times!

Tell us about the player.

Like all of the fans, I was watching him closely when he started with the Canadiens. His enthusiasm for hockey was what struck me. Guy had one thing in common with his captain, Henri Richard: He would have liked to have spent forty hours a day on a hockey rink. Both of them were truly passionate about their sport. And their involvement with the Canadiens was exceptional. Guy had a fluid skating style, excellent hands, and he was tireless. He was a total athlete, who barely broke a sweat.

What was your relationship like when you became president of the Canadiens? And how did it evolve?

It was excellent. I adored Guy, as a player and as a human being. Like everyone, I saw him slowing down and I knew that it affected him deeply.

I never interfered in hockey management; I gave Serge Savard 100 percent autonomy. But I tried my best to give Guy some encouragement when I saw him—when I went to train in the team dressing room gym, for example.

One day in November 1984, Serge told me, "Guy wants to retire." As the president and as a fan, I would have loved it if he could have played even longer at his maximum ability, but it was no longer possible. So he announced his retirement. After that, I made a couple of mistakes. But thankfully, we had a chance to mend fences during the 1990s and went a long way together from then on.

What do you mean by "mistakes"?

First of all, I should have stuck with my plan to ease Guy much more gradually into his role as ambassador for the Canadiens, by giving him some time to make the transition. But he wanted to start right away. I should have resisted—he was not yet emotionally ready immediately after his retirement.

Second, when he complained in the newspapers that he was being paid like a secretary, I shouldn't have fired him. It would have been better to let the dust settle, explain myself, and be more patient with him.

As president of the Canadiens, I made a lot of decisions,

always in the best interest of the team. Some of the decisions were emotional because I had to terminate people I loved. For example, I dismissed two former athletes and men I loved very much: Guy Lafleur and Serge Savard. I know those decisions hurt both of them, and I deeply regret that.

Fortunately, I was able to bring Guy back to my team, and we worked together for the last five years of my mandate. Over time, my relationship with Serge Savard became harmonious again. I'm very grateful to him for helping to bring about that reconciliation by inviting me to his golf tournament. We had some wonderful moments together, and it's because of him we have our two Stanley Cups.

What did you think of Guy's return to the game after his first retirement?

I was happy for Guy when he returned to the game. Hockey was still in his blood, and it gave him satisfaction.

When he returned to the Forum wearing a Rangers sweater and he scored two goals, it was the first time I ever spontaneously stood up to applaud a player scoring against the Canadiens. The atmosphere was electric.

Then he played for two years with the Nordiques. I found it even more bizarre to see him wearing their sweater than the Rangers'. But it was a homecoming for him—he'd loved Québec in his youth.

I have to mention that Guy did something that very few people would have done in his place a few years after a dismissal: He came behind the Canadiens' bench and shook my hand, on the occasion of his last career game at the Forum. I was very moved by that gesture.

Tell us about his return to the Canadiens after his second retirement.

In 1995, when Réjean Houle was my general manager, he suggested Guy return to the team as an ambassador. I immediately said yes. Guy had ended his second career with New York and Quebec and, along with Réjean, I thought that Guy ought to come back with us.

There was unanimous support for his return to the Canadiens. His endearing personality, his humour, and his love of the fans made him very much appreciated as an ambassador. And after I'd left, my successors renewed the partnership, which lasted over twenty-five years.

When he returned to the Canadiens, he was more ready to assume the role. By the time he'd retired from hockey a second time, he had really matured. He was with me for the last five years of my mandate and it was very pleasant. He didn't have a job in our offices. I created a role that suited him much better, out in the world with the fans. That was where he was most comfortable and at his best.

There were a few appearances in particular that I asked him to make. For instance, public hearings were being held when the Canadiens wanted to build a new amphitheatre in downtown Montreal. I asked Maurice, Jean, and Guy to come with me. Their role wasn't to present the project in all its detail, but to show that the entire organization was behind the plan. It had the desired effect!

What kinds of initiatives did you engage in with former Canadiens players?

In 1982—the year I became president of the Canadiens—the Nordiques were getting a lot of exposure in different markets in

Quebec, with players going out to meet the fans, for example. I immediately wanted to do something similar to bring our team closer to members of the public who were far away. And the best way to do that was to spread out farther afield.

One of my strategies was to target our team's former players, who embodied the wonderful memories in the hearts of the fans. But before I could hope to count on a group of ambassadors who would go and meet them, I had to reconcile the players with the organization. Several of those who had built the Canadiens believed they had been underpaid during their careers and no longer felt welcome at the Forum. At Maurice Richard's suggestion, I had an Alumni Lounge built in the entrance to the Forum. It was small, but we did the most that we could with the available space.

And so, starting in 1982, I gathered three of the most significant players in the affections of Canadiens' fans—Maurice Richard, Jean Béliveau, and Guy Lafleur—to form a group of ambassadors, along with Réjean Houle, Yvan Cournoyer, and other important players in our history.

One day, I had the opportunity to chat with George Steinbrenner, the owner of the New York Yankees. I told him about what the Canadiens had done to re-create the bonds between the organization and its former players. I thought he seemed a little jealous since, despite the Yankees' dynasty, there were a lot of unresolved conflicts with their former stars.

Tell us an unforgettable story.

In 1984, I was at the airport in Rome, on my way to the Sarajevo Olympic Games to see some of the players in action. Claude Ruel had gone there ahead of me.

The airport was completely deserted, apart from a crowd of soldiers. After asking them some questions, I found out that there had been a shooting a few days earlier. Everything was at a standstill and very few planes were taking off, except for the ones from the company my flight was on.

In the distance I saw a crowd—they were making a lot of noise. With all the cancellations, agents were trying to find other flights for passengers. It was chaos. When I came up to the desk, the airline representative noticed I was wearing a Canadiens pin on my coat. He said, "Hey! Montreal Canadiens, the Flower! The guy with the blond hair!"

He told me he used to work in Calgary and that Guy Lafleur was his favourite player. Let's just say it sped up the process for me to find another flight! All the same, it was fascinating to see that Guy Lafleur was known even in Italy. And I'd gotten some special treatment all because of Guy.

What were your last moments with him?

We always stayed in touch. I called him up when he had his heart troubles, and also at different times when he was fighting cancer. They were always good conversations.

All of the members of the public—myself included—were upset to hear of his health problems.

A few months before he died, I organized a lunch with Guy and his two friends Pierre Bouchard and Réjean Houle. Naturally, Guy arrived before the others. He was stressed out, having just started a new round of treatments. I took him in my arms and said, "*Je t'aime, mon chum.* We are all with you in your battle." He was very touched.

Guy called me the next day to thank me for the nice lunch. We talked about having another lunch outing, just the two of us this time. I said, "I'd like for us to spend some time together, Guy. We have so much to say to each other." He replied, "Good idea. And this time, I'm paying!" Sadly, that lunch never took place, as his health failed him. At that time, he was starting a new cancer treatment, and it was tough for him. He didn't get the results he was hoping for.

A few weeks before he died, he called me. His voice was barely recognizable. He said, "I'd really love for us to go out to eat, but I can't. I want to live! But I'm dying." I was able to say to him, "I love you, Guy. And one more time, I'm sorry for having made a decision too quickly." It was an emotional goodbye.

After he died, I went to pay my respects to him at the chapel of rest at the Bell Centre. But then I tested positive for COVID-19 and was unable to attend his funeral. Fortunately, I could watch the ceremony on television and experience the emotions of the day.

What is his legacy, the most beautiful memory he left behind for the hockey world and for society?

I hold on to the memory of an exceptional athlete who was universally respected. He was the greatest of his generation, without a doubt.

Guy was also an endearing person, always ready to help out, who was unanimously appreciated by his teammates, by other players in the NHL, and by the public. I never hear any negative comments about him.

And he'll also be remembered as a citizen who was very much involved in different causes, including the CHUM, which he supported right up until the very end of his life.

Steve Shutt

Born in Willowdale, Ontario, in 1952, Steve Shutt was a left winger who played twelve complete seasons with the Canadiens. When he began playing for the team, in 1972–1973, Guy Lafleur had been there for a year. Over time, they were paired with three centremen who would be instrumental to their careers: first, Peter Mahovlich, then Jacques Lemaire, and finally Pierre Larouche. He ended his career with the Los Angeles Kings.

Steve Shutt is ranked eighth in the history of the Canadiens for goals scored (408) and also eighth in points (776). A member of the Hockey Hall of Fame since 1993, he had his name engraved on the Stanley Cup five times.

What is your oldest memory of Guy Lafleur?

It goes all the way back to the peewee tournament in Quebec. We were playing in the same edition and he was absolutely sensational. Since I was a year younger than Guy, I played at the same tournament the next year, after he'd moved on. After that, we played in different leagues—him in Quebec and me in Ontario. We only really got to know each other after I was drafted to the Canadiens: him in 1971 and me in 1972.

I'm convinced that every hockey fan in Canada had seen Guy Lafleur play or heard about him before he joined the Canadiens.

You came to the Canadiens when they were a true powerhouse in the NHL. What was the atmosphere like?

I started playing with the Canadiens in 1972–1973, a year after Flower. It would be any hockey player's dream at that time to go into an NHL dressing room and to have Henri Richard as captain, and for teammates, Serge Savard, Ken Dryden, Frank and Pete Mahovlich, Yvan Cournoyer, Guy Lafleur, and all the others. I'm still struck by what a privilege it was to be on a team with all of them.

I realized pretty quickly that I hadn't been drafted to sit around and be intimidated by these legends—I was there to use my youth and talent to help them out. There I was, just into my twenties, watching our captain, Henri Richard—who was sixteen years older than me—crushing it every time he went out on the ice. As a young guy, how could I not give just as much?

The Canadiens team I knew was a winning team built on humility. This great quality was shared by Maurice Richard, then Jean Béliveau, and then Guy Lafleur. They were aware of their talents, but didn't have oversized egos. They embedded that into our family DNA—because we really were a family. That was immensely important throughout our careers. If players who were in a class by themselves could be humble despite their successes, how could anyone allow themselves to wear the Canadiens sweater and not be?

Guy and I, like all of the players on the Canadiens, played to win. Money was not as important in professional hockey as it would become over time. And the more fun we had, the more we won. To this day, Guy and I are the only two Canadiens players to have scored sixty goals in a season, but those are individual honours. As far as I'm concerned, our Stanley Cup victories were much more important, and Guy felt the same.

Tell us about his early days.

He scored almost thirty goals in his first year, which was terrific for a rookie, but a lot of fans in Quebec were expecting more.

When players start their careers in the NHL, without exception they are trying to find their bearings. Guy was looking for his by relying on what had always worked best for him—that is, dodging around to power through and score with his lightning-fast shot—all while adapting to Scotty Bowman's game system.

Guy and I were quick to connect. We got along very well before being brought together on the same line; I believe it was his third season and my second. At first, we played with Pete Mahovlich at centre. Pete was a star and a veteran who took great care in developing newer players. He would put his long arms around our shoulders and say, "All right, it's all right, young guys!" He gave both of us enormous confidence in our ability to make progress.

Pete used to take off like a train towards the attacking zone. He often managed to shake off a few players, but he could lose the puck along the way. So it was up to me and Flower to always be ready to recover it. As Guy gained experience in the NHL, he became excellent at carrying the puck—that meant that both Peter and Guy like to carry the puck. It was one too many, which is why Jacques "Coco" Lemaire became our centreman.

Coco was quite different: not as tall and solid, but he could skate better. Basically, Jacques thought of the plays and set them in motion, then he'd pass the puck to Guy, who handled it skilfully before passing it to us. Very often, one of us would score.

That's how I spent the bulk of my Canadiens career, on the same line as Jacques—definitely the most cerebral player on our team—and Guy, who was the most intuitive among us.

My job was simple: not to look like an idiot next to Guy. So I always had to think fast and play outside the box.

He would say to Jacques and me, "I never know what I'm going to do before I've got the puck on my stick." When I would ask him, "So what do you want me to do?," he'd say things like "That's your problem," or "If all three of us play our best, we'll score."

The way he played was impressive for his teammates, too. I think about all the times he outwitted an opponent and kept on charging like a rocket to complete a pass or shoot on net. He was so fast that our opponents needed to take a second to get back on track. But for Guy, one second's advantage was all he needed to stand out even more.

What impact did he have on your career?

Guy made me a better player—no doubt about it—for two reasons that show very well what kind of person he was. First, I don't remember a single game where he didn't give 100 percent, which made everyone else play to their full potential. As well, on our line, Guy drew all the attention of our opponents, who often pursued him two or three at a time to try to slow him down. And because Guy was such a team player, he would pass the puck to me or Jacques.

Our styles were quite different: He carried the puck and I finished the plays. Before I'd come to the Canadiens, I had carried the puck, too. But I adapted my game when I was on a team where many other players did that very well.

Guy and I didn't step on each other's toes. We each had an objective, but there was no playbook. We played "à la Lafleur," which is to say that while Guy was skating and the opponents had all their attention on him, he knew I was on my way. That was key. We often crisscrossed in the middle of the ice, and that messed up our checkers.

Scotty didn't have a big ego, either. The proof? After a while, he let Guy do his thing because it meant the team would win. For him, winning was bigger than egos.

Following Guy's death, I took a trip down memory lane—including another look at our stats. I'm still impressed to see that Guy and I formed the duo who contributed the most to each other's goals in the rich history of the Canadiens. I scored 184 goals from passes from Flower, and he scored 110 from mine. It's very rare to see such cohesion between two wingers. Off the rink we were both right-handed, but I shot from the left and Guy from the right. That meant his stronger hand was lower on his stick, which maximized the power of his shots and passes.

How did he carry himself, in general?

Like the genuine article. Because that's what he was.

Back in our day, we slept two to a room when we were on the road, and he and I were roommates for four or five seasons. The way he acted was the same in the hotel room as in our dressing room, on the players' bench, or with the fans. He was always himself: simple, humble, focused when he needed to be, and very funny, too.

It's obvious Guy was influenced by Henri Richard. We never talked about it; I don't know if he realized it himself. They were men of few words. Their longest speeches in the dressing room were usually the three words "Let's go, guys!" But it was their actions that always spoke for them.

Where Guy was more talkative was with journalists. He made statements that got him into trouble with the Canadiens' management on a regular basis. And then he'd do it again. Even when he was the team's ambassador, he criticized players who weren't doing enough to justify their high salaries. But no one was surprised—it was Guy Lafleur they were talking to!

Like all athletes, you had a period of growth and eventually a period of decline. Tell us about that.

Unfortunately, it's inevitable. When you're young, you push yourself to the maximum to become the best you can be, and to maintain that for as long as possible. But a moment comes when we all start to decline, and it's hard to accept.

Guy went through two of those shocks: at the beginning and at the end of his time playing for the Canadiens. In the first case, he wanted to be performing at a higher level, but there was a gap between the results he wanted to achieve and what he was able to do. He was growing. Towards the end, the gap was reversed, between what he'd achieved in the past and what he was able to do.

The fraction of a second that he was missing was due to the decline of the human body's mechanics. It's frustrating for all athletes, without exception—I remember how it felt. And I had a front-row seat when it happened with Guy.

Guy and I both were slowed down a bit when Jacques Lemaire became the Canadiens' coach and implemented his defensive style, which we weren't comfortable with. We were playing less and less.

When the Good Friday Massacre happened, several of our players were ejected from the game. With a smile on my face, I looked back at Lemaire and said, "Now you have no choice but to play me!" I scored two goals and we won the game.

Later that year, I asked Serge Savard to trade me, which he kindly agreed to, sending me to the Los Angeles Kings. But he refused to trade "the idol."

I wasn't really surprised when Guy retired. But I will keep to myself some of the conversations we had.

1951

Guy at eight months, with his older sister, Suzanne.

1953

Little Guy, three years old.

1961

The young hockey player at eleven poses with his father and his peewee coach, Brother Léo Jacques.

1964

Team captain Guy (back row, far left) proudly poses with his peewee team, the Thurso Idéal. Assistant captain Jacques Massie is near him.

1970

Guy playing in the first of two seasons with the Québec Remparts, part of the brand-new Quebec Major Junior Hockey League. André Savard (on Guy's right), Réjean Giroux (on his left), and Jacques Richard were the other key players on the team.

1975

On December 31, the Canadiens hosted the Red Army at the Montreal Forum. The teams were facing each other three years after the Summit Series, and at the height of the Cold War. Guy Lafleur and the Russian goalie Vladislav Tretiak met for the first time. They would play against each other again in 1976 and in 1981.

1977

Serge Savard (interim captain) and Yvan Cournoyer (injured captain) celebrate their teammate's winning of the Conn Smythe Trophy, awarded to the most valuable player in the playoffs.

1978

Guy Lafleur and Steve Shutt greet the crowd on Sainte-Catherine Street during the Stanley Cup parade.

1978

Guy Lafleur was determined to bring the Stanley Cup to Thurso, setting it down on the precise spot where his father built a skating rink. With him are his niece Stéphanie Aubin and his son Martin. Right before the photo was taken, he'd washed Lord Stanley's Mug with dish soap!

1979

Friends for life: Réjean Houle and Guy.

1981

On March 4, Lafleur earned his 1,000th point in the NHL. On his left is Pierre Larouche, who had beaten Lafleur's QMJHL record of 209 points. Looking on intently in the front-row seats of the Forum, just behind Guy, is a young Mario Lemieux—who would go on to beat Larouche's record, with 282 points.

1984

Guy Lafleur retires, for the first time. The expressions on the faces of (from left to right) general manager Serge Savard and team president Ronald Corey show they were aware of how unpopular this decision was.

1985

On February 16, the Canadiens retire Guy Lafleur's sweater. The illustrious number 10 waves to the crowd alongside his wife, Lise Barré-Lafleur, and their older son, Martin.

1985

On February 28, shortly after announcing his first retirement, Guy seems content, posing with members of his family. In the back row, his sisters Suzanne and Gisèle and their father, Réjean. In front, his mother, Pierrette, is flanked by his sisters Lise and Lucie.

1989

The Lafleur family, at home in the Big Apple.

1989

Guy Lafleur and Steven Finn (this book's coauthor), as opponents on the ice in March. In July, they would become teammates.

1989

The Flower officially becomes a Nordique, as he shakes hands with Coach Michel Bergeron, who had coached him with the Rangers. Looking on is general manager Martin Madden.

1990

Guy loved to have fun with his teammates. To celebrate the holidays at the end of the year, he invited the Nordiques to his sugar shack just west of Québec City. In this photo, he shares a laugh with Lucien DeBlois.

1991

The end of an era: Lafleur definitively retires from the NHL. He is accompanied by his wife, Lise Barré-Lafleur, Martin, and, in the arms of his father, Mark.

2011

Guy and Joe Sakic, one of his teammates for his two seasons with the Nordiques, at the Colisée de Québec, during the last friendly match with Lafleur.

2015

Guy loved flying helicopters and sharing those moments of freedom with his former teammates. Here he is with (from left) Guy Lapointe, Yvon Lambert, Chris Nilan, and Yvan Cournoyer on their way to the funeral of their former coach, Claude Ruel. All together, the five men have twenty-six Stanley Cups to their credit!

2020

Grandpa Guy and Sienna-Rose, Martin's daughter.

2020

All in for the CHUM Foundation: spokesman Claude Meunier and Guy with their friend Robert Charlebois.

2021

Réjean Tremblay with an athlete and man he admired.

2021

On September 20, some of Guy's closest friends from the realm of hockey marked his seventieth birthday. Beside Guy is his son Mark. Behind him, left to right: Réjean Houle, Geoff Molson, Bob Gainey, Rick Green, son Martin Lafleur, Guy Carbonneau, Pierre Boucher, France Margaret Bélanger, Mario Tremblay, Serge Savard, Guy Lapointe, Yvan Cournoyer, and Yvon Lambert.

2022

During his funeral, Guy was surrounded, as always, by his teammates. Along with his sons, Martin and Mark, his pallbearers were Steve Shutt, Yvon Lambert, Mario Tremblay, and Guy Lapointe. Pierre Bouchard walked behind the casket carrying a cushion covered in medals. Flower's casket was—most fittingly—draped in the bleu-blanc-rouge Canadiens flag.

You were reunited as teammates for the Canadiens alumni games, right?

Yes, not long after his retirement, we played in about fifty games a year to benefit charitable causes. The magic returned—in his case, anyway. His skating, his shot: You would have thought he'd just played in the NHL the day before. He played with us up until he went to the Rangers.

He spoke to me about wanting to return to the NHL and I said to him, "Do it!" And the rest is history. When he returned to the game, he was ecstatic.

Tell us an unforgettable story.

In advance of the 1981 Canada Cup, Scotty asked a YMCA trainer to prepare a high-performance training program for the Canadian team. It was much more physically demanding than what players from the Canadiens and other NHL teams were used to.

On the first day, we had to run several miles outside the Forum. No surprise, the goalies didn't get very far, and the other players were sweating buckets. By the end, we are all in the same pack—except for Guy. He was already back at the Forum, smoking a cigarette in the dressing room. "The phenomenon" was ready to play the Canada Cup from day one!

What was his greatest quality?

To choose just one is difficult, but one of them does encompass the others. Like they say in French, Guy was a "*maudit bons gars*"—a hell of a guy—with his teammates and in the NHL. And also, of course, with the fans and in the community.

Every star in the world, in every field, should have had the privilege to know him, so they could realize you can be a superstar and still be humble.

What were your last moments with him?

We didn't see much of each other in the last year because I live far from Montreal. But I know he had serious health problems for four years and he suffered enormously. I also know that he never complained about his fate, and that he preferred to share kind words with others who were also suffering.

I went to see him at his place two weeks before he left us. I was with my son. A bed was set up in the living room. His speech was clear and assured, as usual. After we talked for around half an hour about hockey and other things, he left the room and came back with two bottles of his wine, for my son and me. Then he asked for my address because he wanted to send me some of his gin and vodka.

He seemed to be doing fairly well, given the circumstances. I said to myself that he still had a few months to live. But something that gave me pause was when I said to him, twice, "Ninon and I have rented a cottage in Hudson for the month of August—we'll see you there." He didn't respond, and it was as if he knew he'd no longer be with us.

What legacy did he leave us?

His high-speed rushes to the attacking zone, his hair flying behind him, inspiring the crowd to cheer with pride.

Lanny McDonald

Born in Hanna, Alberta, in 1953, Lanny McDonald is a right winger who played sixteen seasons in the NHL, mainly with the Toronto Maple Leafs and the Calgary Flames. A first-round draft pick in 1973, he was one of Guy Lafleur's teammates in the 1976 Canada Cup. Inducted into the Hockey Hall of Fame in 1992, Lanny McDonald has served as the institution's chairman of the board since 2015.

What is your oldest memory of Guy Lafleur?

When I was growing up in the '50s and '60s in Alberta, the Calgary Flames didn't exist yet. I was mostly a fan of the Maple Leafs, and I dreamed of playing for them. And my dream came true: I got to wear their uniform for six and a half years.

Guy Lafleur came to the NHL two seasons before I did. It was the beginning of one of the most glorious decades in the Canadiens' rich history and he made a huge contribution to the team.

Back then, what kind of career did you think he'd have?

Guy was always going to be an exceptional player; it was just a question of time. From his first year, his raw talent was remarkable—the Canadiens just needed to add some polish. He was already strong, and he became more muscular over the years.

It's important not to compare career starts from the 1970s to those of today, because the context is very different. When Guy and I made our debuts, the World Juniors championship and other high-calibre international competitions didn't exist. We played in the Memorial Cup and then went to the training camp of the teams that had drafted us. Today's players are much better prepared to make the leap to the NHL than we were.

What was true in our time and that hasn't changed to this day are the extremely high expectations for the highest draft picks. When players are in juniors, you see the best scorers filling the nets, and the defence and goaltenders making all kinds of spectacular plays—and the journalists and fans imagine those feats being replicated when players arrive in the NHL. It's not realistic. Guy and I both needed time—about three years—to find our place in the NHL.

One of the things that helped Guy to break out was all the time he spent training out on the ice. I have memories from game days, particularly ones at the Forum. During morning practices, he was the first one to jump onto the ice and he'd work on shooting, shooting, and shooting some more. Even though it was just practice, he did all he could to defy his teammates with all sorts of manoeuvres. He'd fake out his goalie, too, shooting pucks into the high corners of the net. It was amazing. Scotty Bowman had a whole sequence of plays for his players to carry out. I'd say to myself, "Yup, it's quite the team we're going to be facing tonight."

I wasn't surprised that Guy managed to stand out in Montreal, a hockey market where the pressure is phenomenal, because he had a personality that was built for that: He was calm.

Talk to us about that era.

Back then, the rivalry between the Maple Leafs and the Canadiens was very intense. Players didn't hang out with each other off the ice the way they do today, and they often stayed with a team for a very long time. When you were a Maple Leaf, you were bonded to your team. And it was the same if you were with the Canadiens.

For every game, you'd jump on the ice with fire in your eyes, and for sixty minutes it was war. No smiles, no fooling around. But that didn't prevent us from being intimidated by the most talented of our opponents. And Guy was one of them, ever since the first time I found myself playing against him in 1973.

During my seven years with the Leafs, we faced each other in the playoffs twice. Toronto had an excellent team and we said to each other, "We are so close to the ultimate goal. If we can just beat the Canadiens . . ." But they had so much depth! Unfortunately, the Canadiens managed to win both times. The rivalry was just as intense on the benches between Scotty Bowman and Roger Neilson as it was on the ice.

What memory do you have of the first time you met him?

I got to know Guy during the 1976 Canada Cup. One word described him very well: "cool."

Flower had earned his spot on a team that, without a doubt, brought together the best Canadian players to play in an international competition. Just think about it: Eighteen out of our twenty-five players would later be inducted into the Hockey Hall of Fame. It felt like I'd found myself inside the Canadiens' dressing room during the selection camp, which took place in Montreal. I was in the dressing room of the players who were normally my sworn enemies, and of the organization that had won more Stanley Cups than any other.

The story I'm about to tell shows just what kind of person Guy was. During the training camp, we played a game between members of the team. Serge Savard was playing against me and Guy, and he did one of his 360-degree turns that he pulled off so often, the move that sportscaster Danny Gallivan named the

Savardian Spin-o-rama. I had anticipated the move and checked him as he was coming out of his turn. Serge reacted by grabbing me with his two hands, and he was given a penalty. In the dressing room, Guy said something to me like, "Don't change the way you play, kid. You did what you needed to do." I had been expecting him to yell at me for going after his teammate, but no. While that game was happening, I had become his teammate and Savard was our adversary.

Those few words he said stuck with me. I'm not sure if I spoke with him again about it. But one thing's for sure: The moment he said those words was the beginning of a lasting friendship.

What type of player was he on the ice?

Even though we were both offensive right wingers we had very different styles. Guy was all over the ice, whereas I was more up and down—that is, more linear. My line often went up against his. Whether he was on the ice or on the players' bench, I kept my eye on him constantly because he was a real pest! In a split second he'd achieve top speed and, with the wind in his hair, he would change the course of the game in no time with his skating, his moves, and his powerful shot. It felt like he was hurtling through our zone at nine million miles an hour.

There was no such thing as a game pattern that worked for him. Guy was Guy, and he operated 100 percent on instinct. Very often he started from his own zone and bolted towards the attacking zone. He was the one who dominated the play, forcing the defenders to retreat.

Flower and Shutty's partnership was as rare as it was effective. For the fans it was incredible to watch them in action and unsettling for the teams that had to play against them. Add Jacques Lemaire to the mix and it was "Oh! My! God!" I played for sixteen seasons in the NHL and the trio of Lafleur, Shutt, and

Lemaire was one of the hardest ones to play against. Neither Roger Neilson nor my teammates and I could ever say, "If Flower does this, we'll do that." We would have needed to have a thousand different plans. And so we were constantly in react mode whenever their line was on the ice.

Guy's feats in hockey made him one of the best players in the world. He made everything he did on the ice look easy—but that isn't possible in the NHL. There's no doubt whatsoever he had a huge natural talent. In fact, he was so talented and played with such intensity—he would rush to the corners to recover the puck—that he was nearly impossible to stop or slow down. And also, his status was such that no one would have wanted to hurt him.

How did you react when he announced his retirement, and then when he later returned to the game?

I was surprised, and also disappointed for the fans, for his teammates, and for the opponents who admired him. And, of course, I was disappointed for Guy.

I don't know the whole story of what led him to that retirement. But I was convinced he could have kept on playing for a long time because he still had the passion, energy, and ability to do it.

I've asked myself, should he have made his return with the Rangers or with the Canadiens? The best answer I've come up with is that, whatever sweater he wore when he returned to the game, he made significant contributions to the Rangers and the Nordiques, and he was happy. That was easy to see.

There's nothing natural about returning to the NHL after almost four years away. The likelihood of succeeding is very low. However, that's what Guy did, with an ease that looked natural, just like his style of play always was.

Personally, I never would have been able to do that. He was two years older than I was. I retired at thirty-six and, despite my passion for hockey, I knew it was time for me to do something else. However, I did retire in 1989 after the Flames won the Stanley Cup against, of all teams, the Canadiens—the team that robbed me of my dream at the end of the 1970s and in 1986, when they beat us in the finals.

How did your relationship evolve?

After having almost always been opponents—other than in the 1976 Canada Cup and in All-Star games—we played together very often in Legends games, whether on the same team or against each other.

When Guy played in the NHL, it was a well-known fact that he liked to be the first one in the dressing room. He kept to that habit even for casual, friendly games. If the game was scheduled for 7:00, he'd arrive at 3:00. One day I arrived at the same time, just to be alone with him. For the next game, he arrived at 2:30 so he would be first again. I realized that he needed to have time to himself in the dressing room.

For Flower, it didn't matter if it was a friendly game with the Legends or one in the NHL: It was important for everyone to bring the same serious attitude to the game, and to have just as much fun playing it.

What was he like with the fans?

Guy had a special relationship with the public. Fans adopted him as soon as he came to the NHL, and he responded to all that love with a devotion that was almost unique. I say "almost unique," because I had the privilege to experience a special moment with one of the greats in the history of hockey.

At the beginning of my career, I was invited to an NHL event where Jean Béliveau was in attendance, and I watched him closely. I saw how he behaved with the fans, how attentive and how patient he was with each one. I took it as a lesson. I know how much Guy Lafleur was inspired by Mr. Béliveau. It was from him that Guy learned how to be an unforgettable idol in the eyes of the fans.

During Guy's funeral, it was one more chance to see just how much he was loved by the fans in Montreal and by the entire hockey world. The cathedral was full, and the nearby streets had been closed off because thousands of fans had come to be there for him. It was the first time I'd ever seen priests go outside and give communion to people on the forecourt of a church.

Do you remember your last moments together?

Yes, very well. It was in Toronto in 2018, for the seventy-fifth anniversary of the Hockey Hall of Fame. Many players and managers were there, representing all of the teams. Our spouses were there, too. We chatted for a bit.

I remember there was a special ambiance at the Canadiens' table. The guys were very happy to see each other, like the members of a family who've been far away from each other for too long. At one point the guys from the Leafs and the Canadiens brought their tables together to make things even more fun! The rivalry was behind us. Guy was especially animated—I don't think he had health problems yet—and he was laughing, loudly.

In June 2022, the Order of Hockey in Canada recognized three former athletes who contributed to the game: Kim St-Pierre, Guy Lafleur, and you. What was that evening like?

Despite the pride Kim and I felt, it was a sad occasion because Guy died between the announcement of the honour in March and the date of the ceremony.

As soon as I found out that I would be receiving this honour at the same time as Guy, many beautiful memories from the 1970s came flooding back. Two of those memories were associated with great Canadiens players. The first was Bob Gainey, because the two of us were drafted the same year and we were both inducted into the Hockey Hall of Fame in 1992. The second player was Guy, as we were both receiving the Order of Hockey in Canada.

Even though we felt a great absence during the ceremony, Martin Lafleur accepted the honour on behalf of his father. He spoke about Guy with great pride, assuredness, and emotion.

What is his legacy, the most beautiful memory that he left the world of hockey and all of society?

Guy was constantly sharing his love of hockey. Fans were able to appreciate his feats on the ice, and have quality moments with him in public.

Gaétan Lefebvre

Born in Montreal in 1959, Gaétan Lefebvre first met Guy Lafleur as a teenager, when he began working part-time as an assistant trainer in the Canadiens' dressing room.

He went on to obtain a commerce degree with a minor in athletic training at Concordia University, continuing to work part-time during his studies, and became the Canadiens' head trainer from 1989 to 2000. Gaétan Lefebvre is one of a select group of athletic trainers to have been inducted into the Hockey Hall of Fame.

What is your oldest memory of Guy Lafleur as a player?

It was the summer of 1974, when I was sixteen years old. I was a big fan of the Canadiens and my family lived in Pointe-Saint-Charles, in Montreal. Thanks to a set of circumstances, I found myself working as the assistant equipment manager for the Montreal Québécois lacrosse team, whose home games were also played at the Forum, and whose team members included the Canadiens' John Ferguson. At the end of the summer, he tipped me off that the Canadiens also needed an assistant equipment manager. I was hired.

There are various duties that come with the job, including collecting the sweaters and washing them, tidying the players' lockers, and opening up the dressing room. At that time, the Canadiens played almost all of their home games on Wednesdays and Saturdays at 8:00 p.m. at the Forum. The trainer, Eddy

Palchak, usually arrived at 5:00 p.m., and his assistant, Pierre "Boom Boom" Meilleur, got there at 5:15. As for Guy Lafleur, he counted on being there at 3:45. So Mr. Palchak told me, "Make sure you get here at 3:45, because Guy Lafleur is always on time."

There was just one small problem: On weekdays, school finished at 3:30. So my father wrote a letter to my principal, requesting that I be able to leave school at 3:15. When I told Mr. Provost, "It's because Guy Lafleur is going to come and pick me up at 3:15 on Wednesdays," he didn't believe me, obviously. So, on the first day I was to leave early, I proposed that he come and see for himself. "If Guy Lafleur doesn't pick me up," I said, "you can give me detention." Guy showed up at 3:15 on the dot, behind the wheel of a big car—an Oldsmobile Toronado, I believe—calling out to me, "Hurry up, *tabarnak*—we're going to be late! We've got a game at eight o'clock." The principal went back to his office, speechless.

In the time it took me to get changed in the dressing room, Guy already had on his shin guards, hockey pants, and unlaced skates. Then we'd spend half an hour playing backgammon.

When he wasn't happy with how his last game had gone, he could spend an hour or more alone on the ice practising his shots before his teammates arrived. And he'd take smoke breaks! I would do my homework in the equipment room. You couldn't make this stuff up. That was how our relationship began.

How was he with the team staff?

Unlike many players I've encountered over my career—whether in the Canadiens' dressing room, at the Canada Cup, or at an NHL All-Star Game—he treated everyone the same. For Guy, the equipment personnel weren't just junior staff, but integral members of the Canadiens.

When I was riding in his car on the way to the Forum from

my school, I could sense his nervousness. He'd ask me, "How's it going with school? How's it going with hockey?" The closer we got to the Forum, the less he spoke. I could sense his feverish anticipation of the upcoming game. He was getting into the zone.

He was always respectful towards my colleagues and me. He would never toss his sweater onto the dressing room floor. He'd get up and put it in the laundry basket. Passing by the infirmary, he'd pick up a coffee cup a teammate had left behind and tell him, "Next time, throw out your cup. I did it for you this time."

He used a lot of sticks, but made almost no demands of our dressing room team. I remember he would have one pair of skates restitched several times over a number of years. And since he wanted to feel light out on the ice, he wore small shin guards and no shoulder pads: We sewed shoulder caps onto the suspenders of his hockey pants. He protected himself with his speed!

Guy was always very generous towards the trainers, whether it was Eddy Palchak, Pierre Meilleur, and René Lavigueur with the Canadiens, or Jacques Lavergne and René Lacasse with the Nordiques. He would pass on to us a lot of gifts that he'd received: watches, sweaters—all sorts of things he knew we'd appreciate. He made sure to be fair, and he did it discreetly.

When it came to praising our work, though, he was far from discreet. On Saturday nights after the games, guests would show up in the dressing room. If one of us had to walk past him, he'd put his hand on our shoulder. He could be chatting with Pierre Elliott Trudeau, Robert Bourassa, Gilles Villeneuve, or Mireille Mathieu, and he'd stop and ask me, "So, Gates—how's it going?"

Guy was at home at the Forum—he knew all of its nooks and crannies. I remember that on the morning of practices, the players and trainers went into the Forum via Atwater Street, walking straight on to the dressing room. Two players happened to notice that, to the right of the entrance, there was a break room reserved for maintenance staff, the Zamboni driver, and others. Jean Béliveau and Guy Lafleur would drop in now and then to have a coffee with them. Pure class, passed on from one legend to another.

The Forum was Guy's kingdom, where he could let his guard down. He was among his people, no matter their individual role. As soon as he jumped onto the ice, he was onstage—he owned it!

Before he entered the Forum and as soon as he left it—and it was the same thing at away games and everywhere else—he set a very high bar for himself when it came to fulfilling his fans' expectations. That's why he was more available than anybody else. If he saw a father and son waiting in the rain or the snow, he said to himself, "If they were willing to get wet to wait for me, I have to take the time to talk to them."

What kind of teammate was he?

A guy who was adored by his teammates. They admired him and followed his example, because he made them all better. Guy was the other captain, the one who didn't have a "C" on his sweater.

For instance, before Yvon Lambert ended up scoring the winning goal in the 1979 Stanley Cup semifinals versus Boston, first there had to be the tying goal at the end of regulation time. I saw the heads of the players behind the bench following Guy's every move, all of them saying, "Go, Flower!" They were sure he'd pull it off.

What drove him?

His fans. Hockey wasn't a job for him. He played hockey and wanted to transfer the pleasure of playing to the fans—and in the process, make them happy at every game. That's why he never did anything by half measures. It's why the rough play and violence in the games against Philadelphia and Boston went right over his head. Guy knew that if he concentrated on doing what he could do better than any of the other players in the NHL—which was to score spectacular goals, hair flowing in the wind—his teammates, whom he deeply respected, would take care of the rest.

During training camp, teams normally send their B squad to play exhibition games on the road and keep their A team to play local games. During the era when he was the best player in the world, Guy volunteered to be sent out on the road because he adored the game and because he knew it would delight his fans.

Now that I think of it, I don't believe that Guy Lafleur played "for" the Canadiens. He played *with* the Canadiens but *for* his fans. It explains why he acted the way he did in certain situations—his outbursts that shocked the team management. It was a form of tough love.

Did you foresee that he would announce his retirement in 1984?

Not at all. It was clear he was unhappy, but I hadn't predicted that he would hang up his skates. I cried on that day. Later on, he surprised me by returning to the game, but it was no surprise that he played so well.

How did your relationship change?

Over the last years, we crossed paths in the Alumni Lounge at the Bell Centre, at the Canadiens golf tournament, and at various events. We'd chat for a bit and then I'd move on, since he was always very much in demand. Like everyone associated with the Canadiens, I'd heard he was battling cancer and that he was staying positive. But I had no illusions about how things would turn out.

The news of his death really shook me up, and it's not hard

to understand why. I was a fan when I first met Guy, in the early 1970s. And then I had the privilege of being around him constantly. He had an effect on my life for fifty years.

The tribute paid to him by the Montreal Canadiens and the fans was fitting for the athlete and the man that he was.

Tell us some unforgettable stories.

Guy was very kind to me.

One winter's day he looked at me and said, "What is that coat you're wearing?" I told him it was the coat I could afford to buy. A few days later, arriving in the equipment room, I find a superb otter coat in my locker. Inside the coat there's an embroidered message: "De Guy à Gaétan." I was uncomfortable, and so I went to speak with him. He said, "I'm giving it to you—it doesn't fit me anymore." I replied, "Come on, Flower—you're six feet tall and I'm five-eight!" I'm convinced he had the coat altered to fit me.

Another time, as the Christmas holidays were approaching, he asked me about my plans. I said, "I'm going to see my girlfriend in Québec City for a few days, and then I'll be back on the twenty-fifth, since the team's going out west." On the first day of my vacation, I went to the Alexis Nihon Plaza, where my car was parked. Guy had taken my old Toyota away and rented me a beautiful car for my trip. The parking lot attendant, who was Flower's accomplice, handed me the keys. On the car seat was an envelope, and he'd written "Enjoy Québec!" on it. Inside was a hundred dollars.

What was his greatest quality?

He was good. That says it all! Guy was a good person. A real person.

One day I heard someone say, "Kindness doesn't kill." It's so true because, on the contrary, kindness makes life better. And that's what motivated Guy: living a life by bestowing kindness on others, whether it was those he loved most or complete strangers.

Guy was good on the ice, but he was even better off of it, whether it was giving to charities, to his teammates, or to staff. I was low on the food chain; I never scored a single goal. But he often told me, "What you're doing is important."

What is his legacy?

He showed the people that you have to have a dream. And, above all, to always pursue your dreams and convictions.

His dream was to dominate in the NHL. And among his convictions was the need to defend and protect his son Mark. Looking back at the images left behind, many show Flower scoring magnificent goals, hair flying back in the breeze, but there are also those of a father—so sad, but with his head held high—standing by his son at the courthouse.

Martin Lafleur

Born in Montreal in 1975, Martin Lafleur is the older son of Guy Lafleur and Lise Barré-Lafleur.

When did you first become aware that you were "Guy Lafleur's son"?

I was quite young; probably about five. I saw that people looked at us differently. When we went to a restaurant, usually only one person there was being approached for an autograph or a photo.

I didn't brag about going to Canadiens games and practices when I was growing up, or about getting to do the kinds of things my friends didn't get to do with their fathers.

Even though I was "the son of," I didn't dream about becoming a professional hockey player the way my father did when he watched Jean Béliveau play. I didn't idolize any of the Canadiens players—probably because I hung around them, whereas usually idols are far removed from us.

Did you find it irritating that your father always paid so much attention to his fans?

Irritating? No, because my brother and I were used to it from a very young age. We were also used to the fact that he was often away twelve months a year, because of away games and all kinds of other activities.

We appreciated the fans. They often took our father away

from us, but we didn't resent them. It was a positive thing: a photo, an autograph. For sure I would have liked to have had our father all to ourselves in a restaurant or public places like other kids. It was like that a little in New York, but never in Québec.

Fortunately, when he was home, he was completely present for my mother and my brother, Mark, and me. We had fun and did all kinds of activities. In the summer, for example, he would often bring us along to Canadiens softball games. From a very young age, I'd tag along with him to the golf course.

How did he get relief from the pressure? He couldn't have always been running on adrenaline, right?

As much as he needed to be in constant motion and to have a lot of things on the go—during his hockey-playing days or during retirement—he was able to unplug when he was at home. He liked to have dinner with friends. And smoking—that did help him to relax.

How was your day-to-day life different from that of your friends?

From a very young age I would go to the Canadiens practices at the Forum on Saturday mornings. My father liked to arrive very early. There were usually just two people in the dressing room: Eddy Palchak, the equipment manager, and the physical therapist, Gaétan Lefebvre. My father would put on his gear, smoke a cigarette with Eddy, and then walk all around the Forum and talk to different people, including the Zamboni driver.

I'd grab the gloves of one of the players—which were way too big for me, of course—and a stick that Eddy had cut down to my size. He'd empty a bucketful of pucks onto the ice and I'd spend a huge amount of time skating and taking shots. I was usually the only kid there. Then, when the team came out on the ice, I'd go back to the dressing room and Eddy would go to the McDonald's across the street from the Forum and buy me a Happy Meal.

All of that was normal to me. It was only as I got older that I realized what an incredible privilege I'd had. Even though my father wasn't demonstrative with his affections, I could tell how proud he was of me. I saw that he wanted me to be part of the team.

Practising on my own on the Forum ice, and with the Canadiens players and their sons, was something I did until my father's first retirement.

During those practices or on other occasions, was it your father who taught you about the game and showed you how to skate or to score?

Quite frankly, my dad was not a good coach!

For example, I was an adult before I found out that he hadn't paid much attention to my equipment. I've played hockey my whole life and it was during a Legends game that Stéphane Richer noticed the skates I was wearing were too big. They were the same size as my shoes. In front of Stéphane, I asked my father:

"What size shoes do you wear?"

"Eleven."

"And your skates?"

"Nine and a half."

I'd always had skates the same size as my shoes, and my father had never noticed. I said, "Dad, it never occurred to you to tell me?"

Did you feel pressure when you were young and playing hockey?

Yes, but it didn't come from my father at all. He'd say to me, "If you want to play hockey, play hockey. You like tennis? Play tennis." The pressure came from the parents of other players who expected me to be another Guy Lafleur. But I didn't have a tenth of his talent. Besides, it almost never happens that the son of a great athlete becomes as talented as his father.

The only condition my father imposed on me was that I couldn't be a goalie. I never really understood why. Still, he bought me some superb DR-brand goalie equipment that I damaged on the first day playing in the street. I played in goal with my friends outside, but on my teams in organized hockey, I was a forward.

Do you have memories of your father playing for the Canadiens?

I mostly have memories of when I was around the team's entourage, either in the dressing room or at games with my mother. For my whole life, I've seen my father's most spectacular plays on television or on the Internet. I don't remember seeing images of him in his later days with the Canadiens, when things weren't going as well.

Much later, I understood that he'd been preoccupied by how he was playing, which was disappointing for him. And he wouldn't have wanted to disappoint us: not me or my mother, and not the fans, who were very important to him.

You were around ten years old when your father left the Canadiens. Do you have any memories of that time?

Yes, and they're quite specific. One day when I got home from school, my mother was very upset because my father had been fired by Mr. Corey. I later understood she was worried because my father would no longer be earning money. And she knew that he would feel demoralized, since hockey was his whole life. I remember my father had tried to reassure her, saying that we wouldn't want for anything. And we didn't—he made more money off the ice than he did when he was playing.

My father continued to play a lot of hockey with the Legends' teams. He'd be on the road for even longer stretches than when he'd been with the Canadiens, sometimes as long as thirty days. He played almost every day: in Alaska and the Northwest Territories and in all the cities and towns all over Canada that had invited them. I remember that he came back exhausted and often with a bad cold or flu.

When you were thirteen you experienced upheaval when he decided to return to the game and your family had to move to New York.

The biggest disruption for me at the time was the move to New York. It meant leaving my friends and changing schools after the school year had begun. For the rest of it, our lives were very much the same, because my father was just continuing to play hockey. Before he accepted the offer from the Rangers, he already had a very full schedule with the Legends. We even spent several weeks in Marseille in 1985 when he played for the Français Volants team.

The Rangers were very important for my father: They allowed him to be at peace with himself when he ended his career. It's a paradox: He felt betrayed by some former teammates, and yet he received a warm welcome from strangers in a different country.

As for me, I loved New York. At my high school, football, baseball, and basketball were very popular. But I quickly found my niche, doing quite well in hockey. Over there I was Martin Lafleur, not Guy's boy.

At home, my parents were happy. Mark was four or five years old. My mother adored living in New York and in our area, Rye, and she also loved the mild weather.

One year later, you moved again. How did your years in Québec City go?

Yeah . . . my mother and I would have liked to have stayed in New York or to have gone to Los Angeles. But my father chose Québec. That city had treated him well when he was in peewee and junior. For him, it was a kind of homecoming, a way to come full circle.

He had slowed down on the ice but he was happy to be playing all the same. He became a kind of mentor for the next generation of Nordiques players, including Joe Sakic. But I'm quite convinced he didn't have to say too much to them. He led by example, on and off the ice.

It didn't take me long to love Québec: my school and my new friends, our house, the neighbourhood. However, just like in Montreal, my father couldn't go anywhere incognito!

What kind of a relationship did he have with money?

My father was very preoccupied with the need to always be accumulating revenue so that he and my mother and my brother and I would have enough money later on. Luckily, my mother was an excellent "minister of finance"!

For my father, it was as if he knew that there was value attached to his status as an exceptional player and a personality very much in demand by sponsors, but inside he was still the timid little guy from Thurso. He thought that Quebec sponsorships didn't pay big sums because it was a small market.

It was René Angélil who negotiated the first ten-year contract my father signed with the Canadiens as ambassador. Later on, I was his business partner in the last years of his life and, among other deals, I negotiated his last contract with the team. For that agreement, the Canadiens were very respectful towards my father, knowing that he was ill and would not be as available to go and meet different groups of fans.

When I was negotiating contracts on his behalf, he would tell me the amount he was hoping to get. I would respond, "No, I'm going to ask for more," and name the figure. I often was able to sign an agreement at the desired level. He and my mother were very proud of that.

One difference I was able to make involved certain types of promotions. Companies will often have items made and ask athletes to sign them. As an example, a star hockey player I know charges $250 to sign a puck. My father's fee was . . . five dollars! I made some considerable changes to his fees for promotions like those. But of course, my father always signed personal items for free, such as slips of paper, photos, jerseys, pucks, etcetera.

Tell us about the restaurants your father owned.

They were two experiments that were very rewarding professionally, but rather the opposite financially. We learned a lot about things in business we should do—and things we shouldn't.

The Mikes franchise in Berthierville was the most profitable one in the whole chain. But there was a price to pay: My father was there almost every day. We were living about 100 kilometres away in Île-Bizard, in the west of Montreal, so it wasn't easy. A lot of times we spent the night at the Days Inn in Berthierville. We sold the restaurant after a few years.

The Bleu Blanc Rouge in Rosemère was a "white tablecloth" restaurant. It was always very busy and everything was perfect—except the size. My dad and I had said to each other that we had to go big or go home. The restaurant ended up being too big, and therefore too expensive to run to earn enough profit. We sold that restaurant, too.

He started having health problems when he was around sixty-five. How did you react?

Yes, he was quite young.

The lung cancer was very aggressive. And we all know how it ended for him—even though many other patients under the care of the same superb medical team at the CHUM had similar treatments and got better.

He was himself right up until a week before the end, when he asked the staff at the palliative care home if he'd be able to go home and they told him no. Up until that moment, he was combative, courageous, and sure that he'd pull through. He never complained. He worried about my mother, my brother, and me. About what we'd do without him.

Tell us about what the CHUM meant to him.

He got very good care. But not any better than any of the other patients who weren't well-known like him. He adored his medical team and learned the importance of research, which was why he suggested he could help.

The Guy Lafleur Fund is very much reflective of my father: original, simple, and effective, and a great benefit to others. He was well aware that the fundraising efforts he was supporting would not be able to help him, but that the advances in research would help many people he didn't know.

My father didn't ask me to take over for him in running the Guy Lafleur Fund. One day, I woke up and it seemed to me the most natural thing to do. Obviously, I'm not able to obtain the same kind of results that he would have because of his fame, but I do the best I can. This research fund will continue to grow, one donation at a time.

What is it like to have a loved one die when the public is also deeply grieving the loss?

The pain is no less intense. But to feel the enormous wave of love is comforting.

First, the announcement went out that he had died, early on Friday, April 22, 2022. The media prepared their reports, and in the space of a few minutes, special programs were airing on the radio and on television. Everywhere in the press, in Canada and abroad, and on social media, of course, thousands of fans shared photos and memories.

Then there was the lying in state. For two days, the Bell Centre was constantly full of fans. There definitely has never been an occasion with more people in the same place wearing the number 10 jersey. People of all ages, even children, were wearing it. And almost all of them were autographed!

It's no exaggeration to say that many thousands of people came to place flowers at his statue at the Bell Centre, and to offer us their condolences. A lot of them were Montrealers, but there were also people who made the trip specially from elsewhere in Canada, the US, and Europe. They wanted to gather together in his presence and thank him for everything he'd done.

My family and I were very moved to hear thousands of people, one after another, barely mentioning their memories of the hockey player but instead speaking much more about who he was as a man. They would repeat to us the words he'd said to them, like the time he urged a complete stranger to go and see someone from their family who was dying. They told us about the strength he gave them to fight an illness. Many people saw themselves in the difficult moments we'd experienced.

Those individuals who were so sad in our presence were the same happy people who constantly approached my father. I saw an enormous number of people during the national funeral for my father, but I will never forget any of those faces.

Then there was the funeral. That morning, I arrived quite early at the Bell Centre to park my car and meet up with the large Canadiens family before proceeding to the Cathédrale Marie-Reine-du-Monde. Already, hundreds of people were waiting outside, in silence. Streets were blocked off. I couldn't believe it.

The prime minister and the premier, the commissioner of the NHL, innumerable personalities from the world of hockey and beyond, F-18s flying above the overflowing cathedral, and hundreds of people outside shouting "Guy! Guy! Guy!"—it was surreal.

What was his greatest quality?

My father had many qualities! But if I have to pick one, I'd say it was his authenticity.

When he had something to say to journalists, my father spoke the truth. But it shook things up. He said, for example, that Scotty Bowman should cut them some slack because he was putting too much pressure on his players. His teammates were thinking it, but he was the one with the courage and the stature to speak up the way he did.

What is his legacy?

His performances on the ice, along with the CHUM Guy Lafleur Fund, are probably the ones that stand out the most.

On a personal level, a great legacy is the love shared between my father and my daughter, Sienna-Rose—he was a very doting grandpa.

They had so many wonderful times together at my parents' and at my place. She saw pictures of him playing hockey. She knew that when people wore the bleu-blanc-rouge jersey with the number 10 on it, it was because they loved her grandpa, too. In restaurants, she'd do drawings while he signed autographs. When they walked beside each other, she'd put her little hand in the immense hand of my father. I'm sure that these moments will stay with her forever.

Réjean Tremblay

Born in Saint-David-de-Falardeau in the Saguenay–Lac-Saint-Jean region of Québec in 1944, Réjean Tremblay taught Latin and Greek before starting his journalism career at the *Progrès-Dimanche* and *Quotidien* newspapers. Then, from 1974 to 2011, he was part of the sportswriting staff at *La Presse* before moving on to the *Journal de Montréal.*

Réjean Tremblay's notable credits include covering twelve Olympic Games, and writing the teleplays for numerous television series, including *Lance et compte* (*He Shoots, He Scores*). He was a go-to journalist for many of the scoops about Guy Lafleur.

What is your earliest memory of Guy Lafleur, the hockey player?

It was in 1971, when the Remparts won the Memorial Cup. I really liked that a team of francophones that had only been around for two years had given a thrashing to the Anglos from western Canada! It was already obvious that Guy Lafleur was hugely talented. And that year, it was written in the stars that the Canadiens would choose him first in the draft.

Tell us about your very first meeting with him.

It was Flower who allowed me to report my first big sports story, in February 1975. The Canadiens were on the road in Atlanta and Guy had stayed behind in Montreal because he'd injured his finger. He was on the ice at the Forum, training alone with the goalkeeper Wayne Thomas.

With my skates in tow, I had no problem going through the Forum entrance right up to the dressing room. Times certainly have changed—no journalist today could do that. Guy, the ultimate superstar, the greatest player of the 1970s, welcomed me and my photographer colleague, Armand Trottier, and we took some pictures. He loaned me Steve Shutt's stick and showed me all sorts of moves on the ice—which he executed marvellously, unlike me. Still, I was able to score on Thomas!

A week later, I covered one of the standout games of Ti-Guy's career where he scored his fiftieth goal in a season. He scored on Denis Herron, at the Forum.

How did you get to know each other?

When I started covering the Canadiens, I spoke a mangled version of the English I'd picked up in three days of Berlitz courses. Scotty Bowman, Yvan Cournoyer, the great Savard, and Flower were very forgiving of my English. One day, the defenceman Don Awrey was making fun of my Saint-David-de-Falardeau accent and Guy said to him, "You, when you're in Boston, do you speak French? Right, so leave him alone and let him learn English!" Flower took me under his wing, because he remembered his early difficulties with speaking English and he didn't want anyone to mock me.

For a while, I didn't do interviews with Bowman and his players—like other journalists did—because I didn't have the ability to ask questions. Instead, I was an observer, taking note of the relationships in the dressing room, how different players acted, who the leaders were, etcetera. Guy noticed that I had my own way of working and he told me he liked what I wrote. It was from that moment that we started building a very special relationship, very solid. We understood and respected each other.

How would you describe your "very special relationship"?

We never had to say anything was off the record, because for him, everything was on the record!

The first big story I wrote about Guy was during the 1975 playoffs. For some background, I had quickly become extremely plugged in to what was happening in the World Hockey Association. The Nordiques were founded in Québec City in 1972 and they did everything they could to throw the Canadiens off-balance, both by stealing players like Jean-Claude Tremblay and Réjean Houle and by establishing themselves as a Québec nationalist team in the hearts of the fans. Roger Barré, Guy's father-in-law, was a Nordiques shareholder.

I knew the truth: In 1973, Barré had tried to recruit his son-in-law with a contract of one million dollars for five years. He even came to the Forum with a certified cheque for that amount in his jacket pocket. But he arrived a couple of hours too late with this final offer from the Nordiques, because Guy had just signed a new deal with the Canadiens: one million dollars—for ten years. Guy had been alone with Sam Pollock in his office, and Sam had said to him, "You're not leaving here without signing." He signed.

The team was staying in retreat at a hotel in the Laurentians, which is what they used to do during the playoffs. The team bus had left after the game against the Sabres, so Sam brought Guy with him in his car to the hotel. He patted Guy's thigh and said, "You must be happy, Guy," and Guy replied, "Oh, yeah," without enthusiasm. He'd just learned the amount of the Nordiques' offer and that he had been royally swindled.

Guy recounted the whole saga to me right after it happened. And he gave me permission to print it during the playoffs. The headline on the front page of *La Presse*: "I Felt Like Bawling."

Imagine what waves that made on the seventh floor of the Forum, in the Canadiens' offices. He took responsibility for what he'd said.

Guy's love for hockey and the Canadiens allowed him to rise above all that. But later, he became livid when he found out Don Awrey was making $165,000 a year while he was earning around $90,000. Pierre Bouchard was also making more than he was. But the kicker was when he found out Ken Dryden made $275,000. He had to threaten to go on strike in 1978 for the Canadiens to start paying him $350,000 a year.

Guy was aware that his declarations would become big headlines in the next day's papers. He told me, "You can write about everything, but try not to hurt anyone." I learned to decode what he said and to tell the difference between "Don't hurt anyone" and "That's too bad, but it is what it is."

What was he like with journalists?

Candid. And fair. I wasn't the only journalist he gave big scoops to. My competitors, Bertrand Raymond, Bernard Brisset, and Yvon Pedneault, got some of those big stories, too.

It was known in the NHL that I was close to Guy. That's why, when I arrived in different cities with the team, local journalists would approach me and ask, "So, Regeeeeen, what's new with Laflooor?" The star of the show had landed in their city. When we went to Detroit, I'd throw them a line or two and, in exchange, they'd fill me in on whatever was happening with the Red Wings. And it worked in St. Louis, too! In the days before the Internet, I could get a fair bit of mileage out of what I had to offer to keep getting new information on other teams.

Tell us about the player on the ice.

He'd weave around at an incredible speed, his blond hair flying in the wind, adding a romantic air to his spectacular game. I can't say that he was better than Gretzky or Lemieux, but he was more electrifying.

You have to remember that apart from his offensive game, Flower could make some spectacular defensive plays. I'm thinking of a game at the Forum against Kansas City. He took off from the point, where'd he just shot from, so he could catch an opponent who was on a breakaway. We could hear the power of his skates cutting into the ice all the way to the press box. Guy easily got the puck back from the player. The crowd reacted loudly, as they did whenever he did anything at all. The Canadiens were leading by something like 5 to 1, but Lafleur had decided it was important to execute that play. There were no half measures with him.

What kind of athlete was he?

He was an extremely committed athlete.

We most often associate Guy with qualities such as his passion, his exceptional talent, and his desire to win. One day I asked him where it all came from. He must have told me the story at least ten times. His father used to leave his job at the factory in the afternoons, travelling from Thurso to Québec to see Guy play with the Aces or the Remparts. The journey would have taken him five hours to get there, and then five hours to return home to sleep for a couple of hours and then get up to go to work. While Guy was warming up on the ice, he'd catch a glimpse of his father in the stands. A little smile and that was all it took for him to be motivated. He didn't need a pep talk from the coach—he'd just gotten all the motivation he needed.

Would you say that Guy was disciplined?

For his time, yes, but—only now and then!

I saw him smoking constantly and drinking often. At a steak house in Denver, the night before a game, he put away a thirty-two-ounce steak, fries, and four crèmes de menthe. He said, "If my tongue isn't green, then I'll be fine." The next day, he played a very good game.

Even on the occasions when he'd overdone it in the evening, he would be on time and effective at the next day's practice at 10:00 a.m. And not long afterwards, he'd be scoring big goals.

If Guy hadn't smoked, and if he'd kept away from the "CC"—champagne and cognac—he most certainly would have had seasons in his early thirties where he scored forty or forty-five goals, rather than experiencing a decline and retiring at thirty-three. But the only thing he relied on was his instinct to perform.

Of course, there was the car accident he had in 1981 that could very well have killed him. I believe it was a tipping point between Lise and Guy—she was ready to give him the boot. It wasn't easy being the wife of Guy Lafleur.

What do you mean?

Especially in the 1970s and 1980s, Lise was an extremely resilient and patient spouse. She lived with a very successful man whom everyone was fighting over, who started getting into the party scene, and then someone who was humiliated by the Canadiens in a one-two punch: first as a player, then as an ambassador. After that, she had to live with a reluctant retiree. Fortunately, there was Guy's return to the game in New York and in Québec, which lifted their spirits. And later on, Guy was often absent, participating in various activities or tooling around in a helicopter.

On top of that were the significant family problems they had and that—as the price of fame—were covered extensively by the media. In particular I'm thinking of the madness that was the arrest warrant issued for Guy.

It was a well-orchestrated media circus, complete with images of Guy in handcuffs. Not just in Québec, but all over North America, front pages used the same headline: "Lafleur Wanted." Come on! If the police wanted to question him, a simple call to his cell phone would have sufficed. Guy Lafleur was not exactly Billy the Kid or Jacques Mesrine. Did anyone really think Guy Lafleur could have passed through customs incognito and fled Canada?

Why do you think Guy Lafleur was never captain of the Canadiens?

I am certain that it never interested him. He knew he would have felt constrained by rules and regulations.

Besides, the players usually voted for a guy who didn't speak much. Maurice Richard, Doug Harvey, Jean Béliveau, Henri Richard, and Yvon Cournoyer were all men of few words. Serge Savard talked more. And then management named Bob Gainey, a man who didn't say one word. They were all less expressive than Guy. I don't know if it was done consciously, but the players voted for captains of few words, knowing that Guy would compensate by saying everything he thought out loud.

Scotty Bowman ruled his players with an iron fist—without the velvet glove! He knew that the best way to unite these guys was for them to be united against him.

Whenever the players had had enough, Guy became their spokesman. In the Canadiens dressing room, or often on flights between Montreal and Los Angeles or between Montreal and Vancouver, the guys would grumble and whine but never really stick their necks out. Then Flower would supply a journalist with a couple of colourful turns of phrase, like when he said that Bowman had to "*slaquer la poulie*" [cut them some slack]. It turned into an automatic front-page headline the next day. Guy was the only one who could get away with outbursts like that, because he was untouchable.

Despite all of the remarks to the media that Lafleur made against him, Bowman loved Guy. He said, "You can't be as passionate as he is and always play by the rules." When he needed a big goal, he turned to Flower.

In your opinion, why did things end so badly between the Canadiens and Guy Lafleur?

First, he was betrayed by his coach and friend Jacques Lemaire.

The night before what would turn out to be Flower's last game with the Canadiens, against Detroit, he and Lemaire went out for coffee. According to Guy, Lemaire promised him a lot of ice time. That evening, over supper with Lise, he said to her, "Jacques understood me—tomorrow will be a new start!"

During the game, Lemaire not only did not give him any more ice time than in previous weeks, but he sent him to the penalty box when the Canadiens were ruled to have too many men on the ice. That's when Guy understood that it was all over with Coco, and he did not accompany the team to their next game in Boston.

At the press conference announcing his retirement, Guy was devastated. From that day on, he made me think of a thoroughbred who'd been put out to pasture without even having anywhere to run.

And then Ronald Corey hired him to do public relations. But what was his thinking? That he could fit Guy into a cookie-cutter role? And a poorly paid one on top of that? Guy shared an outburst with the media and, just like that, he was fired. It was the second big blow Flower suffered at the hands of the Canadiens in the space of two years.

Throughout the club's history, the team has treated its larger-than-life players—such as Maurice Richard, Guy Lafleur, and Patrick Roy—as disposable.

As for Guy, he showed that he had class: On Forum ice, wearing an opponent's uniform, he was the one to offer a handshake to Corey. We saw who the king was.

Tell us about his relationship with the fans.

For Flower, the fans came before the billionaire owners of the team.

Maurice Richard was so revered he brought people out into the streets. Jean Béliveau was admired. As for Guy, he was loved. Loved unconditionally, in the true sense of the word. In all of his magnificence. Guy raised up the Québécois people, playing a part in making them proud and believing in what they could accomplish.

I saw Guy interact with the fans in all sorts of settings. All over North America, during different eras. I remember the 2003 Winter Classic in Edmonton. The night before the game I was having dinner with Lise and Guy in the hotel dining room. From the moment we sat down until we left, the fans came up to us nonstop, asking for an autograph or to take a photo with an Instamatic camera. When I had to take on the role of photographer to immortalize these encounters between Flower and his fans, I even started to wonder if it was a setup for the hidden-camera television show *Surprise sur prise*! Lise told me, "It's always like this." Guy's best years were more than two decades in the past. But for the fans, it was yesterday.

Flower was an idol who loved the people who loved him. And Ti-Guy loved people: the rich, the famous, the ordinary, those down on their luck—everyone. Even when he was ill, he responded to people. And up until the end, he took care when signing autographs. So that a kid could show off the signature in the schoolyard without someone saying it was fake.

Did you benefit from some scoops because of your relationship with Guy Lafleur?

Yes. And out of several, there are two that stand out in particular.

The first was in 1988, when he returned to the game, which was announced in two stages. My colleague Tom Lapointe and I made the announcement of Flower's return to hockey. And a few days later, I confirmed that he would be playing for the Rangers.

Guy had gone with his agent and friend Yves Tremblay to New York to meet with Phil Esposito. That's when he got confirmation that he was invited to the Rangers' training camp. That evening, after landing in Montreal, they met me at Bocca D'Oro, an Italian restaurant at the corner of Saint-Mathieu and De Maisonneuve Boulevard. At the end of the evening, I shut myself up in the office of the restaurant's owner to write and file my report with *La Presse*. Flower was so happy to be returning to the game, it was as if he were walking on a feather duvet three feet off the ground!

It was important for his own peace of mind that he make a return to the game. He knew he was no longer the best player and that he'd no longer be scoring the big goals. But he was back doing what he loved best: playing hockey.

The second story was the very last. It was told over the course of four years, until his death. When there was an important development in the state of his health, Guy would say to his son Martin, "Call Réjean. He'll know what to do." I would write my piece, protecting both father and son by camouflaging my source so they wouldn't be pestered by other journalists jealous of the scoop. And I admit, I would invent sources: a nurse, a doctor, etcetera. We hadn't agreed on it beforehand; that's just how it was.

How would you describe your relationship?

I loved Guy Lafleur. He's in my top five of the people I've loved the most in my life.

I didn't socialize with him. He was a superstar and I was a journalist. But I spoke with him a lot. He knew about my problems and I knew about his.

He influenced the man I am. And the writer, too. The character of Marc Gagnon in *He Shoots, He Scores*, played by Marc Messier, has a lot of Flower in him. His intense will to win, right up to the last episode—that came from Guy.

What were your last moments with him?

On August 4, 2021, in the middle of the pandemic, he granted me an interview, at least two hours, to be used in an eight-hour documentary on the rivalry between the Canadiens and the Nordiques. He had had a chemotherapy treatment the day before, and yet he arrived early, as usual. It was clear to him and to me and to our technical team that this would be his last in-depth interview.

The very last question my colleague Mathias Brunet asked him was "How would you like people to remember you?" He thought for a while and he was about to speak. But he started to cry, for about five minutes. Everyone on set was uncomfortable. And moved. Imagine that: this force of nature who had become so vulnerable.

After all this time that felt like an eternity, he apologized. And then he answered, "That I gave everything."

How did his funeral affect you?

When Guy died, I was harsh towards the Canadiens. One more time! Because it was the people who brought honour to Guy

Lafleur. It was the people who got the party started. It was the people who gave you shivers as they proclaimed their unconditional love.

I'll go further: The Canadiens attempted to pay tribute to a fallen great, but it was Guy Lafleur who truly celebrated the Canadiens by reminding us that the torch had to be passed on for an institution to rediscover its greatness.

What is his legacy?

He showed us the importance of being real.

Everyone knows that Flower smoked, drank, and drove too fast. He was loved because he was, in fact, imperfect—but real. Imperfect as a man and also a proud father who stood up for his children. Even when everything was going badly.

Guy also went from the red sweater of the establishment to one that was the colour of the Québec flag. Almost no one else has done that. He reconciled the irreconcilable.

Vladislav Tretiak

Born in Orudyevo, USSR (now Russia), in 1952, Vladislav Aleksandrovich Tretiak is a goaltender who was dominant on the international scene from the end of the 1960s to the mid-1980s. Thanks to his performances in the legendary 1972 Summit Series between Canada and the USSR, he was the first Russian athlete to become an idol in Canada.

In 1983, Serge Savard and the Canadiens used their seventh-round pick to try to secure his services, but they were not able to come to an agreement with the Soviet government. Tretiak was the first Russian player to be inducted into the Hockey Hall of Fame, in 1989.

Note: Mr. Tretiak responded to our questions in writing.

What kind of relationship did you have with Guy Lafleur?

It was very pleasant. I met him for the first time in 1975 at the Montreal Forum, for a game that pitted the Canadiens against CSKA Moscow. We quickly had great respect for each other. It was obvious even with the language barrier.

Guy Lafleur always showed respect for international competition. He was happy and proud to be part of his national team.

He was a magnificent and dignified man. Among all my opponents, he was the player who was the most intelligent, the most spectacular, and the most athletic of all. Right from the start, we had a warm relationship, based on mutual respect, despite the fierce rivalry that reigned on the ice. And we always communicated well with each other, both during our hockey careers and afterwards.

I'll always remember the events of 1989, when I was inducted into the Hockey Hall of Fame in Toronto. It was Guy Lafleur who introduced me at the ceremony. He put a ring on my finger, awarded me with a commemorative medal, and said many beautiful things about me. I was truly moved and honoured by his speech. After all, the person paying me tribute was a real hockey hero in Montreal and all over Canada—an idol for millions of people in his country.

How would you describe him?

Guy Lafleur didn't really look like a hockey player. He was slim, had a medium build, and an expressive face. I would say he looked more like an actor!

On the ice, he did incredible things. His speed, the way he could read the game, the way he handled the puck—all were top-tier. Guy really was different from the Canadian players of his generation. Most Canadian players relied on their physical power to win possession of the puck, and their ability to beat someone with their speed. Lafleur focused on other talents. He skated very fast and his skating had a surgical precision. His puck handling was impeccable, enabling him to execute very complicated plays. And his shot? A cannon!

I would say that Guy's style was more like a star Soviet player from that era than a Canadian player.

When Guy jumped onto the ice he made an impression. No helmet, his hair flowing in the wind. Slim, no shoulder pads, invisible behind his teammates. When he got the puck and skated right up to my net, the whole Montreal Forum shouted, "Guy! Guy! Guy!"

Tell us about the athlete.

I quickly realized that Lafleur liked to take low shots, with no warning, and so I prepared myself for those—but it was hard because the shot was still lethal. Like a cannon shot, the puck came at me at top speed.

In 1976, during the Canada Cup, he took a particularly good shot. With difficulty, I was able to deflect the puck with my pads. Guy skated slowly towards me and gently tapped my pads with his stick. Without uttering a word, he was saying, "Good work, well played." In those days, it was unusual to communicate with opponents during a game. But Lafleur appreciated my skill, just as I always appreciated his talent.

As for his style of play, it was similar to that of Wayne Gretzky and Igor Larionov—one of the best Russian players ever. True masters, strong, able to score at any moment. But his shot was clearly more powerful and sharper than Gretzky's or Larionov's. And he could make very precise passes. During the New Year's Eve game in 1975, when CSKA Moscow played the Canadiens at the Forum, Yvon Lambert scored the second goal off a superb pass from Guy.

I remember when he played in the Ice Hockey World Championships in Stockholm in 1981. He was badly injured during a game against the Netherlands. Everyone was surprised—how were the Dutch, not the most imposing team, able to injure a pro NHLer? At the time, Canadian players seemed invincible. Lafleur performed very well at the Canada Cup in 1976 and 1981. It's a fact that in 1981, Canada didn't win the tournament; our team won in the final, 8–1.

Did Guy Lafleur enter the popular imagination of hockey fans in your country?

In the Soviet Union, the most popular player of the 1970s was probably Bobby Hull. He also came to play here for the Izvestia Trophy. During the 1974 Summit Series, Hull was remembered for his gentlemanly conduct: he didn't fight and he didn't try to intimidate his opponents. On the contrary, he was polite and treated the USSR national team very well. Lafleur didn't play for the Canadian team that year.

Lafleur's style of play had an effect on the young people of our country. He didn't fight—he made use of his main assets, which were his skating and his hands. When they watched him in action, many young players saw that they could become stars by improving their technical skills.

Tell us a story.

In 1987, I was invited to Québec City, for the Rendez-vous 87 series, and I went to the Québec Winter Carnival. On that trip, we spent a whole day with Guy. They asked me what I'd like to visit in Québec and my reply was, "An art gallery, please." Everyone was surprised that a professional hockey player was interested in art. We went to a gallery, and Guy came with me. And we even met with the celebrated Canadian artist Jean Paul Lemieux, who gave each of us a painting!

What memory of him stays with you?

I always liked meeting up with Guy, whether at the centenary of the Montreal Canadiens or at other events. We would talk about our personal problems, and recall the moments we played against each other.

It is sad that he died so young.

Lucien DeBlois

Born in Joliette, Quebec, in 1957, Lucien DeBlois was the recipient of the Michel Brière Memorial Trophy for the most valuable player of the 1976–1977 season in the QMJHL, playing for the Sorel Black Hawks. The eighth pick in the 1977 draft, he was one of the earliest Québécois to be picked in the history of the New York Rangers. He played close to one thousand games over seventeen seasons in the NHL, as right wing and centre, for six different teams.

He is the only player to have been Guy Lafleur's teammate in Montreal, New York, and Québec City.

What is your earliest memory of Guy Lafleur as a player?

I knew about his achievements in juniors. But he was no longer with the Remparts when I arrived in Sorel in 1973–1974, the year Pierre Larouche beat his points record.

In Joliette, when I was captain of the parish cathedral team, I wore the number 4—not because Guy had that number and had worn the "C" with the Remparts, but because I wanted to be like my idol, Jean Béliveau. Guy admired him, too.

Then, for seven years, I played against him when I was with the New York Rangers, the Colorado Rockies, and the Winnipeg Jets. I was impressed by his immense talent and his absolutely unpredictable style of play.

Tell us about the first time you met him.

Before I even met him, I first became acquainted with one of his sticks! Around 1975, I was playing in a game against the Moscow Selects at the Montreal Forum. Our team was using the Canadiens dressing room and the players were all allowed to take a couple of sticks from the storied team. I took one of Guy's, and I scored!

The first time we played together was in 1981 at the Ice Hockey World Championships in Sweden, playing on the same line. Not long after the tournament began, I made an imprecise pass to Guy. Guy juggled with it a bit, an opponent took advantage and elbowed him violently to the head—he was wearing a helmet, which was mandatory in the tournament. It's probably the only time Guy had a concussion—provoked by a teammate, no less!

We spent two weeks in Sweden. The practices and tours allowed us to get to know each other more. I could tell right away what a good guy he was. The Europeans who were following the competition already knew Guy Lafleur very well; he was one of their stars. One thing that started for me in Sweden, and then later with the Canadiens, the Rangers, and the Nordiques, was spending crazy amounts of time waiting for Guy, who was constantly signing autographs.

In the NHL, you first played with him in Montreal. Tell us about that.

I was traded to the Canadiens before the 1984–1985 season. At the training camp, he outpaced us all on the ice and in the gym. He said he found it tough, but he was faster and stronger than everyone. There wasn't a drop of perspiration on him while we were all sweating buckets. At thirty-three, it was phenomenal.

He had scored thirty goals in the previous year and I had no reason to believe he'd be retiring just two months later.

The season began. Jacques Lemaire liked to use the trap, which meant that players had to play a defensive and reactive game. You needed to be patient. Guy, as everyone knew, was an instinctive and emotional player. He found that system hard, and it was suffocating him.

During the previous season there had been a few clashes between Lafleur and Lemaire—Guy spoke about it in the media with Paul Arcand. Lemaire supposedly had asked him if he was going to keep slacking off or if he was going to play for real. Guy had been the Canadiens' best scorer. Lemaire had replaced Bob Berry as the coach near the end of the season, and he shook up the team, which performed well in the playoffs. But Guy was playing less and less, and scoring fewer and fewer goals. Not a single goal in two playoff series! And then the following season Jacques had me playing on the power play a few times instead of Guy. It didn't make sense.

Jacques could have implemented his trap system for everyone else on the team and allowed Guy to play his way, which he was still able to do at thirty-three. That's what Scotty Bowman had done, eventually. Besides, at the beginning of his career, when things weren't going so well for Guy, his captain, Henri Richard, had said something to him like, "Stop playing the way everyone tells you to play and just play like Guy Lafleur!" That would explain how he had exploded on the ice afterwards.

During his final game playing with the Canadiens, Guy played for roughly two minutes. On the players' bench, he said to me and Chris Nilan, "I've had enough of this bullshit. I'm done." After the game he didn't get on the plane with us, and he retired.

Guy was very good at handling the pressure of being in Montreal. He just needed ice time. Anyway, he went on to play a huge number of games with the Canadiens' alumni team. He still skated a hundred miles an hour and no other player on any of the teams of retirees had a shot like his.

Tell us about his return to the game in New York. Did that surprise you?

Yes and no. Flower still had hockey in his blood, and he had things he wanted to prove to himself. And to the Canadiens, too!

I was very pleased that he came to the Rangers. He was in exceptional shape for a thirty-seven-year-old, and if he hadn't gotten injured, he certainly would have scored around thirty goals.

The Rangers' fans were very happy to see Lafleur wearing the Blueshirt because he was an international star. Just like in Montreal, you'd hear the fans shout "Guy! Guy! Guy!" at Madison Square Garden.

We had a young team. The next generation centred around Brian Leetch and Tony Granato. I was thirty years old; Marcel Dionne and Guy were the oldest. All the younger players looked up to Guy, who was already in the Hockey Hall of Fame, and Marcel, who would soon follow.

Tony Granato was a sponge when it came to Guy. He was a very talented right winger, and Guy gave him a thousand and one tips on the ice. He was also influenced by the way Guy conducted himself in all areas: He was a passionate player and a man of integrity.

What was life in New York like for him?

In Montreal, Guy wasn't able to take a walk on Sainte-Catherine Street without being recognized. But he could be almost incognito on Broadway or Fifth Avenue. I think that the anonymity helped him fall in love with hockey again.

One day we went with our families to Jones Beach, a public beach on Long Island. He couldn't get over how we could be on a white-sand beach and be so close to New York. If Bergie [Michel Bergeron] had stayed longer with the Rangers, Guy and I would have stayed with him.

Tell us about the impact Guy had with the Nordiques.

I used to tease Guy, saying, "After the Canadiens and the Rangers, here you are with the Nordiques. You keep finding ways to follow me!" But really, I was the one who was privileged to find myself on his turf.

It was a special thing to get to witness his return to where it all started for him in Québec. For the Remparts and Guy, it was "till death do us part." And even when he played for the Canadiens, a lot of people in Québec City liked him and followed his career. For the fans, it was a consecration when he went to the Nordiques to finish his career. The team was not great in its last two years at the Colisée, to say the least. But he still contributed to the organization, with his presence and his passion for the game, up until they moved to Colorado in 1995.

What was he like as a teammate?

Flower was one of the most charismatic and spectacular players I ever played with. Despite his superstar status, he was very easy to get along with in the dressing room and outside of it. He loved to laugh and tell jokes. Two of his strengths that stick with me most were his mental fortitude and the way he prepared for games.

Guy had an aura about him, twenty-four hours a day. We players saw it, just like the fans did. But he always acted like one of the boys, plain and simple. Around us, it was as if his celebrity didn't exist.

Tell us an unforgettable story.

There were three or four players, including Guy Lafleur, who smoked in the Canadiens dressing room. One fine day, Jacques Lemaire decided that it would be a no-smoking zone. So Guy would go into Eddy Palchak's little room between periods and tell him, "Pretend you're sharpening my skates and wave the vacuum cleaner over your machine!"

What was his greatest quality?

Guy was a combination of Jean Béliveau and Maurice Richard. He had the class of Mr. Béliveau and the fire of the Rocket, but his charisma was all his own. He was so spectacular! He was definitely one of the most electrifying players in the NHL, along with Bobby Hull.

He also always had integrity, with his unsparing opinions—in particular when he was playing for the Canadiens—and he paid a price for expressing them.

What were your last moments with him?

We saw each other at a golf tournament sponsored by the CHUM Foundation. Robert Charlebois and a few other of Guy's good friends were there. We chatted for fifteen minutes or so. We also spoke on the phone and texted a few times in 2021.

Then, on April 24, 2022, the Canadiens organization paid tribute to Guy, before a game against the Boston Bruins, and I was there. Réjean Houle, the president of thc Canadiens Alumni, had invited me, and I considered it a privilege to be there. It was very sad in the Alumni Lounge before and after the ceremony. When I saw Yvan Cournoyer and other former teammates crying, that's when it hit me. To see an icon of our own youth go through so much suffering really brings it home.

What is his legacy, the most beautiful memory that he left the world of hockey and all of society?

In my opinion, his greatest legacy is that he did not act as if he were God's gift, even though there were a lot of people who considered him to be, both on the ice and off of it.

Guy was a human with his faults, his limitations, and his problems. That's what he presented to the public and it explains why people saw themselves in him. He stood tall, for the sake of his family, his teammates, and himself. That is a tremendous life lesson.

Pierre Larouche

Born in Taschereau, Quebec, in 1955, Pierre Larouche is a centre who was the first-round draft pick of the Pittsburgh Penguins in 1974. He moved on to Montreal for the 1977–1978 season and became the pivot between Steve Shutt and Guy Lafleur. Two years later, he finished the regular season with fifty goals, just like his celebrated line mate.

What is your oldest memory of Guy Lafleur as a player?

I grew up in Abitibi. I remember that on television they talked about him a lot more than they showed him in action. Later, I briefly played with the Remparts—where they talked about him even more—before my two seasons with the Sorel Black Hawks.

In 1973–1974, for my last year in Sorel, my wingers were Michel Déziel and Jacques Cossette. I beat the record that Guy had set with the Remparts of 209 points in a season—I had 251. Obviously, I hadn't started the season thinking about that record, which I'd thought was unattainable. But the closer I got to 200 points, the more I started to hear about it in our dressing room and in the media. I reached 209 points, then 210, and so on until I'd set the new record. And then, exactly ten years later, in 1983–1984, Mario Lemieux set new records, with 133 goals and 282 points.

At the time, I didn't know Guy or Mario. It wasn't like today, where, with social media, you'll often see an athlete reach out to the person who broke his record—the older one congratulating the younger. Back in my day, I didn't receive a phone call from Guy and later, I didn't call up Mario. But fortunately, over time, I became excellent friends with both of them.

At first, Guy and I played against each other in the NHL. I was with Pittsburgh and he was with the Canadiens. I remember the first time I faced him. I watched him closely and said to myself, "So that's how you make your plays!" His speed impressed me, because he was even faster on the ice than fans could appreciate watching from the stands or on television.

During the 1977–1978 season, you were traded to the Canadiens. What was your reaction?

What Quebecer wouldn't have been very happy? My family and friends were, too. I was just a kid born in Taschereau who grew up in Amos, pretending to be a Canadiens star when I played street hockey. And now here I was, spending every day on the ice and in the dressing room with those guys.

Very soon after I arrived, I noticed an enormous difference between the cultures of the Penguins and the Canadiens at that time. In Montreal, professionalism was at the heart of everything we did, at every moment. The practices were short, but intense—our simulated games were just as intense as our real ones. The mentorship of the younger players by the veterans came naturally. In the dressing room, the power play guys sat together, the defensive players were in their area, etcetera, so that everyone could talk to each other. Nothing was left to chance. It's little details like those that make for winning teams.

Sam Pollock ruled his club with an iron fist. When my contract had expired I had fairly high expectations. Pollock met with me, and when he gave me back my contract, I saw that the annual salaries were a fair bit lower than what I'd been hoping for. Seeing my disappointment he said, "That's the salary. You know, we won twenty-one Stanley Cups before you came to play for us." Guy Lafleur was also squeezed in the same way by the Canadiens; he never earned the salaries he deserved.

The day came when you became the regular centre alongside Guy Lafleur and Steve Shutt. Tell us about that.

Yes, it was a wonderful challenge that Scotty gave me. Jacques Lemaire had just retired and they needed a centre to complement Flower and Shutty. I joined the trio, without putting any pressure on myself, and we had chemistry right away.

I was recently looking at some clips from our games. We were really fantastic! One of us three would go into the offensive zone with the puck, a couple of opponents would go after him, and that created space for the other two. Flower, Shutty, and I moved the puck rapidly and, very often, the goalie didn't know which way to look. And whoever finished the play found himself in front of an empty net. In hockey speak, that's called tic-tac-toe!

In 1979–1980, Guy and I each scored fifty goals, and Steve scored forty-seven. At the end of the season, we tried really hard to have him get fifty, too, but he hit the post a couple of times. It was superb teamwork.

What kind of player was he?

I never had the impression that Flower was coming to work. Guy "played" hockey. He did it with seriousness and professionalism, but he *played*. He was very demanding—of himself, enormously, but also of his teammates. It was perfect because he pulled the team up.

I remember one night in Toronto when I made a pass to his skates. He recovered the puck and scored. When we got back to the bench he said, "Skates are for skating. Sticks are for receiving passes!" I don't remember ever sending him any more passes to his skates.

It's important to keep in mind that, as a player, Guy was even more exceptional than what we saw and what his statistics show. There's a simple reason: He was a target for hooking and other interference game after game—from the beginning of the season to the end—because the rules were not rigorously applied. In the playoffs it was even worse. If our opponents had received penalties, the way they do today, he would have been even more dominant.

Tell us what he was like as a teammate.

Any way you look at it, he was a leader. He would have done anything to help his teammates—and I'm convinced that there were a lot of things he did, discreetly.

As a personality, he influenced us. We bought nice suits because that's what he did. One time I bought a large leather pocketbook and my wife was really surprised. I said to her, "Didn't you notice? Flower has one like it." And, by the way, I still have it.

Every time he went to the media—which happened a lot—it was always in the interests of the team or a teammate. Never for himself.

I remember that in 1980–1981, we were having a rocky season. Guy spoke out in the media about the cliques that were dividing the team. He said too many players were acting like coaches, and that only the defensive players on the team were happy, because they were playing forty minutes per game. He stated clearly that they should be playing Pierre Larouche more often. It's the only time in my career I've seen a player speak like that to the media.

The thing that Guy did more and better than other players was that he didn't play only for the Montreal Canadiens. He played for the people. In our era, the players belonged to the people. The Canadiens should have been called "The People's Team of Montreal"!

In 1981–1982, the Canadiens traded you to the Hartford Whalers. What's the story behind that?

Irving Grundman had become the general manager, Scotty Bowman had left, and several players had retired. I wanted a better contract and Grundman told me, "Wait your turn." I replied, "Turn for what? I just scored fifty goals, and a hockey career is short. I don't have time to lose." He didn't want to hear it.

At the next training camp, our line had been dismantled. Guy and I were no longer roommates on the road. The team was using a defensive style of play that was exasperating to us both. It was feeling like the end—for him and for me—of our time in Montreal. I was traded to Hartford, and we all know how it ended between Guy and the Canadiens.

Were you surprised when his retirement was announced?

Oh yeah, like everyone else. Because he had several good years of hockey still in him. The proof was that he played pretty well when he returned to the game in New York and in Québec, despite being away for four years. It showed he wasn't yet finished expressing himself on the ice.

When we were in Montreal, I remember we said to each other that it would be good to play in New York with the Rangers. We spoke about the city and the ambiance at NHL games. We compared the worlds of hockey and golf, saying that the Montreal fans were as noble and contained as if they were on the green at St. Andrews in Scotland. At Madison Square

Garden, the party atmosphere was more like the Scottsdale golf course in Arizona.

In our era, the pressure you had as a Montreal Canadien was not at all like what it was playing for the Rangers. In Montreal, it was a requirement to be constantly talking to journalists and to fans. I remember that when the Canadiens won, my postman would ring the doorbell. When we lost, he left my mail in the snow!

Of course, nothing would have led Guy and me to believe that we'd both end up wearing the Rangers' Blueshirt. And yet it happened at almost the same time.

Tell us about choosing sweater numbers.

In Sorel I wore 16, but in Pittsburgh one of my teammates already had it. So I chose 10. When I arrived in Montreal, the equipment manager, Pierre "Boom Boom" Meilleur, told me, "Henri had 16 and Guy has 10. But I'll give you 28 since 2 plus 8 equals 10." I really liked the idea.

In New York, I was number 10 again. When Flower arrived, I'd been seriously injured in the hip and I knew I wouldn't play again. In the preseason games, I saw he was wearing 44—a nod to his old number and that of his idol, Jean Béliveau, since Ron Greschner had number 4. I went to Guy and said, "Take the 10, it's yours." He didn't want to take it and I insisted: "Don't be ridiculous—you're getting it back. You'll be insulting me if you don't take it. You're Guy Lafleur!" I was very proud from the first day that he wore it.

How did your relationship evolve?

Flower was my best man when I got married. That's all you need to know. He was like a brother to me. I would have done anything for him and I think he'd have done anything for me as well.

Tell us an unforgettable story.

In Montreal, there were a number of us who lived on the West Island. I often went to practices and games with Guy, Bob Gainey, Yvan Cournoyer, and Larry Robinson.

One day, Larry, Bob, Guy, and I were all injured, but we still went to the Forum to train, only without any intensity. A friend of mine from Amos, Michel Boilard, was visiting me in Montreal. He had played at the junior level, and Guy knew him. Michel came into the dressing room with us and we loaned him skates and equipment. When he jumped on the ice and Guy started making passes to him, the GM, Irving Grundman, asked everybody, "Who's that guy over there?" So Flower replied, "I've just recruited him and he's very good!" That was a day Michel would never forget.

What was his greatest quality?

His generosity with the public. I know of only one other great athlete who was as generous as he was with the fans: Mario Lemieux. Mario's idol was Guy, and he probably was a positive influence.

What were you last moments with him?

The terrible scourge of cancer appeared at the same time in my personal life and in the lives of my close friends, including Mario Lemieux and Flower.

The public must have imagined Guy was invincible, and we, his teammates, also wanted to believe it. We all thought he would beat it. Even Guy must have believed it, too.

The last time I texted him to ask him how he was doing, he replied with two words: "Not strong." I understood then that he wouldn't be with us for much longer.

Chris Nilan

Born in Boston in 1958, Chris Nilan is a right winger who played for thirteen seasons in the NHL. A teammate of Guy Lafleur's for five seasons with the Canadiens, he was a member of the Rangers when the Démon Blond made his return to the game.

Known chiefly for his reputation as a fighter—he racked up 358 penalty minutes in a single season with the Canadiens—"Knuckles" always did what he had to do for Guy Lafleur to allow his talent to shine.

What is your oldest memory of Guy Lafleur?

My first memory was that I hated the guy!

I grew up in Boston. In the 1970s, like every Bruins fan, I hated the Canadiens, a talented team that beat us too often. I really hated the way Guy skated, his shot, how he looked. But deep down, I could recognize he was an exceptional player.

I believe that among all the excellent players on the Bruins, the Canadiens, and everywhere else in the league, two towered above them all: Bobby Orr and Guy Lafleur. As soon as either of them touched the puck, they had an exceptional ability to energize the crowd at every arena in the NHL.

Tell us about the first time you met Guy.

I had two "first meetings" with Guy. And there's a whole story behind how we became buddies.

In 1978, I was playing at Northeastern University in Boston.

I was drafted by the Canadiens in the nineteenth round, number 231, to be precise. Imagine how I felt: drafted so low, by the team I hated the most!

The next spring, during the Montreal–Boston playoff series, a friend and I went to see the Canadiens practice at Boston Garden. Afterwards, we were driving away and saw Guy Lafleur, Jacques Lemaire, and Gilles Lupien standing in front of the Garden waiting for a taxi. I said to my friend, "Let's go—we'll offer them a lift to their hotel." When we approached them, they gave us a look, like, "Should the winners of the Stanley Cup get into this old car with a couple of weird guys from Boston?" They gave each other a look, and then they said yes!

During the ride, Guy asked us if he could light a cigarette, and we said, "Sure!" Then my friend pointed at me and told them I'd been drafted by the Canadiens the previous year. "Yeah, I'm going to be playing with you next year," I said, all proud. One of them asked what round I'd been picked and I replied, "Nineteen." The three of them then burst out laughing.

We dropped them off at their hotel. That series ended up being decided in game seven at the Montreal Forum. Obviously, my heart would be broken when my passenger Lemaire made a perfect pass to my passenger Lafleur to tie the game right at the end of regulation time. And then Yvon Lambert scored in overtime.

So, to finish the story, a few months later I was at training camp, and I found myself playing on Guy's team for a practice game and of course was with him in the Canadiens' main locker room. He takes a long look at me and finally, he says, "Hey, you! *Tabarnak*—it's you, the kid from Boston." And with the same confidence I had back in the car with my friend, I replied, "I told you I'd be coming to play with you guys!"

Something happened between us that day. Then, the Canadiens sent me to the Nova Scotia Voyageurs and I came back to finish the season in Montreal. My arrival on the team was a story worthy of a Hollywood movie.

What do you mean by "worthy of a Hollywood movie"?

In 1980, I'd just been called up. Between a Thursday game in Atlanta and the next one in Philadelphia on the Saturday, the team was back in Montreal and had the day off from practice. I still wanted to train, though, so I went to the Verdun Auditorium, where only one other player had shown up: Guy Lafleur, who was getting over an injury.

So we were the only two players in the locker room and on the ice. Obviously, I was intimidated—but he treated me like a real Canadiens teammate. Even though he skated very fast, I think he cruised a little so I wouldn't feel too bad. He never stopped shooting, and kept passing to me, even though he didn't have to do me any favours—never mind after we were done practising.

Still, after we got out of the shower he said, "Let's go get lunch." I got into his beautiful Corvette and we went to Thursday's, on Crescent Street, which was packed. We parked, and as we crossed the street, I could see everyone turning their eyes his way. We went in and up to the second floor. I could see he was in his element. Everyone there was looking at him, too, with Montreal's most beautiful women coming over for an autograph or a photo. But he shared the spotlight, introducing me as his new teammate, and he had me sign the first autographs of my life!

It really struck me to realize what was happening. A year before, I was playing university hockey, I hated the Canadiens, and I was eating sandwiches. And here I was, just called up by the Canadiens, and the world's best hockey player had invited me out for lunch. From that day on, Guy made sure I was a part of the team.

I loved having Flower as a teammate. He didn't speak much, but he took care that all of the guys felt good in the locker room and on the road. With his talent, he did everything he could to help the team win. And all of the players, each in his own way, contributed to the team's success. For example, I wasn't there to make pretty plays. My role was clear: to stay on top of our toughest adversaries and protect Flower. After all the games in which I'd taken on opponents who'd tried to mess with Guy, he thanked me. He told me, "Chris, you don't have to do that." But I sensed that he appreciated my contribution.

What was he like on the ice?

He was successful at everything he did. But he worked harder than he let on.

During practices, he fully applied himself when doing all the required drills. But there was one thing he practised more than any other teammate I've had on the Canadiens, the Rangers, and the Bruins: his shot. If he was a superstar in juniors and became one in the NHL, it was because he devoted an inconceivable amount of time on his shots: making them powerful, working on angles, targeting high-percentage areas in the net, rebounds—everything. He left absolutely nothing to chance. That's why he spent so much time practising on his own before the rest of the team arrived—day in, day out.

You played with Guy during his best seasons and also when he was slowing down. Tell us about that.

By the early 1980s, Guy was slowing down. It happens to all athletes, even the best ones. All the same, he was still a dominant player.

Other things were going on that didn't help Guy. The team ended its streak of Stanley Cup wins at four—not exactly shabby!

Scotty had left, and so had some key players like Dryden and Cournoyer. The team was in the midst of a rebuild and had four coaches in the space of a few years: "Boom Boom" Geoffrion, Claude Ruel, Bob Berry, and Jacques Lemaire.

Jacques Lemaire was my favourite of all the coaches I had during my career. But he experienced the same problems that 100 percent of coaches have who are in charge of their former teammates.

He put a system in place that truly made the team better and enabled many players to improve their performance. I was one of them. I understood that he wanted all of the players to follow his rules and he was inflexible about that. But Flower was never a systems guy. With him, it was "Give me the effin' puck and I'll charge the net!"

As a coach, Jacques enforced discipline with a capital "D," which was nonexistent before he arrived. I can think of two examples.

We were playing in Boston. Lunch breaks weren't open-ended like they had been before, but took place at a specific time, with everyone together. I arrived ten minutes late. Jacques didn't say anything in the moment. But that night, he made me sit on the bench for the whole game—in my city, in front of my friends!

I also remember during one of Guy's last games he played with the Canadiens, Lemaire called him back to the bench with something like three minutes left to play in the game. Guy started to remove the tape from his pads—he thought his game was over, because he hadn't been getting much playing time. Jacques saw that, and quickly sent Guy back out onto the ice. If looks could kill, Jacques would've been dead on the spot. Lemaire shouldn't have done that.

All of that background contributed to the breakdown of their relationship, which had been excellent when they were playing together on the same line. Luckily, through all of it, there was one thing that never changed: Guy's commitment to the team, every day.

How did things unfold when he left the team and announced his retirement?

We had just finished a game against Detroit at the Forum, and the players were heading to Dorval Airport to get a flight to our next game in Boston.

Guy was driving me and Chris Chelios. I was sitting in the front and Chris was in the back. Once we got to the airport, Guy didn't drive to the parking lot, but instead stopped at the departures entrance.

"Why are you bringing us here?" I asked. "We've got to park and walk over, like we always do."

"It's because I'm not going to Boston," he replied.

"What are you talking about? You're not injured."

"It's over. I'm done playing. I'm taking my retirement."

Chelly and I were in shock. We tried to get him to change his mind. It was no use. We walked into the airport—none of our teammates had any more understanding than we did about what had just happened. But we all had to face the facts: Guy was going to announce his retirement. In the meantime, we were told by team management that the official reason was "Lafleur has a groin injury."

What kind of relationship did you have with him afterwards?

Guy became the Canadiens' ambassador, so we would see each other from time to time during games. He was always very well-dressed. He often came to see the team, and didn't really look like a happy retiree.

Later, I was heartbroken when the Canadiens traded me to the Rangers. As someone who had previously detested the Habs, I had now become a full-fledged member of this organization, and I loved it. But chance can play some funny tricks: Guy chose my new team to make his comeback!

Before inviting Guy to the Rangers training camp, the general manager, Phil Esposito, said to me, "Guy Lafleur wants to come back to the game and we're in talks with him. Do you think he could score twenty goals?" I replied that I had no doubt he could. In fact, he would finish that season with eighteen, but he'd missed several games due to injuries.

I remember the day he arrived in the dressing room for the first time with us as if it were yesterday. It was in Trois-Rivières. We welcomed him with open arms.

What was Guy's life like in New York?

It was different from anything he'd experienced since he was born.

It was the first time he'd lived outside of Quebec. The first time, too, that he lived in a place where he wasn't asked for a photo or an autograph every second of the day. For him, living in the Big Apple, one of the world's most bustling cities, was more relaxing than it was in the Belle Province!

What stays with you about the kind of man he was?

He was unique. Unique because of his personality. Unique because of his passion for hockey. Unique in everything he did.

Like all athletes, Guy had an ego. But what always surprised me was even though he was one of the best in the world, his ego was no bigger than mine, or than anyone else's in our locker room. And his charisma—that's something you either have or you don't. Flower had charisma coming out of his ears!

I don't know how he managed to find the time for his family, his teammates, the fans, or charitable causes, but I never heard about him saying no to any request whatsoever.

Guy was born to play for Montreal, because it's in the team's DNA to pass the torch from one generation to the next. As far as I'm concerned, Guy was the flame.

Flower also embodied Quebec culture: He was passionate, friendly, proud, a bon vivant, and humble. He taught me a lot!

Chris Chelios

Born in Chicago in 1962, Chris Chelios (born Christos Kostas Tselios) is a defenceman who had an impressive twenty-six-season career in the NHL, with the first six of those playing with the Canadiens. He played 1,651 games in the regular season, which ranks him ninth in the history of the NHL, and 266 games in the playoffs, the most of any player in history.

A teammate of Guy Lafleur's in 1984–1985, Chris Chelios remained close to the Blond Demon.

What is your first memory of Guy Lafleur as a player?

It seems to me that it was in 1971, when he came to the NHL. I was nine years old and my family lived in Chicago. In those days, the Canadiens and the Blackhawks—my favourite team—regularly faced each other in the playoffs, and I watched the games on television. I remember two heartbreaking goals scored by Henri Richard in game seven of the finals in Chicago in 1970—and the imposing presence of Serge Savard and Guy Lapointe on defence.

Guy Lafleur joined the Canadiens the following season. He quickly stood out with his powerful shot and his skating skills that allowed him to keep his opponents off-balance. And with his hair flowing behind him, he had a unique look.

Do you remember the first time you met him?

Yes, like it was yesterday. In 1983–1984 I joined the Canadiens after the Olympics in Sarajevo. I played twelve games in the regular season, and fifteen games in the playoffs. On my first day Guy came up to me in the dressing room, shook my hand, and welcomed me to the team. I remember it was a good squeeze, the first contact of my rookie's hand crushed in his immense one. He told me not to be nervous and to have fun. I'll never forget the way he welcomed me to the club.

I realized quickly that there was a lot of pressure to win for the Canadiens, and Guy knew that very well. When I came into the dressing room I saw Flower, Bob Gainey, Larry Robinson, and the head coach, Jacques Lemaire, and so on. All around there were plaques featuring history-making players. And high above the ice were all the Stanley Cup banners.

To play in the NHL with the Canadiens was like getting a degree from Harvard. You were representing the most successful team in history and you were surrounded by true leaders like Guy, Larry Robinson, Bob Gainey, and Steve Shutt. And then there were the alumni who gravitated around the team like Henri Richard, Yvan Cournoyer, and others. I learned how to win from the best in the game.

What was he like as a teammate?

Whether it was on the bench or in the dressing room, Guy always had a kind word for me. He also liked to see my puzzled reaction to his deadpan jokes—and then he'd laugh really hard. I remember the first time I set foot on the ice in an NHL game, our opponents scored a goal on us and Guy made light of the situation, saying to me, "Welcome to the big league!"

On game days he would arrive in the dressing room around

3:00 p.m. Chris Nilan and I also liked to show up early, but it was hard to be there before Flower. And it was crucial that we didn't disturb his routine. Sometimes I would call the security guard to make sure I didn't get to the Forum before Flower. I watched Knuckles and Flower having fun like kids, and I heard them talking—sometimes about serious things. They'd take their time getting ready for games. After the game, Flower was the first one to be in the shower and ready to leave, so he could go and meet his fans.

What was his playing like during the lead-up to his first retirement?

Flower arrived at training camp as if he hadn't stopped playing since the previous season, as if he hadn't taken a summer break. He was in great physical shape, even though he hadn't been training. It was his genetics.

I didn't play very long with him: a dozen games in the regular season, followed by the 1983–1984 playoffs. And then, about fifteen games into the beginning of the next season, he announced his retirement. But it was long enough to leave a huge impression on me.

Flower was tough on his body. During the 1984 playoffs, in a game against the Islanders, our teammate Ric Nattress injured Flower on his shoulder during a practice. It was obviously a fluke accident, but Guy played for the entire playoffs all the same—because he wanted to—even though he wasn't in the best of shape.

Were you surprised when he retired in 1984?

Yes, and devastated.

The team was in transition. Jacques Lemaire was managing the "young lions" coming in, along with his former teammates.

It's never an easy situation. Guy hadn't lost his desire to win, but he had lost opportunities to play.

I experienced an unforgettable moment with him—Chris Nilan was there, too. We were in Guy's car after what had been—unbeknownst to us at the time—Guy's last game in a Canadiens uniform, against Detroit. After the game, we were flying to Boston to play the Bruins the next day. Guy drove us just as far as the airport in Dorval, and there was no indication that anything was wrong. He was a little quiet, but that felt normal because Chris was always talkative and Guy liked to listen to his stories.

When we got to the airport, instead of going to park his car as usual, Guy drove right up to the departures area. He looked at us and said, "I'm going to leave you here, boys. I'm not going to play anymore. Good luck." We tried to persuade him to change his mind, but it was no use. He had made his decision.

Chris went into the airport to tell our teammates. We were all in shock. On the plane to Boston, you could have heard a pin drop.

It's possible that Flower made his decision during the game against Detroit. He'd had very little playing time.

Did you stay in touch afterwards?

Yes. Right after he retired, he became the Canadiens' ambassador for a while, so we ran into each other at the Forum. A few times he came to lunch with us at Yvan Cournoyer's restaurant.

Were you surprised when he returned to the game?

With hindsight, it's easy to imagine that when Jacques Lemaire left his job as the Canadiens' coach in 1985, Guy could have arranged for his return to the game. But it never occurred to me at the time, and it didn't come up in dressing room conversations. For everyone in Montreal—not least of all for me—his return was a total surprise. For about two weeks, it was *the* biggest topic of conversation in our dressing room, in the media, and in the NHL.

It's impossible to forget his return to the game at the Forum wearing a Rangers uniform, and scoring two goals against us. The fans in Montreal were so proud to have Flower back. I watched that game recently, and Guy's smile fills up the screen, from start to finish.

Flower was happy that night, but he must have had mixed feelings. There he was on Forum ice, but wearing a sweater that didn't belong to the Canadiens. I would find out what it was like to leave Montreal—a city I loved—and to find myself in the opponents' dressing room at the Forum that first time. I had to go through a different door of the Forum than the one the Canadiens used, and I had to remember to return to the correct players' bench at the end of my shifts!

I was playing for the Canadiens and then the Blackhawks during the three years of his return to the game. We'd find opportunities to chat, but the second the puck was in play, we became adversaries, and his desire to win came before everything else.

Talk to us about the athlete with his fans.

During the whole span of my career, I was truly impressed by two great players and their special relationships with fans: Flower and Wayne Gretzky. It wasn't just that the fans were very happy to be meeting them, but that they gave back their genuine attention. When I went to play in Boston, the Bruins fans would yell at me. But Flower and Gretz didn't get that at all.

I remember Guy was always very stylishly dressed. Custom-made suits, shirts that were always unwrinkled, shined shoes, and a perfectly knotted tie. He often preferred to remain standing so he wouldn't get creases in his suits. I never saw him wear jeans. What's more, he'd shave before games, even though it burns your skin when you sweat. But he always wanted to look his best for the fans, on the ice or afterwards. I followed his example, always shaving before games myself.

Did Guy Lafleur have an influence on you?

Oh yeah. On the ice, in the dressing room, and with the fans. Whatever Flower did, so did I.

When I first started with the Canadiens, I didn't have the money to dress the way he did, or the habit. But as soon as I was able to, I took inspiration from his sense of style when he was out in public. Guy played with Sherwood sticks and so I changed sticks and used Sherwood. I ate the same pregame meals as he did. He liked downtown Montreal, so often that's where I went. He was there for his teammates, and it became important for me to have that role, too.

How did your relationship evolve?

Whenever I came back to Montreal, Guy was the first person I'd call. We got together as often as we could, except in the last years—he didn't want people to see him when he was ill.

However, I was allowed to be an exception: I went to see him about a month before he died. We discussed a business opportunity, to have my tequila distributed by his wine and spirit company. He was also quite motivated for us to join forces for a business partnership, calling me a few times in the following days to discuss how to move things along.

Wayne Gretzky and I had a FaceTime call with Flower, about two weeks before he died. We were playing golf in Florida, and Wayne, who wanted to talk with him, said, "Call Flower." Our first idea had been to go and see him in Montreal, but his health had gotten much worse, and we'd run out of time. They had a lot of fun reminiscing about playing in the Canada Cup in 1981. Guy was so happy to be chatting with Gretz, he didn't want to hang up. And it was the same for Gretz because Guy had been one of his idols, along with Gordie Howe.

Do any unforgettable anecdotes come to mind?

I have a lot of them, but there is one in particular. Sometime after Flower announced his first retirement, we were talking and he said to me, "When you win the Stanley Cup, I'll go and celebrate with you." And then, that's what happened not too long after, in 1986.

A few days after our victory over the Calgary Flames and the parade in the streets of Montreal, a few of us friends ended up in a bar downtown. Gathered there were Larry Robinson, Chris Nilan, and I, who had just won the Cup, and our friends Steve Shutt and Flower. It was important for Larry, Chris, and me to celebrate that great victory with Shutty and Flower, since they had made such an enormous contribution to the success of the organization.

What was his greatest quality?

Flower was always himself. And by being true to himself, he was larger than life. He was genuine, and considerate of others.

What is his legacy, the most beautiful memory he left behind for the hockey world and for society?

He showed us what it meant to have class. Flower was classy in everything he did: on the ice, in the dressing room, in the community.

Mark Lafleur

Born in Montreal in 1984, Mark Lafleur is the younger son of Guy Lafleur and Lise Barré-Lafleur.

When did you first realize you were "the son of Guy Lafleur"?

I must have been about six or seven. My father took me to Nordiques games when he was playing in Québec, and later to Canadiens games after we moved to Montreal. I went to all kinds of other activities with him, like softball games.

He stopped playing for the Canadiens in 1984, a few weeks before I was born. He always told me I was his retirement gift!

I remember that my friends' parents were impressed by my father. And it was the same thing with strangers in restaurants and other places. Wherever we went, people would whisper, "Look, it's Guy Lafleur!" as if we wouldn't hear them. My mother, my brother, and I would always have people around us whenever we were with him.

I was extremely proud to see how people looked at him or approached him to ask for an autograph or a photo. When we were at a restaurant and the food would arrive, there was always someone around—and so his food would get cold. It didn't bother him—the people would leave our table happy. When you hear about someone being so popular they can't even go to the toilet in peace—for my father, it was his reality.

What do you know about his glory years with the Canadiens, even though you didn't witness them?

The Canadiens were "his" team ever since he was little, in Thurso. It was the team of his idol, Jean Béliveau. Every time I watched clips from his games in the 1970s, I could see the happiness on his face.

I also watched the media coverage of his retirement in 1984 with him. He was really sad. He told me just how hard it was for him to leave "his" team. Later, he told me—and I saw for myself—how much joy it gave him to return to the Canadiens as their ambassador.

Did you play hockey?

Yes, for a few years. I was a left winger.

The parents of the other players said I skated like my father, which was a great compliment. But at the same time, they had high standards: Several expected me to be "another Guy Lafleur," which was impossible. It was extremely heavy pressure to have on me as a kid.

Fortunately, my father always said to me, "Never mind what other people think. Do what you want; do what you love."

I stopped playing hockey when I was a teenager, when I started taking Ritalin to help me concentrate at school. From that moment on, my game wasn't the same, and I didn't have the same level of energy.

Besides hockey, what did you have in common?

My father had said in public that he was also hyperactive. He was like that his whole life. From when he was very young, and right up until the end of his life, he always had to be active. That's probably why he understood my situation so well.

He was always moving a lot and couldn't stay still. He had several projects on the go at the same time, he was full of ideas, and he was always going all over the place to meet people. That's the way he was until it became truly impossible for him to continue on.

All families have their troubles. In your case, they were all laid out in the media, right?

Yeah. That came along with all of the positive aspects of having the name of Lafleur. Even when I was stopped by the police for something minor, it would be publicized.

What kind of father was he?

An excellent father, the kind of father I'd wish for anyone.

He taught me how to live in the moment. He lived life to the fullest and devoted a lot of time to his activities with the Canadiens and his other projects. It meant he wasn't home that often—but when he was, we always had quality time with him.

My father was preoccupied with the financial future of all four of us. He always told me, "Save your money." Which was a good idea in theory. . . . Luckily, in practice, my mother was in charge of the budget!

It's well-known that I've had ups and downs. The media showed my father standing by my side during my worst moments. But there was much more to our relationship that was not covered by the media, thankfully. I could always count on him at any hour of the day or night.

There were times when he was really mad at me, and he told me so. But he was always there for me, no matter what.

It would have been easy for him to cut me loose. But no, he called me every day. Often, several times a day. He wanted to know how I was, what I was doing, who I was with. He told me often, over and over, how important it was to make good choices. I didn't always listen to him.

When I ended up in different penitentiaries, he came to see me. I imagine that wasn't easy—in the eyes of the other prisoners and of the guards, he was no ordinary father.

When my family welcomed the public to the Bell Centre for my father's lying in state, and later to the cathedral for his funeral, many of my father's friends told me what he'd said about me. He told them that, despite my mistakes, he would always be there for me. He kept his promise right up until the end of his life, which still touches me very deeply.

Your father got in trouble protecting you . . .

He wanted to protect me so I could get through it. It was his way of encouraging me, of having faith in me. Contradictory testimony is something that happens all the time. But unlike in other cases, he found himself in handcuffs and it made headlines just about everywhere.

His health problems started when he was around sixty-five years old, right?

Yes, too early, as it always is . . .

The first signs were when he started having chest pain when he was at home, whenever he lifted heavy things. He then underwent some stress tests, and that's when the doctors decided to do an emergency operation to open up his arteries, which were almost completely blocked. Even so, he had been functioning "normally" up until that moment, despite the problem. He had quite the constitution!

He recovered, but then the doctors found a spot on one of his lungs. We were told it was a "small spot." He was in good hands with the CHUM, so I wasn't too worried. And since he's always survived worse situations—his 1981 car accident, among them—while always being optimistic and not complaining, I really believed he'd beat cancer, too. Sadly, we know how things turned out.

You were with him in his very last moments. Would you be able to tell us about that?

My mother, brother, and I stayed close to him at the palliative care home. On the Thursday afternoon of the day before he died, I went to join them after I'd finished work. They were worn out and went to get some rest in the evening. My dad was having more and more trouble breathing.

I spent the evening with him and Carmen Lampron, a close friend of the family who's a doctor. I stroked his head and his arm, and told him we'd see each other again. I kept thanking him, so many times, for having loved me so much.

In the previous few days, he wasn't very comfortable with all of the times I said "Dad, I love you" to him. Now, it was like he had let go, and I could say it as many times as I wanted.

I know that my father and his dad loved each other a lot, but they didn't say it very much, because that's how it was back then. For my dad and me, it was different—we said it often. Before he passed, I told him everything I wanted to.

My father had said I would be a support for him as he aged. As it happened, I was the one who was there with him until he passed. I'm convinced that I would be having many more problems today if I hadn't experienced those last moments with him. It's important for me, and also for my father, my mother, and my brother that I stay focused on making good decisions. I want to make them proud.

Would you say that the public loved him both as a hockey player and as a man who was generous with his time outside of the arena?

Yes, those two sides of him could not be separated.

He participated in a huge number of fundraising activities for sick children and other causes. Later, he founded the Guy Lafleur Fund at the CHUM, and he took the time to send notes or make calls to people who were in need of some words of encouragement.

When he died, it was the good guy as much as the hockey player that people came to salute. For the two days that the public were allowed to come and pay their respects at the Bell Centre, it was quite special to experience. For us, we had lost the leader of our pack. But the public had lost their idol. It was a great pain we all shared.

The wave of love was so immense it could have crushed us, but instead, it lifted us up. It really helped me get through it.

What struck me during that time was the huge number of young people who had never seen my father play, but who came to pay their respects. All they'd seen were clips of games on the Internet. It showed just how much he had influenced people from all generations.

Tell us an unforgettable story.

I was always a troublemaker! When my father went to play with the Nordiques, I was five years old, and for a while our family lived in the Château Bonne Entente hotel in Québec. One day I took my father's lighter and set a rug on fire. When I realized what was happening, I ran to tell my parents. My dad put out the fire, and then I got a smack on the behind. That slap from my father's big hand is something I still remember, thirty years later!

What was his greatest quality?

The immense confidence he had in the people closest to him.

With all of my bad behaviour and everything people said to him about me, my dad could have cut me out of his life. But instead, he was always there for me, because he wanted me to be happy. Right up to the very end.

I still talk to him, every day. When I'm feeling good or bad, I "connect" with him. And I have dreams where he feels just as present for me as before.

Maybe one day we'll see each other again—and have a gin!

What is his legacy—the most beautiful memory he left behind?

His presence. Guy Lafleur will always be associated with a thousand and one beautiful things he did for his loved ones and for strangers.

Hope and ambition, too. He always said to me, "Nothing is impossible in life." So many people, from many different walks of life, told our family just how much he had inspired them in their successes.

Stéphane Richer

Born in Ripon, Quebec, in 1966, Stéphane Richer is a left winger who played in the NHL for seventeen seasons, about half of them in a Canadiens uniform, between 1984 and 2002. A talented player, he was often compared to Guy Lafleur, both when he was in minor hockey and as a Canadien. He was the first—and to date, the most recent—member of that team to score fifty goals in a season after Lafleur had notched that achievement. In their respective careers, Richer had two seasons with fifty or more goals, while Lafleur had six.

What is your earliest memory of Guy Lafleur as a hockey player?

I grew up watching him play hockey on television. Guy and I were both from the Outaouais region: He was from Thurso and I was from Ripon. The two villages are just thirty kilometres apart, and I played lots of games in the Guy Lafleur Arena when I was in minor hockey. The day that I found out that Guy Lafleur's mother was serving hot dogs at the arena I was very impressed! Obviously, like everyone, I was proud that a guy from our area was one of the best hockey players in the world.

On the minor hockey teams in our region, all the players wanted to be Guy Lafleur, so much so that none of the teams had a number 10, to avoid creating feelings of jealousy.

Do you remember the first time you met?

Of course! Flower was at my first training camp with the Canadiens. It was close to the end for him, since he retired not long after the start of the season. But I couldn't have guessed it, because he trained and played with a lot of determination.

In 1983 and 1984, the Canadiens had selected several good prospects in the draft: Claude Lemieux, Sergio Momesso, Petr Svoboda, Shayne Corson, Patrick Roy, and myself, players who would go on to have very good careers. The general manager, Serge Savard, wanted the veterans to mentor the best recruits. From the beginning of training camp, not only was I wearing the same colours as Guy Lafleur, we were playing on the same line. I learned later that Serge wanted me to experience how that felt right away, and to quickly get comfortable with Guy. Maybe he also suspected that Guy wouldn't be with the team for long.

I'll never forget how he treated us rookies. He was a good veteran player who cared about how we fit in. A few months earlier I was playing in juniors in Chicoutimi, and now here I was at the Montreal Canadiens training camp! Guy remembered what it was like to be a rookie in the dressing room of this great club.

Flower was proud to have a local boy from his part of the world on the Canadiens—I could tell from his encouraging smiles and winks.

How would you describe him?

Flower was a simple guy—with a sarcastic sense of humour that made an impression on the rookies.

During that training camp in 1984, I played centre a little, between Steve Shutt and Guy. I was eighteen at the time. Imagine how I felt. One day, Flower said to me, in front of Shutty, "You have to keep going to the net and then get back to our zone quickly because, at our age, we're a little less likely to retreat."

In Ripon, did you grow up with people mentioning his name to you or comparing you to him?

For sure! In minor hockey, there were a lot of people who imagined me as the next Guy Lafleur. It was a heavy burden to carry, especially because it all goes very fast—for a kid who had to leave his little town to stay with a host family in a bigger hockey market. Guy had experienced that, and so did I.

A lot of the time the public sees only the "glamorous" aspect of the Canadiens uniform and the NHL, without knowing about all of the sacrifices young people and their families have to make. Those kinds of sacrifices were made by Guy, by me, and by a great number of young people who made it to the professional level, or who didn't.

Have hockey lovers made comparisons between your styles of play?

Yes, very often, because we were both strong skaters with a powerful shot. It started in the minors and it continued in the NHL. The first season that I scored fifty goals, people felt obliged to tell me that Guy had had six.

Do you feel he had an influence on you?

Oh yes, without a doubt. His work ethic spurred everyone on the team to excel. And he was able to motivate me using a few well-chosen words.

One time, Guy took me aside to say just three words to me: "Shoot to kill." What he meant was that I needed to shoot with as much power as possible, either near or at the goalie to either hurt him or throw him off-balance. He hung on to that same intensity even after he retired. When we were playing in a Legends game, he'd yell, "Shoot to kill!" in the dressing room or on the players' bench.

Speaking of intensity—that was in the Canadiens' DNA. There were a lot of times I'd make the effort to work twice as hard, including during the season I first got to fifty goals. To get there, I had to score five goals in the final two games of the season, in Montreal and Buffalo, even though I'd injured my thumb. They'd taken my cast off just before those two games. When we got back to Montreal, Guy congratulated me. With his sarcastic humour, he said, "Bravo, but . . . fifty goals doesn't mean anything anymore. The counter restarts at zero in the playoffs!" Later, Mr. Savard met me in the hallway outside our dressing room. Maurice Richard was with him. He looked me with those unforgettable eyes and said, "Welcome to the club. I'm really happy for you." The encounter lasted ten or fifteen seconds, but I was shaking!

Were you surprised by his retirement, and then by his return to the game?

Yes, very surprised. From that day forward, you could feel that the organization was in mourning. It affected me because we were losing a big piece of the team.

When he returned to the game it was like a movie. Guy had been gone for close to four years, he'd already been inducted into the Hall of Fame, and he scored twenty goals a season, despite injuries—and smoking probably two packs a day.

I was still playing for the Canadiens when Flower made his return. At his first game back at the Forum wearing a Rangers uniform he scored two goals against Patrick Roy. On one of them he completely outmanoeuvred Petr Svoboda!

From the start of the game, I played left wing against Guy's line. Denis Brodeur, Martin's father, took a magnificent photo of number 10 and number 44 facing off, which I treasure to this day. For that first face-off, Mats Näslund gave me a little tap on my pads with his stick to encourage me, because he knew what that moment meant to me. It shows what an excellent mentor Mats was.

What was behind your famous declaration that "there's more to life than hockey"?

It was after my second fifty-goal season. I even asked to be traded because I found it hard playing with the Canadiens and having to deal with the constant comparisons to the Lafleur–Béliveau–Richard lineage. Guy handled the pressure in Montreal better than I did, even though his early and later seasons were difficult.

I'm going to say this publicly for the first time, and I waited until after he was gone to say it: Guy was there for me during my most difficult moments. If anyone could understand the pressures on a Québécois playing for the Canadiens, it was absolutely him. He also knew what it was like to live with the outsized expectations of both management and the public. He listened to me more than he spoke, and that helped me a lot.

Larry Robinson was never far away. They were friends, and they both wanted what was best for me. Also, Larry and I had an agreement: He helped me speak English and I gave him the chance to improve his French.

In 1991, Serge Savard did me a favour by trading me to the Devils, and playing hockey in New Jersey suited me much better. Jacques Lemaire and Larry Robinson were behind the bench. I had my best years in the NHL playing for the Devils. What's more, Flower made a habit of calling Larry in his office on game days in New Jersey, and I often joined in on the conversation.

Afterwards, we stayed in touch. We saw each other at different activities associated with the Canadiens, and he always participated in the annual golf tournament I put on at my golf club, Montpellier, in the Outaouais region. When Guy would arrive early in the morning—by helicopter—to have coffee with our volunteers, he made everybody extremely happy. When he took off again, I was afraid the power of the wind from the helicopter would pull up the greens!

Why do you think he was so devoted to the fans?

It was part of who he was, as natural for him as playing hockey.

In a great number of the cities and towns where we went to play with the Legends, it was always the same thing: After the game, all the players would be on the bus—except Guy. One day, in the Gaspé town of Chandler, the temperature must have been minus thirty. He was outside the bus, wearing a light aviator jacket, patiently and carefully signing each autograph. His autographs all looked the same.

He always said about his fans, "I owe them that. I wouldn't be where I am today without them." I still reflect on the significance of those very simple words—because Guy didn't say much, and he never spoke for the sake of speaking. There's a lot of meaning in that sentence.

It was in his nature to be close to the people, in a simple way. The boy left the countryside, but the countryside didn't leave the boy! You could see that he always stayed rooted to his family and to Thurso for his whole life.

Did you play in a lot of Legends games with him?

I played at least fifteen years with Guy. He was right wing, of course, Normand Dupont was centre, and I played left. As often as possible, Normand and I would pass the puck to Flower because we knew he was the one the crowd wanted to score the most, so they could shout "Guy! Guy! Guy!"

Even for those games, Guy kept to the routine that he'd had in the NHL, arriving three hours before the game. Marc Verreault and Sylvie Gladu, who took care of our team, sometimes had to arrange for the local arena to open early just for him, since it was so much earlier than the manager's schedule. When the players arrived, he'd already be suited up, a coffee in one hand and a chocolate bar in the other. And there'd be a cloud of smoke in the dressing room, since he'd probably just smoked half a pack. He had fun, but he still played with the same intensity. If his shot missed the net, he'd be so frustrated he might even break his stick. He still believed in "Shoot to kill"!

When Flower announced that he was playing his last year with the Legends, it cast a pall over everything. Both within the team and in all of the places we went to play, everybody knew that it wouldn't be the same without him.

I'll always remember the last game Guy played with the Legends at the Bell Centre. It was 2010 and there were fifteen thousand people. Several former opponents and teammates from different eras decided to come and play with us: Darryl Sittler, Eric Lindros, Luc Robitaille—who had tears in their eyes—and many others. It was emotional at the brunch we had before the game: Everyone knew that nothing would ever be the same again.

Tell us an unforgettable story.

I have a ton of them! But I'll tell you two that will illustrate who the real Guy was, at two different times in his life.

The first one goes back to the late 1970s, at the Thurso elementary school, during a regional minor league hockey awards banquet. Players and teams were given awards in various categories. Mrs. Lafleur had arranged for Guy to make an appearance. When he arrived, he was smiling, stylish with his long sideburns and at the wheel of his white LeBaron. Flower didn't come empty-handed either—he walked into the school carrying the Stanley Cup! Imagine the reaction of the kids, the parents, and the volunteers. Naturally, he appeared in all of the photos taken that day. It was crazy.

The second anecdote is from when Guy was playing with the Legends. We often would play a game on Mother's Day. One time, we were playing at the Robert Guertin Centre in Hull. Guy said to me, "Bring your mother—I'm bringing mine." I mentioned that I'd also invited the team from my golf club, which included many mothers and grandmothers. He found out how many would be coming and greeted them all with his arms full of flowers to give to each one. That was Guy Lafleur.

What was his greatest quality?

His greatest quality was having remained . . . Guy Lafleur, the shy little guy from Thurso. He was larger than life and as simple as can be.

I've known athletes who acted very differently when playing their sport, when they were in the dressing room, and with the public. But for Flower, there was just one way of conducting himself—and that's why the public was so comfortable being around him.

What memories do you hold on to?

Mr. Béliveau and the Rocket were monuments in the Canadiens' history. Flower was a phenomenon who lived his life as if it were a movie.

I hold on to the memory of a childhood idol who became a friend. A true friend. Because when I needed help, he came to me.

And even though I'm not a big collector, I have two hockey sticks that are precious to me: Mike Bossy's red Titan Turbo, and the stick that Guy used during his last game with the Legends, which he signed for me. In the space of just a week, in April 2022, Mike and Guy were both gone.

What were your last moments with him?

The truth is, we hadn't seen each other for a while because his health had deteriorated considerably. Our last contact was through texting. My wife, Lisa, and I wrote to him to wish him well and he responded "Merci." His thank-you said everything.

After his death, it made me laugh to hear about the enormous number of people—including those in business—who boasted, "We talked on the phone; he sent me texts." I don't believe that. A lot of people wanted to make themselves look important at Guy's expense and it pissed me off. The reality was that Guy was suffering, and his entourage was protecting him to help him conserve his energy as much as possible.

The morning he died, I was getting ready to play golf. My father-in-law sent a text to his daughter, "Please tell Stéphane that his friend has passed." He hadn't written his name, just the number 10. I was so shaken up that I cancelled my golf game; I wasn't capable of functioning that day. It really got to me.

What would you like the public to remember about Guy Lafleur?

In Ripon, in my corner of Outaouais, Guy's death showed the young people just what kind of success he'd had. It made them realize that we can achieve our dreams.

On top of being an elite hockey star who played and lived one hundred miles an hour, Guy Lafleur was a model citizen. We all know he wasn't perfect, but he was a model of surpassing oneself, of generosity and integrity.

Tony Granato

Born in Downers Grove, Illinois, in 1964, Tony Granato is a right winger who played for thirteen seasons in the NHL, mainly for the Los Angeles Kings and the San Jose Sharks. When he started as a rookie with the New York Rangers in 1988–1989, he could count on Guy Lafleur for support.

What is your oldest memory of Guy Lafleur as a player?

When I was around ten years old, I was a fan of the Chicago Blackhawks. Which meant the performances of the Canadiens during the 1970s were hard on me—and Guy Lafleur was a big part of that!

He was the kind of player who could embarrass the Hawks and enrage the fans, but also earn their admiration. I believe the fans of the Canadiens and of other teams would have seen Stan Mikita the same way, when he was dominating for the Blackhawks in the '60s and '70s.

Were you surprised by his retirement? And by his return to the game?

I was around twenty years old when Lafleur left the Canadiens, and so I didn't really grasp the impact of that decision.

But fortunately, I had the privilege to play alongside him when he returned to the game with the Rangers. For example, I was at the Forum the first time he returned to his city wearing the Blueshirt on his back. The excitement wasn't limited to

Montreal—it spread across Quebec, Canada, and the whole NHL. He hadn't even hit the ice for the warm-up period before the crowd started shouting "Guy! Guy! Guy!" Every time he was in action, it was crazy.

Thinking back on the smiles of the fans at the Forum that night, I can imagine how profoundly it affected Flower. Those smiles were their way of telling him, "Thank you for everything, Flower, and welcome home." I'll never forget that, and it was definitely one of the standout games of my career.

Tell us about the very first time you met.

It was in Trois-Rivières, at the Rangers training camp ahead of the 1988–1989 season. It was my rookie year, while Guy was attempting to return to the game. Of course, the public wanted Guy to succeed just as much as he did.

When he arrived at training camp, he was in great physical shape and he'd stopped smoking. Unfortunately, later on he took up that bad habit again.

For our group of rookies—and for me in particular—it was really remarkable to be around this superstar who was actually a very unaffected and humble teammate. I quickly realized that the fans loved him both as a star and, also, as a man.

With Flower as the veteran and me the rookie, both of us were there to secure a place in the Rangers' lineup. Even though he was in the NHL players' dressing room and I was in the one with all the other rookies, both of us had to work really hard. I was fascinated by how present he was—he was so intense during every second of practices and games.

What was he like as a teammate?

With his big, warm handshake and his smile, and his ability to build relationships, he quickly made his teammates and his fans feel comfortable. He was impressive and cool at the same time.

As a teammate he also looked out for others, and me in particular. On the players' bench, he'd nudge me in the ribs and tap on my helmet, my shoulders, or my shin pads, always with words of encouragement. When he put his arms around one of the rookies after a nice play, I'm sure he knew the effect that had on us. For him, rookies like me or Brian Leetch were important to the team, just as Marcel Dionne was. He made a huge contribution to the atmosphere in the dressing room and on the bench because he always had a look, a tap on the back, or some other little encouraging gesture to make sure everybody felt good.

I learned a lot by watching him. I thought, "That's how hard you have to train to succeed; that's what you do to be liked by your teammates; that's how you have to act to be loved by the fans."

I also had the privilege of playing with Wayne Gretzky. He and Flower both learned how to channel the enormous pressure they were under so that when it was time to put on their hockey gear, they could concentrate on having fun, "playing" like kids.

Lastly, Flower had a complete picture of his team. He had excellent relationships with his teammates and dressing room staff, as well as with the coaches and management. In New York, he was very well regarded and respected by Michel Bergeron and our general manager, Phil Esposito, for what he'd accomplished in his career, and because they saw how much he contributed to a healthy dynamic in our group. One of the reasons they appreciated him is that he didn't complain when they asked him to sit out for a game. I think I was more disappointed than he was when that happened. Flower understood it was important to keep giving the rookies more ice time.

What was he like on the ice, at the age of thirty-seven?

Like a kid! From the second Flower entered our dressing room and hit the ice, he was one happy athlete. Whether it was in exhibition games or regular ones, he had his uniform on and was ready to play three hours before the start. I've never had a teammate who got ready so early. Even though he was in his late thirties, his passion was remarkable, and an inspiration for the rookies.

I remember how Bergie broke the ice at the beginning of training camp by getting me to play left wing with Guy. It was a great vote of confidence. I was young and energetic, and Flower had just as much energy and seemed much younger than he was. During the season that we were teammates in New York, I played around twenty games on the same line as him. It always made a big impression on me and I wanted to keep on playing alongside him.

On the ice was where he was at home. One time, we jumped on the ice for practice and he said to me, "Watch this, Tony—here's a knuckle slapper!" He proceeded to move the puck quickly on his stick with the same effect as a baseball pitcher's knuckleball. He hadn't lost any of his dexterity. He really impressed me that time, and on many other occasions, too.

With Flower, everything was always fun, even when he was concentrated on the serious work of playing hockey. He was also at home in the dressing room—he loved to joke around with his teammates, and sometimes there was some shaving cream involved. I can still hear his laugh!

Were you ever roommates?

Yes, for a while. And I only recently found out that it was Flower who'd asked Bergie if we could room together on the road. He wanted to show me the ropes of the NHL. I was extremely touched by that.

That request was typical Flower: a discreet gesture intended to give an extra boost to a teammate—and, by extension, to the team.

Tell us about his relationship to the fans.

When I got to know him when he was in his late thirties, he was still patient with the fans. He took time to sign autographs in New York and everywhere in the NHL.

What was Guy Lafleur's greatest quality?

His intensity, because it was an integral part of the intensity of our whole team. Guy was intense in everything he did. For him, there was only one way for him to play his best on the ice: It was with his hair in the wind, with just shoulder caps attached to the straps of his suspenders. No full shoulder pads! Still, he was constantly being fouled by his opponents. I don't think the fans realized just how strong and muscular he was, and also how hard he was on his body.

The idea of the team was also extremely important to him. He took great care to pay it forward, to pass on the torch to the rookies. That's what he did with me, and I always took care when it was my turn to pass on the torch as best I could to the rookies I played with in the NHL.

Guy Lafleur's passion—his star power—was something I recognized in one of the players when I was coaching the University of Wisconsin Badgers: Cole Caufield. I can't predict exactly what kind of career he's going to have with the Canadiens and in the NHL, but I'm convinced of one thing: That player has some Flower in him. He is a born goal scorer who has the same passion for the sport, the same joy in playing—you can see that from his smile—and the same mutual respect between him and his teammates.

How did your relationship evolve?

Sadly, we lost touch over time—that's often the way it goes when a player changes teams or retires and the other one bounces from one city to another. It was thanks to our mutual friend Chris Nilan that I heard about what was going on with Flower when things were good, and also when he was having health problems.

About six months before he died, I texted him to tell him he'd been a positive influence on me, that I was thinking of him and praying for him. He responded with a very touching, very Lafleur-style message, showing that, even with all that he was going through, he still took precious moments to give comfort to others.

Tell us an unforgettable story.

Even though it wasn't very far into the season that we played together on the Rangers, I was already running out of hockey sticks. I have to say that rookies don't receive many sticks from the suppliers! Flower, who got as many sticks as he wanted, said to me before a practice, "Take this one and try it out." That's what I did, and I preferred it to mine. That season I must have played seventy games using Flower's sticks, and I scored thirty-six goals. For the rest of my career, that was the type of stick I used.

I still regret not having asked Flower to autograph one of my sticks. I was too embarrassed. Fortunately, shortly before he died, I searched for—and found—a stick of Flower's for sale on eBay. I looked at the photos from various angles and could tell it was authentic. I bought it without hesitating, and treasure the keepsake.

What is his legacy, the most beautiful memory that he left the world of hockey and all of society?

The legacy he left us was love. It was essential for Flower to love not only those close to him, but also his teammates and the members of the club. He showed us by his example that it's important to love the work we do, every day. For athletes, he showed us the importance of loving the fans.

Michel Goulet and Peter Stastny

Born in Péribonka, in the Lac-Saint-Jean region of Quebec in 1960, the left winger Michel Goulet was the first choice of the Québec Nordiques at the 1979 draft, the year they entered the NHL. He played fifteen seasons in the league, with the Nordiques and the Chicago Blackhawks. In 1995 the Nordiques retired his number 16, and in 1998 he was inducted into the Hockey Hall of Fame.

Born in Bratislava, Czechoslovakia (now Slovakia), in 1956, Peter Stastny is a centre who wore the colours of the Nordiques at the same time as his brothers, Anton and Marian. The three brothers, who first made their mark with Czechoslovakia's national team before fleeing their homeland, had a firework effect on the Nordiques club. Peter Stastny had the second-highest points total in the NHL during the 1980s, after Wayne Gretzky. Stastny achieved the 100-point mark seven times, six of those in consecutive seasons.

Goulet and Stastny played on the same line as Guy Lafleur at the end of his career, and they were inducted into the Hockey Hall of Fame on the same day in 1998. Together, they talked to us about "their" Guy Lafleur.

What is your oldest memory of Guy Lafleur as a player?

Peter Stastny (PS): In the 1970s, Guy was a scoring machine. Plus, he had charisma! All over the hockey world, he was one of the most well-known and respected faces of the Montreal Canadiens—in addition to Phil Esposito and Bobby Orr, who were among the most well-known players in the whole NHL. They were true idols for every hockey player and fan.

Guy will continue to be remembered as a winner and one of the best in the history of hockey. Along with Maurice Richard and Jean Béliveau, he was one of the three best players in the history of the Canadiens, the most victorious franchise in North American hockey.

Michel Goulet (MG): My seven brothers and I were hockey maniacs. We watched Montreal Canadiens games on television and, like all the young boys in Péribonka, we pretended to be Guy Lafleur, Gilbert Perreault, and Marcel Dionne. We were spoiled having those three enormously talented Québécois players to look up to. They were huge inspirations for us because they played with intensity and made the game exciting. Even better, not many attacking lines had nicknames, but theirs did: There was the French Connection with Gilbert Perreault in Buffalo, Marcel Dionne's Triple Crown in Los Angeles, and Guy Lafleur's Dynasty Line in Montreal.

In the 1970s, Guy Lafleur was certainly, in Quebec and in Canada, *the* player par excellence in the NHL. In 1979, his equalizing goal, coming at the very end of the seventh game in the Stanley Cup Final against Boston, has remained one of the best memories of Canadiens fans of that era. Everyone in our family was jumping for joy in the family room.

Guy stood out above the rest, with his combination of flair, talent, energy, and motivation. He had everything going for him. When he was on the ice, the pace of the game changed.

Were you influenced by his playing style growing up?

MG: By his intensity, yes. I believe that his passion for hockey certainly gave a lot of young people the desire to play the sport, and persevere. But we had very different playing styles. Guy had an exceptional talent for moving the puck and he was much flashier than I was.

He also influenced me in another way. When I played for the Québec Remparts, it had been five years since he'd left. However, the team's management still spoke about Guy and his exploits, and all around there were photos of him. He still had a great presence for the Remparts, and it spurred us on as players.

You both played against Guy Lafleur and were also teammates playing on the same line as him. What was that like?

PS: I first played against Guy when he was on the Canadiens, and then with the Rangers. And also later, when the Nordiques traded me to the Devils. It's always hard to play against players who are that smart, talented, and fast, with a powerful and unpredictable shot. Guy had all of that, and more.

MG: I played against Guy starting in 1979—when the Nordiques moved from the WHA to the NHL—up until his first retirement. I often faced him since I played left wing and Guy was right wing. He wasn't easy to cover! I remember how proud I felt the first time I played in a game against him, side by side in the face-off circle.

We were still opponents when he came back to the game to play with the Rangers. It was impressive to see how a guy his age could still make it in the NHL after being absent so long. Once again, he demonstrated what an exceptional athlete he was.

The next year, he came to Québec. Unfortunately, it wasn't a great period for the team when we played together: He was at the end of his career, the Nordiques were last in the standings, and I was on the trading block, leaving for Chicago at the end of the season. I played against him for a little more than one season with the Blackhawks before he stopped playing for good.

In Québec City, Guy quickly realized there weren't too many talented players for him to play with. But he still brought energy and passion to the Nordiques. Even though he'd slowed down, he was still a role model for all the players on our team.

Were you surprised by his first retirement, and then by his return?

MG: Like everyone in the hockey world and like the fans, I was surprised both by his retirement and his return to the game.

He'd had some injuries, Montreal had a new coach, and from what people were saying, he was more or less happy. He still scored twenty-five or thirty goals on a team that had become very defence oriented. It was like the ticking of a time bomb—and it went boom when he stopped playing at the age of thirty-three.

How was Guy perceived at the end of his career?

PS: I was close enough to him to recognize his human and personal qualities. Guy possessed something extraordinary: He was truly appreciated everywhere. Not just in Quebec and in Canada, but everywhere on the hockey map.

MG: At the end of his thirties, he was still quite the athlete. And he was respected by all the players, both by his teammates on the Nordiques and by our adversaries.

His contribution on the ice remained important, and his leadership in the dressing room made a difference for a team that, all the same, was going nowhere. I remember once hearing one of the guys complaining, "Another practice . . ." Guy responded, "What do you mean, complaining that we have a practice? It's our job! And looking at the standings, I think we really need it."

What's more, it's incredible just how much he was known and admired. He had fans in all of the NHL cities.

I've only met one other athlete who had a similar aura of importance: Michael Jordan. When I came to the Blackhawks, Michael was playing basketball with the Chicago Bulls. One evening, after a Bulls game, we went out, and I noticed similarities between him and Guy in the way they related to their many fans. Obviously, when they engaged in their sports, both played with great intensity—they were winners! It was because of their charisma that they each made a lasting impression on their cities, their countries, and their sports.

After Guy retired from the NHL for good, he played a lot of games with the Legends. He kept his athletic appearance right up until the end of his life. Unlike many retired hockey players, he didn't put on a few pounds around the middle!

Tell us about the rivalry between the Canadiens and the Nordiques, from the point of view of this athlete who had played for both teams.

MG: The Canadiens–Nordiques rivalry was born on the day the Nordiques joined the NHL. If anyone understood that, it was him. But Guy was also above all that.

For him, it didn't make any difference who the opponent was.

The only thing that mattered was winning. It didn't matter if he was playing against a tough team like the Flyers or whether it was against another team like the Sabres. He'd start to focus on the game early in the afternoon and at game time he'd jump onto the ice full of confidence in his abilities.

Guy and I never really talked about the 1982 playoffs, when the Nordiques beat Montreal. But I'm certain that it was painful for him. It was a change in the dynamic between the two teams: The little one was now able to beat the big one. With Dale Hunter's overtime goal, the rivalry between the two teams and their fans became very intense.

What was his greatest quality?

MG: He was a good guy who was simple, candid, and honest. Guy was an excellent teammate who led by example, and who always said exactly what was on his mind.

He brought people together. Throughout my career, I knew captains who were excellent players but not necessarily unifiers. But Guy was one, and he loved to make big gestures. For example, he bought a sugar shack in the Quebec countryside. One day, he invited the entire Nordiques organization, and some others as well. There must have been two or three hundred people there. We were very warmly welcomed, and he just lit up around everyone, because he was as pleased to be hosting us as we were to be there.

What are you best memories with him?

PS: Playing on the same team as Flower, on the same attacking line, remains one of the best memories and experiences of my career. Guy, Michel Goulet, and I were probably the oldest trio in all of the NHL: added together, one hundred years old!

Still, our stats were among the best in the league, especially in the first half of the season. It was such a joy and an honour.

I will always consider it a privilege to have been able to call Guy Lafleur my teammate and my friend.

What is his legacy?

PS: The most important aspect of his legacy is his passion for hockey and for the people. The fans had enormous love for him, and Guy loved them back. There really was magic between him and ordinary people. I was able to witness it up close and I've never seen anything like it.

MG: Guy Lafleur left such an impression on hockey and on society that his name will still be known a hundred years from now.

Joe Sakic

Born in Burnaby, British Columbia, in 1969, Joseph "Joe" Sakic is a centre who played for twenty-one years with the same organization: the Québec Nordiques, which became the Colorado Avalanche. At the beginning of his career, he was Guy Lafleur's teammate and roommate for almost two years.

To date, Sakic has won the Stanley Cup three times: twice as a player, in 1996 and 2001, and once as a general manager, in 2022.

What is your oldest memory of Guy Lafleur as a player?

Even though I grew up in British Columbia, my father was a Habs fan. It was the era when they won the Stanley Cup four years in a row. I watched a lot of his favourite team's games on *Hockey Night in Canda*, but we didn't get to see the Canadiens as often as the Maple Leafs and the Canucks. Sometimes we tuned in to the Canadiens games in French.

I would have been about six or seven when I became fascinated by Guy Lafleur. He was truly impressive, the wow factor at the heart of the Montreal Canadiens. Once I really understood the game, I realized just how hard it was to cover him: No opponent could predict what he would do with the puck. Later, I saw for myself how Flower played solely by instinct—which meant even he didn't know what he'd be doing with the puck a fraction of a second later!

Tell us about your very first meeting with Guy Lafleur.

It was in 1989, when he came to the Nordiques. I'd been with the team for one year. I was nervous meeting him because I had two images superimposed in my head: one of my new teammate, and one of my first hockey hero. There were a lot of very talented players on our team, but from that moment on, our dressing room also included the legendary Guy Lafleur.

How did this Hall of Famer behave as a member of the Nordiques?

In the most unassuming way possible. He quickly fit in with our group of players. I have a very clear memory of him coming to talk to me on the first day of the Nordiques training camp. We all looked up to him—after all, no one else in our dressing room was a member of the Hall of Fame. But Flower acted like any other player, without any particular status. He had a great sense of humour, with a loud and hearty laugh.

When he signed with the Nordiques, Guy knew very well that the team was in the midst of a rebuild. Everyone on the team just did their best, whether they were the veterans, like Peter Stastny and Michel Goulet, or the younger players, like me.

Flower was a winner throughout his career: in peewee, juniors, taking five Stanley Cups and numerous individual trophies in the NHL. He was very committed during the Nordiques games. And so it must have been frustrating for a winner like he was to no longer be racking up victories, night after night. But he didn't show it. He was always smiling and in a good mood.

I could see that for Guy, the rebuild of the Nordiques didn't represent an abandoned construction site, but more like the beginning of a new phase of reconstruction, which included leaders who would set an example. And he was certainly one of the most influential among them. Despite his humility, we felt the aura of his presence in the dressing room and on the players' bench.

Even though he was very busy beyond playing hockey, Guy took time for his teammates, all of them younger than he was. It was obvious that he had come back to the NHL for the simple pleasure of playing hockey, being around teammates, and making his fans happy.

Tell us about the player at thirty-eight and thirty-nine. What kind of physical shape was he in?

Flower was in great shape physically. His skating was still sensational and his shot was still dangerous. The opposing team's goalies couldn't afford to be distracted for an instant.

He was very energetic and had as much fun as a kid on the ice. During practices, he was active at least forty-five minutes before all the other players. Just as we were hitting the ice, he was ready to fire! And on game days, when we would arrive at the dressing room about two hours before the puck dropped, he had already been in his uniform for quite a while. He drank coffee and made jokes, but he was already focused on the game to come.

Returning to the NHL after at least three years away is something that probably only Mario Lemieux and Guy Lafleur have managed to do. You have to be a real force of nature to succeed in that. I don't think I ever could have done it.

In Québec, you and Michel Goulet played on the same line as him. What was that like?

It was easy, because a very talented player, even an aging one, remains a very talented player. There was a lot improvisation in our game. But we always ended up finding each other, and I loved that.

Flower was instinctive, which meshed perfectly with our coach, Michel Bergeron, who led with emotion. Game systems were not very developed in those days.

What was he like as a roommate on the road?

We shared a room for a good part of the two years we were teammates. I was intimidated—for about a minute. He knew how to put me at ease. I quickly understood that he didn't want me to look at him as a father figure, but rather a teammate like any other. Like a big brother. All the same, his humility made an impression on me.

Flower was a proud man, always stylishly dressed, even when he came to practices. When we were heading out on the road for several days, he packed a lot of shirts so that he'd always be clean and well turned out. His clothes were never wrinkled.

Tell us about the athlete and his fans.

A true love story.

Everywhere, in all of the NHL cities, Guy had fans who wore his number 10 sweater. He was always surrounded by them, and he gave a few seconds of his attention to each fan. Those fans will always remember that quality time. But when you start adding up a few seconds to a few seconds more, and then a few more seconds, it becomes quite a few minutes—and hours! During the two years that I played with him I would not be able to calculate how much time the team had to wait for him. But we were understanding.

After he confirmed that he would be retiring for good after the 1990–1991 season, he received a real star's welcome on the road, especially in the Canadian cities. I never saw such a thing, for a local team to salute and honour an adversary like that. There would be a video featuring his highlights against their team, they would present him with gifts, and the crowd would give him a huge ovation.

In Winnipeg, he signed autographs for an hour or an hour and a half. In Edmonton, he stayed three or four hours after the game to sign some more. It was something else.

Instead of being frustrated by such delays, I used those moments to really take the measure of his celebrity.

Talk to us about his last games.

He wanted to end his career in Québec, where it all started for him. I remember his last games at the Forum and at the Colisée. That last home game felt like it went on for five hours! You could really feel what Guy represented for Québec. He was nothing less than a superstar.

As soon as he came to the Nordiques he was telling people around him that you were going to be a star player in the NHL.

I didn't know that. That's very touching to hear.

For a member of the Hall of Fame—and not just any member, but Guy Lafleur—to have said that about me when I was only in my second season, I'm very humbled. But it's too bad to find out about that now that he has died, because I would have liked to thank him. And to give him a hug.

What did you learn playing alongside him?

I learned different things that became fundamental in my life.

For example, being a class act when it came to the fans. He made himself available to a level that's hard to imagine. He'd always say to us that the fans paid our salaries when they bought their tickets, and it was the least we could do to give them their money's worth, with everyone on the team making their best effort. Even if the team was in the midst of rebuilding.

Flower wasn't one to give speeches. But one time in particular, he spoke with me and it stayed with me for the rest of my life.

It was after a hard loss in Washington. There were about fifteen games left to play in that miserable season. Flower came to the back of the bus and sat beside me. He said, "You know, Joe, you have to focus on the things you can control. Your effort, your playing, how you prepare before games. Just about all of these guys won't be playing in the league soon. But you're going to be here for a long time. It's going to be your team. You have to stay positive, have fun, and play for the fans." I never forgot those words.

It was also from observing Guy that I learned just how hard you have to work to win. His influence lived on in our team's Stanley Cup victories: first as a player and, five years later, as general manager.

Tell us a story.

The first day that we were roommates, I felt reassured when he said to me, "Joe, I promise you I won't smoke in the hotel room." He kept to his promise faithfully—that is, to not smoke "in the room."

What he neglected to mention was that it didn't include the bathroom. When I opened the door to go in, there was always a cloud of smoke, and he'd have a good loud laugh at that!

What was his greatest quality?

Guy would approach others and often start the conversation, even though he didn't talk much.

One thing we used to say about him was "He cares." He took care of other people, particularly his teammates. All of the fans in Québec and elsewhere could also say "Guy gave me his attention."

In fact, Flower treated others as he wished to be treated: with respect. And in the end, that means giving quality time to other people.

What were your last moments with him?

Since he lived in Montreal and I was in Colorado, we didn't get to see each other often, unfortunately.

But even after he'd retired for good from the NHL, he played an incalculable number of games with the Legends teams. We had the pleasure of playing together occasionally, for example, in Québec during his very last game. It was in 2011, during his farewell tour, and I made a point of being there. The fans in Québec—his fans—gave him many ovations: before, during, and after the game. There was a lot of love for Flower in the tributes from the fans as he played for them one last time.

The next year, in 2012, I was enormously grateful that he came to the Hockey Hall of Fame when I was inducted. We also saw each other there on several other occasions.

It was probably two or three years before he died that I learned about his health problems. I know he battled ferociously and that he created a charitable fund for a leading hospital in Quebec.

Even though the Colorado Avalanche began its playoff series in Denver the same night as the funeral, you made a return trip to Montreal that day to attend the ceremony. Why?

I wanted to be there. For Guy, for his family members, and for myself. To remember, in a very sad but also extraordinary setting, the athlete and the man that he was. For his influence on me, which remains to this day.

I saw myself again as a young man, looking up to Flower. And later, to have the honour of being one of his teammates and to play on the same line as him with the Nordiques.

I was very impressed—but not at all surprised—to see just how many people of all ages came to pay their respects. Flower remained very present in their lives, as if he still played hockey—even though he'd retired for good more than thirty years previously.

What is his legacy, the most beautiful memory he left behind for the hockey world and for society?

Hockey, family, fans: He always brought passion to everything in his life, without cutting corners.

From the early 1970s, on the ice and off of it, Guy Lafleur was a worldwide ambassador for the NHL. For all the players, even though they didn't possess his immense talent, he set an example of passion, determination, and being present in a meaningful way for the fans.

Flower was an icon. And I'm convinced he'll remain one, even though he's gone.

Gary Bettman

Born in Queens, New York, in 1952, Gary Bettman has been a sports executive for most of his career: first rising to the level of senior vice president of the National Basketball Association (NBA), and then as commissioner of the NHL since 1993. He got to know Guy Lafleur when Lafleur was the Canadiens' ambassador.

What is your oldest memory of Guy Lafleur?

As a player it was in the 1970s, during his heyday. Later, I met him at the NHL All-Star Game in 1993, my first as commissioner. On that day, it was a fan having a first meeting with a hero of his youth! But it wasn't an event conducive to forming connections because there were so many people and different activities, one after another. Rather, there are two particular encounters I had with him that stand out in my memory.

The first was in 2003, during the Heritage Classic in Edmonton. It was the first time a regular-season NHL game was played outdoors, with the Canadiens taking on the Oilers. It was an extremely cold day, and there were a lot of photos taken outside with legendary players from both teams. I remember his sense of humour: Guy was constantly teasing Wayne Gretzky and Mark Messier, as well as his former teammates and opponents.

The second occasion was in 2017 in Ottawa, at the NHL 100 Classic event. The Canadiens and the Senators played a regular game outside and, just like in Edmonton, there was a Legends game, too. What was original though, was how Guy arrived:

by helicopter! There were former NHL players who became airplane pilots, but I never knew any who had such a great love for helicopters as Guy. I never got the chance to fly with him, but I always heard it said that he was just as perfectionistic up in the air flying a helicopter as he was on the ice. Which is saying something.

What kind of player was he?

Beyond his exceptional talent, Guy understood that he needed to do more than just score goals. It's why he thrilled the fans with his unique style, his hair in the wind. It was obvious he took pleasure in playing hockey, and that joy was contagious, both for his teammates and the fans.

On and off the ice, it was his class that left an impression: He never acted untoward with opponents and he would never turn a fan away. He had an aura about him, which earned him admiration for a very simple reason: He was himself. Guy Lafleur transcended professional hockey.

Were you surprised when he returned to the game in 1988?

Who wouldn't have been? Age—and everything that comes along with it—has always been the greatest obstacle in athletes' careers. There's a slowing down. And despite what Guy had experienced, he came back to the game with passion and pride. His return was nothing less than an incredible physical and mental triumph.

Tell us about what he was like during the years he was the Montreal Canadiens' ambassador.

I know that particularly in Quebec, the fans of the Canadiens and the Nordiques were very proud of "their" Guy Lafleur, who was always stylishly dressed and reflected well on them. But it's important to note that, in fact, he was one of the greatest ambassadors in the entire NHL. Fans everywhere were fascinated by Guy.

As an ambassador, he didn't just shake hands—he was profoundly concerned with the future of professional hockey. For example, some years ago he wrote to me to plead the case for the Nordiques to return to Québec. I can't remember any other former player of his status taking the trouble to put in writing different arguments for a team's return to a particular market.

Taking into account the qualities you recognize in him, would you like today's NHL to have 640 Guy Lafleurs on its 32 teams to "sell" hockey?

In every era of the NHL, there have been exceptional players who distinguished themselves in the sport, and who made a mark on society. Each one had wonderful qualities. Guy was one of them in his time, just as others who are emerging today, and the next generation will produce their own.

But one thing is certain: From 1971 to 2022, the entire NHL was privileged to be able to count on Guy Lafleur, on and off the ice.

Why did you go to his funeral?

I wouldn't have been anywhere else that day. Of course, it's not possible for me to attend every funeral of our ex-players, but on that day, I absolutely had to go to Montreal. I wanted above all to show his family, and the Canadiens organization, just how much respect all of the teams of the NHL had for Guy Lafleur.

I was very impressed by his funeral, both by the meticulous care in its organization and by all the love the fans once again demonstrated for "their" Guy Lafleur. I was impressed and moved, but not surprised in the least.

What legacy did he leave the world of professional hockey?

Guy Lafleur left a legacy that embodied the core values of our sport: passion, honesty, and respect.

Rob MacDuff

Born in Montreal in 1953, Robert "Rob" MacDuff has built a career as a helicopter pilot and instructor. He has flown VIPs all over the world.

Rob MacDuff became the instructor of a very special student in Guy Lafleur, who impressed him with the talent and the seriousness he brought to this new career. They would become great friends.

What is your oldest memory of Guy Lafleur as a player?

It goes back to when he was with the Québec Remparts. I hadn't seen him play yet, but I had read an article about him in *Sports Illustrated*—which shows just how dominant he already was in junior hockey in North America. The journalist asked him how many goals he was going to score that night. Guy jokingly replied that he'd score two, and that's what he did. The journalist wrote that Guy was so good he could score at will. When I mentioned it to him years later, he laughed.

I was born in Quebec, but because of my father's influence, I was a Maple Leafs fan, and I hated the Canadiens! After my father died, in the 1970s, my aversion to the Canadiens faded away, especially once Guy Lafleur became a standout player. How could you not love him? I also figured he would probably be the last of the Flying Frenchmen on the Canadiens, so why not enjoy it?

Tell us about your very first meeting.

It was late in 1996. I was working for Bell Helicopter, in Mirabel. During a meeting, our chief pilot mentioned that a hockey player was coming in that week to take a few courses towards getting his licence, and he asked who had time to take him on as a student. I asked who the player was, and when he told us, I said, "What? Guy Lafleur is coming here to take courses? I'll take him on personally!" Around the table, I was the only one who had played hockey and who was very excited at the thought of him coming to our facilities. My colleagues were mostly pilots who weren't hockey fans. Guy had begun his studies several years earlier in Québec, when he was playing for the Nordiques. But since the school had closed, he'd chosen Bell Helicopter to resume his training.

He came to meet me that week. First, we did a thorough review of theory over several days. Two weeks later, we went on our first flight, and then alternated theory and practice.

The day after our first meeting, a beautiful signed photo of Guy appeared on my desk. Another day, one of his hockey sticks arrived, also signed. He wanted to show me how much he appreciated all the work I was doing with him. Because I did a lot of work!

What was he like as a student?

For about a year and a half, he called me several times a week—often in the evening, while he was studying at home—to ask me extremely specific questions. I realized very quickly that I was dealing with a future pilot who had enormous potential and extraordinary determination. The elite right winger was giving way to the elite helicopter pilot.

He told me, "I'm not brilliant, I'm athletic. It takes enormous concentration for me to study very seriously, and I need help." He often said that studying did not come naturally to him.

Guy was still playing with the Legends when he started his pilot studies. A lot of the time the team travelled by bus, often in cities in Canada's north. He loved learning about meteorology, air regulations, aerodynamics, flight theory, and navigation—and that's what he did on the bus and in his hotel rooms at night.

What kind of pilot did he become?

I'll compare the professions of hockey players and pilots of helicopters and planes: In both cases, a gigantic effort has to be made on both theory and practice in order not only to succeed but also to stand out.

Take the goal that Guy famously scored in the seventh game of the Stanley Cup Finals against the Bruins in 1979. Some might say it was a shot like any other—but no! For him to have scored that goal, he first had to have shot probably a million pucks onto the boards and in nets in order to know all the little details that led to success. It's the same for pilots: Everything that we do to make a flight smooth for our passengers is the result of the enormous amount of work we've put in.

Guy achieved extraordinary mastery as a pilot. Of all of the excellent students I've had over the decades, he was without a doubt one of the best. The proof is that he earned the highest—and most exceptional—grade of 100 percent on his FAA exams for commercial helicopter pilots in 1998. The way the exam is designed, even the very best students will have one or two mistakes, but not Guy. He got a better grade than I did!

It was common knowledge that very frequently he would drive far over the speed limit between Montreal and Québec City. He was completely different piloting a helicopter. I can attest that he was always extremely careful and conscientious.

Where did his passion for helicopters come from?

Guy told me he always liked race cars and speed. So it was no coincidence he was Gilles Villeneuve's friend!

He confided in me that one of his regrets was not having taken a pilot's course during his first retirement. He would have liked to have flown a big Air Canada jet. Imagine how the passengers would have reacted if they'd heard "Ladies and gentlemen, this is your captain, Guy Lafleur, flying you to your destination of Paris." Finally, some years later, after his second retirement, he did become a pilot—of helicopters.

How did your relationship evolve?

At first, our relationship was strictly teacher and student. As with all of my students, I was very demanding. Except that with him, he regularly called me at home in the evening. It became a ritual in my family life. When my wife overheard me talking to him sternly about whatever technical element he was having trouble fully mastering, or if he hadn't got a perfect result on a test, she would tell me I was being hard on him. I would reply, "I'm only as hard on Guy as he can handle."

We had spoken about this approach and he appreciated it. The proof was that our great partnership turned into a true friendship. He was the best friend I ever had.

I was hugely impressed by his success as a pilot. To become so good, after having studied such complex material later in his life—it was phenomenal. All instructors want only one thing: to see their students become excellent pilots, completely autonomous, like the parents of chicks wish to see their offspring flying off on their own. With Guy, it was particularly successful.

After that, we flew together for the pure fun of it. He was an ambassador for Bell Helicopter, so he would fly helicopters manufactured in Mirabel to different company centres in the United States, in Texas, or Tennessee, or Florida. He met with clients and employees, and every time—despite how humble he was—he made an impression on people.

When we discussed his successes as a pilot, he always said the same thing to me: "People think that I became good at hockey because I had a natural talent. It isn't true. I succeeded because I worked extremely hard. You saw how I studied for my pilot's licence? I always put the same kind of effort into hockey."

He owned luxury cars and a boat. Did he also own a helicopter?

No, for the simple reason that a hockey player's salary did not permit him to make that dream come true. When he flew, it was with Bell Textron helicopters, or else he would rent, or had friends loan him theirs.

One day, he had to have emergency heart surgery. Tell us about that.

A heart anomaly was detected during a routine physical exam required to renew his pilot's licence. This "anomaly," though, required an emergency quadruple bypass operation: Three of his four arteries were completely blocked, and the fourth was 85 percent blocked. Happily, he made a quick recovery. But then very soon after, the cancer appeared.

Guy was still permitted to fly, but no longer by himself—he had to be accompanied by another pilot. It meant the end of his freedom as a pilot.

He never brought up his hockey career in our conversations. The past had no interest for him. Instead, he lived in the present, and was always thinking about the future. I think the thing he said most often was, "What's next? When's our next flight?"

Even though he was no longer flying alone, we had fun on two trips to Labrador to go fishing. The first time, I flew; the second time, in August of 2021, we had a pilot. His son Martin came with us. The second time, Guy was too ill to do any fishing. So Martin, our friends, and I shared our fish with him.

I'll never forget Guy's eyes the first time he saw polar bears, or the time when we savoured our freshly caught fish on the beach. On the return flight, he revelled in each moment of the trip and the indescribable beauty of Eagle River in Labrador. He knew, deep down, that he would not be returning.

When guys get together, a lot of things can be expressed without saying a word. Guy was quite aware that his health was deteriorating, but he never spoke to me about it. As for me, I suspected the end was near. But not a word. We always savoured the moment, in silence.

When were your last moments together?

The fishing trip we took in 2021 was the last time we saw each other. After that, it became increasingly difficult for him to see a lot of people while trying to conserve his energy. There were people he didn't see as much, like me, but we spoke on the phone every week. I found that hard, but I respected his wishes as to how he wanted to live out his last months. If I were him, I probably would have been the same way.

Tell us about some unforgettable moments.

First, there was an unforgettable moment among his peers. In 2017, the NHL celebrated its one hundredth anniversary at an event in Ottawa. Guy decided to go there by helicopter and he invited me to come along. Thanks to him, I found myself in the company of the greatest players from different eras: Dave Keon, Frank Mahovlich, Bernie Parent, Bryan Trottier, Mike Bossy,

Daniel Alfredsson, and many others. There were quite a lot of journalists buzzing around them. I can affirm that it was Guy Lafleur—who'd retired for good in 1991—who drew the most attention!

I can think of so many unforgettable moments when people realized that Guy Lafleur was either piloting a helicopter they were in or was a fellow passenger. One time we were tasked with delivering a helicopter to Texas. We left from Mirabel and stopped at the Detroit airport to fill up on gas and go through customs. It was evening, and the customs agent appeared to be in a foul mood. He decided to slow us down by doing a thorough—and totally random—inspection of our helicopter. We certainly weren't going to raise any objections, which would have made the situation worse. Guy and I figured we'd have to cool our heels in Detroit for several hours, and maybe even spend the night.

The customs agent came over to the passenger side. In the same stupid tone he said, "Passport." He took our documents and suddenly cried out, "Guy Lafleur, the hockey player?" Guy nodded. The agent said, "Oh my God!" So I asked him, "Would you like a photo of Guy, and he can autograph it for you?" The agent was thrilled. "Oh yeah, for sure! And could you also sign one for my daughter?" As you might guess, we were able to leave quickly and without an inspection.

What was his greatest quality?

Guy was a real gentleman, in every sense of the word. I spent a lot of time by his side for the last twenty-five years of his life and really—even when I try very hard—I can't think of any major flaw.

Throughout my career as a pilot, I flew all sorts of politicians, kings, princes, rock stars, F1 pilots, astronauts, billionaires, and famous explorers. There's a certain glow that surrounds famous people, and they all treat their fans differently. Guy had an exceptional relationship with every fan he met. Everyone felt special in his presence.

You attended his funeral. Tell us about it.

It was very moving to be there, and I was told that it was the same for the television broadcast.

It was probably the biggest Guy Lafleur rally ever: All of the people in attendance at the cathedral or watching on television weren't there for the Canadiens, but for him.

I think Guy would have been uncomfortable to see so many people praising him and crying over him. He didn't like big crowds of fans. I know that when he did find himself in that situation, he gave each person a few seconds of his time to show them they mattered, as if there were nobody else there.

In fact, despite being in the spotlight for all of his life, Guy was a private person. He did a great job of dealing with the spectacular aspects of his public life. But he was happiest when he was with his family and close friends.

What is his legacy?

Massive!

As a hockey player he was pretty much the perfect embodiment of an idol, with his exceptional talent and his attitude on and off the ice. He showed us how a superstar should conduct himself.

As a pilot, he demonstrated that every challenge has to be taken on very seriously, without compromise. It's an approach we can all apply in our daily lives.

Geoff Molson

Born in Montreal in 1971, Geoffrey Eric "Geoff" Molson has pretty much always had the Canadiens in his blood, as the team and the Molson Brewery have been closely linked for several decades.

In fact, his family, with Geoff at its helm, became owners of the team for a third time in 2009. That was when Geoff Molson became chairman of the board and ambassador of Molson; the following year he acquired the team and the Bell Centre. He became president and chief executive officer in 2011.

What is your oldest memory of Guy Lafleur as a player?

My father, Eric, and my grandfather Hartland set a rule: Even though our family owned the team, the dressing room was a place reserved for the players. And so, even though I went to practices now and again, I only set foot in the players' dressing room when I was invited.

Back when the Canadiens won the Stanley Cup four years in a row, I was just a kid who was shy in front of the players, often unable to talk to them. With all their equipment on, they seemed like giants to me. Guy wasn't intimidating himself, but I was intimidated by his size and the air he had about him.

The most beautiful memories I have are every instant that Guy's stick touched the puck. The crowd would immediately stand up en masse, sensing something was about to happen. I loved hearing their reaction—it was electrifying.

Guy always played hockey creatively, using all of the ice. And we knew he was going to fire off a slap shot. We didn't know where or when, but we could count on it happening several times in a game. Guy often said that even he had no idea when he was going to do it.

Tell us about your very first meeting with Guy Lafleur.

My father and my great-uncle were often around Guy, but I wasn't. He and I would cross paths now and then, either at the Forum or the Bell Centre, in Montreal or in airports—that was it. It really wasn't until 2009, when I took ownership of the team, that we began to have a real relationship.

How would you describe his ties to the Canadiens?

He experienced both highs and lows. And that's to be expected: He was human. He always had a positive relationship with the Molson family. He made the differentiation between the team led by a coach and general manager, and the family who owned the team. He was always respectful.

Talk to us about his relationship with the fans.

From my childhood to the present day, I rubbed shoulders with quite a lot of great athletes in the Canadiens organization. But no one will be surprised if I mention two among them who enjoyed a special status in the hearts of the fans: Jean Béliveau and Guy Lafleur. And Jean was obviously a role model for Guy.

These two men were completely different personality-wise, but they shared some fundamental qualities: the same great generosity and the same understanding of how important the fans were. Jean and Guy were always well dressed and always represented the Canadiens very well. They never left any place without having signed an autograph for the last fan waiting.

Both of them were very devoted to their fans. They made themselves available everywhere in the community when they were needed. But Guy always arrived earlier than necessary—just like he did when he was a player. He often would show up an hour and a half early. We didn't know what to do with him!

But you would agree that Béliveau and Lafleur reacted quite differently in public?

Oh yes. Jean Béliveau spoke from the heart. His words were always carefully chosen and he was probably a little reserved. Guy also spoke from the heart, but without holding back! It was beyond his control; he couldn't be any other way. Our fans appreciated both Jean's diplomatic side and Guy's directness.

Guy's approach was to share his opinions with the media. It affected him deeply when the team wasn't doing well or when the players weren't making the necessary effort. Even though his words touched a nerve with team management, he was often right. But why didn't he come and speak with us directly?

What memories do you have of his retirement from the Canadiens, and of his return to the game?

I was a fan who was surprised by his retirement, like everybody else. I was a teenager at the time. I didn't know it was going to happen; my father never spoke about Canadiens business matters at home.

Later, it was painful to see him wearing a Rangers uniform, and it was even worse when it changed to the Nordiques! I think back to his goals at the Forum, against Patrick Roy, both with New York and Québec. That was Guy, with all of his showmanship and intensity. And the fans showed him their love every time, even when he scored against us.

When the Molson family bought the Canadiens in 2009, eight years after selling to businessman George Gillett, you quickly reached out to Guy—why?

When I arrived, the Canadiens had already had some excellent ambassadors: Jean Béliveau, Henri Richard, Yvan Cournoyer, and Réjean Houle. But there was one key person missing. Relations between the club and Guy weren't ideal, and it was essential that we rebuild bridges.

It was really starting in 2009 when the two of us forged a relationship. I wanted to hear him tell me about his finest moments with the team and also about what had caused him pain. And why. I wanted to figure out how we could successfully bring him back into the fold, focusing in the long term on his passion and his unique personality. It was clear he still had the passion and desire in his heart to see the Canadiens do everything possible to win.

When I proposed a ten-year contract with him, he could tell I was sincere in my intentions to build a solid and durable relationship with him. A lasting trust was established. I remember one day, his wife, Lise, came to thank me for having given this financial security to Guy and, consequently, to his family. I understood that, despite what had happened in the past, she also had made her peace with the Canadiens.

That contract got extended, and Guy remained an ambassador for the Canadiens until his death. Over all those years, he continued to express his views—sometimes too much!—to the media. But there was one thing I understood: He was Guy Lafleur, and you had to appreciate and respect him for who he was.

Beyond the contract, he was an ambassador for the Canadiens 365 days a year, both in the eyes of the public and at the core of his being.

Over time, he didn't let up on sharing his opinions—but fortunately, not just with the media. He would come to my office or call me to share what made him proud or what was bothering him. He also passed messages on to hockey staff. For example, when I hired Jeff Gorton and Kent Hughes, he wrote to them to share his views on the Canadiens. Jeff and Kent were touched by the gesture. He was someone who gave his all right to the end.

Thousands of people have told me that they became fans of the Canadiens because of Guy Lafleur. I hope they still are!

What was his greatest quality?

I would choose a word that isn't usually used as an attribute, but in Guy's case, we're talking about someone exceptional. The word is "electrifying."

That's what Guy was every time he stepped onto the ice, and in particular when he was wearing the Canadiens uniform. He was always electrifying when he entered a dressing room, a restaurant, a hospital, a fundraising gala, and so on. It's hard to explain. He would arrive somewhere and a current would pass between him and the public, no matter what their age. Before he'd even started to sign autographs or pose for photos with people, his mere presence made them feel good.

Also, I absolutely have to mention his candour and his sense of humour. He would always formulate his criticisms in very direct language and, once he'd got his message across, he'd end his speech with a wink. Or he would rephrase his message with a joke and a loud and hearty laugh.

Guy will also be remembered as being synonymous with "passion." Lafleur always had the same approach to hockey—I believe going back all the way to his peewee days: Hockey has to be played with a great deal of passion, never forgetting that it's a game and you have to have fun.

Guy remained a Canadiens ambassador to the very end. Why was that?

For all that he represented for the Canadiens and for all the Canadiens represented for him.

I was very confident that Guy was in good hands at the CHUM. Every time we saw each other or spoke, he told me he was hopeful. He never, ever spoke about the end. He talked about the future. I went to see him about two weeks before he died. He told me he was planning on changing the windows in his house the following summer. And that he wanted to go to Québec to buy a new flag for his property.

Tell us about Guy's seventieth birthday luncheon.

It was held on September 20, 2021, at Manago restaurant in Kirkland, which was a place he loved. I invited Martin, Mark, and the teammates he was closest to. It was a casual atmosphere, and the guys were all very happy to see Guy again. They teased each other as if they were back in their 1970s dressing room!

There were some sad moments, which was to be expected. But I think that on that day, Guy went home a happy man.

How did you react when he died?

On April 22, 2022, I had to manage my own grief while I consoled colleagues and friends. The Canadiens organization took on a key role in planning the funeral, with the support of the family and the Quebec government. Which was fitting.

It was a big shock, even though I knew the end was near. I had prepared myself mentally, of course, but you're never ready to hear that kind of news.

It's something I still notice every day: The Montreal Canadiens without Guy Lafleur just isn't the same. There's a big piece missing.

What is his legacy, the most beautiful memory he left behind for the hockey world and for society?

On the ice, Guy did everything to be the best player he could be. He also had an enormous impact off the ice, in the community.

In the time between his death and his funeral, I was convinced that every member of our organization understood his importance to the Habs. If our young players take to heart Guy's influence as a player and a good person, we'll have a wonderful journey.

Dr. Benoît Coutu

Born in Montreal in 1958, Dr. Benoît Coutu is a cardiologist and electrophysiologist at the Centre hospitalier de l'Université de Montréal (CHUM).

A good friend of Guy Lafleur's, he is also one of the health specialists who treated him in the last years of his life.

What is your oldest memory of Guy Lafleur as a player?

Unlike the majority of boys my age, I wasn't interested in hockey in my teen years. I was focused more on my studies, entering medicine in 1976. I knew that Guy Lafleur was a very good hockey player, but I don't recall having watched any Canadiens games back then.

Tell us about your very first meeting.

In 2010, the Moisson Montréal food bank organized a VIP fundraiser: a fishing trip with Guy Lafleur to Némiskau Outfitter in the La Tuque region. That was the first time I met him, when I participated in that fundraising campaign.

In the fall of 2010, the official presentation of a cheque to Moisson Montréal took place at Bleu Blanc Rouge, Guy's restaurant in Rosemère. My son Philippe had the idea that he could interview Guy that evening for his school's radio station. He went to make the request and came back smiling: Guy had accepted!

Afterwards, the school administration called our house to verify that what my son said was true. The interview was supposed to take place by phone, but the principal asked if Guy could come and do it at the school, and then meet with students and staff. My wife, Carmen Lampron—who admired Guy as a player and as a person—called Guy, and he accepted right away. He came to our house and then she and Guy went to the school.

The students in grades five and six had done research on him and were let out of class to spend quality time with this former athlete. In the gym, the children chanted "Guy! Guy! Guy!" to welcome him. He answered questions for more than an hour and autographed photos for everyone. He spent the whole afternoon there—imagine how the staff reacted!

How did you become his friend?

Not by doing anything special. Our friendship arose out of that encounter with Carmen and from that fishing trip. From one occasion to another, we spoke about many things: life, our kids—but never about hockey.

I would often be around Guy when he was meeting with fans. Whether it was in the street or at a restaurant, people were always starstruck. I realized he was really big—he had a kind of aura around him, all the time. However, I was perhaps one of his rare friends who didn't take much interest in his former career.

We would have dinner at each other's houses. Carmen and I are both doctors. As his friends, we were both by his side right until the end.

What can you tell us about the health of your patient, without betraying confidentiality?

It was under special circumstances that I became involved in Guy's care.

He had to undergo medical exams twice a year, an essential

requirement for renewing his helicopter pilot's licence. I saw him once or twice for certain tests.

On Monday, September 23, 2019, he called me to say his family doctor suspected he had heart problems and he needed to look into it. The next day, very early in the morning, he came to see me at the CHUM. He told me he'd just returned from a fishing trip and he saw a bear up close. So close, in fact, that he abandoned two big salmon and took off! As he was climbing up a sand dune, he had tremendous difficulty catching his breath.

My colleagues and I immediately had him undergo a series of tests, including treadmill and ultrasound. The results were very concerning. At that point I told him, "Call Lise. You're going to be staying at the hospital with me." On that same day, he had a coronary angiography, and we decided to operate on the Thursday. He took it all stoically.

On September 26, 2019, my cardiac surgeon colleagues Simon Maltais and Nicolas Noiseux operated on Guy for three or four hours to clear the blockages in his arteries. They told me the operating room had been completely silent. Because, while all lives are important, this was Guy Lafleur. The open-heart surgery was a great success. He left the ICU "like a shot." During that hospitalization, he received a lot of attention from staff and the patients who crossed his path—he never refused to sign an autograph. The CHUM team took pride in caring for him.

Unfortunately, at that time, a considerable mass was detected on his right lung, possibly cancerous. It meant having another operation in two months' time.

I was in the best position to announce the news to Guy, which I did. Once again, he was stoical. I believe there are two reasons for the way he reacted: He had confidence not only in life, but in the medical team taking care of him.

For the cancer component, I had no role on his medical team.

Thoracic surgeon Dr. Pasquale Ferraro operated on Guy's lung cancer on November 28, 2019. Guy was in a lot of pain after that operation. Then there were tests to assess whether there were any metastases. Everything looked good. When I told Guy he'd been cured "theoretically," he said, "This is the most beautiful day of my life!" From that moment on, he stopped smoking—the cancer had really frightened him.

During his two stays in the hospital, not just anyone was allowed to go into Guy's room. The CHUM provided a twenty-four-hour security guard. I'd never seen such a thing.

What happened after that?

After being treated for cancer, there are regular follow-up tests. In September 2020, a control scan showed that his cancer was back, having metastasized.

A team led by Dr. Mustapha Tehfe, supported by research nurse François Morin, provided the best care to Guy throughout his illness—as is the case for all oncology patients.

Guy insisted I come to his appointment with him to "absorb the shock" and ask questions. My colleague Tehfe told him, "Mr. Lafleur, we can't cure the cancer. But we can treat it and give you a good quality of life." And he added, "Looking at you, you seem to be in great shape. You have some time, so enjoy it." Guy seemed to be encouraged by those words, and he lived the rest of his life like a true fighter.

Tehfe proposed that Guy do two programs at once: the standard one along with a research project focused on immunotherapy. It was a tough combination. Both as a doctor and a friend, I asked my colleague every imaginable question. But I didn't tell Guy what choice to make. It was up to him to make the right decision for him.

Obviously, he was going to have a very busy schedule with

the treatments, which became his top priority. After discussing matters with me, Carmen, and Lise, he quickly signed the documents for the treatments to get underway.

On the mornings of his treatments, we would meet up on the third level of the underground parking lot at the CHUM. Then we'd sit and have a coffee, either in my office or in the cafeteria. We talked about absolutely everything: his worries about his health, what he would be leaving to Lise and his boys, and so on. It's important to underscore what a great respect he had for the fans: Even in the cafeteria they would say hello or ask for an autograph, which he always did happily. Then I would accompany him to his treatments.

Over time—and this happens in many cases—there were periods where he successfully fought the cancer. Then his progress would plateau, and adjustments to the treatments were made. Things would go better for a while and then, less well.

During the summer of 2021, Guy was in a lot of pain, no more so than when he was sitting down. I asked him if he'd like to join our usual group on a fishing trip. But despite the medication he was taking, he was in too much pain. He wouldn't be able to spend several hours at a time in a rowboat. In the following months, things just kept getting worse.

I thought I knew my friend up until that point. However, I started to discover different sides to him. I realized it was in his nature to rush headlong into a cancer research project. He figured he had nothing to lose. He was a model patient, very disciplined. He believed—up until a few weeks before his death—that he would beat it. Until the holiday season, he'd kept repeating his positive messages to everyone, but he was in terrible pain.

What happened in his final months?

By the beginning of 2022, he must have understood he wasn't going to make it. He stood tall whenever he walked; he never wanted to use a walker.

On January 26, he and Carmen had a serious discussion. She said to him, more or less, "Guy, the medical team will never give up and will fight with you. But it's up to you, and only you, who gets to decide what to do next. So that's what you have to think about. And your quality of life has to be part of that." He was in considerable pain while he reflected on her words, despite the medications he was taking every four hours to alleviate it. Not long after their talk, he told me, "It's enough; I'm pulling the plug." He hoped he might recover enough to share some quality time with his family and friends. Guy died several weeks later. He no longer had any quality of life.

At first, he entered the CHUM's palliative care centre. It seemed as if this was the end, but no—he got stronger and was able to go back home. On his arms he had six butterflies, subcutaneous injection sites for medication that Lise had to constantly administer. With our help and the support of home care services in his neighbourhood, Lise enabled Guy to stay at home as long as possible. My wife couldn't stop saying that Lise was her hero.

Several weeks later, when things were going less well, Guy finally entered a palliative care home in Kirkland, on the West Island of Montreal. The home had a new wing, and he was in one of the few occupied rooms. Up until the day before he died, he was eating and making jokes about the food.

And then, his death came very suddenly. Lise and her sister, Martin and Mark, and Carmen and I were by his side. Guy was surrounded by love until his last breath.

The head of the palliative care home asked Lise what music

she would like to have played during the transfer of the body to the funeral home. A few hours after he died, the exit happened with kindness and respect. Guy left the palliative care home to the tune of a song he loved: Frank Sinatra's "My Way."

What was his greatest quality?

Guy was generosity personified. It was also his worst failing, as he was incapable of saying no to anyone.

He had a limitless imagination for how to make other people happy.

Tell us about the Guy Lafleur Fund.

The entire hospital knew that he was our patient. And so the management of the CHUM Foundation asked him in the autumn of 2020 to become one of its ambassadors. Then we proposed the idea of a Guy Lafleur Fund which would include, among other initiatives, the Club des 10, bringing together personalities from the world of hockey. Guy and his colleagues phoned major donors to thank them personally—and he pushed himself to the limits of his energy to do that.

What is his greatest legacy to society?

Probably the CHUM's Guy Lafleur Fund. At the time of his death, that fund had already amassed—in about a year—$1.5 million for research. His son Martin and a dedicated team are following Guy's wish to keep "paying it forward."

Ken Dryden

Born in 1947 in Hamilton, Ontario, Ken Dryden is a legendary goaltender who played for the Montreal Canadiens from 1970 to 1979. He won six Stanley Cups and five Vezina Trophies, becoming one of the most dominant goalies of his era. Dryden was also named the 1971 Conn Smythe Trophy winner as playoff MVP. After retiring, he became a lawyer, author, and politician, serving as a member of Parliament and as minister of social development in Canada.

When and in what context did you meet Guy Lafleur?

I met him at training camp in the fall of 1971. He had been selected first overall a few months earlier, and he joined us in what was a very special year: We had just won the Stanley Cup unexpectedly, with new players like Peter Mahovlich and rookies such as Guy Lapointe, Réjean Houle, and Marc Tardif. For this new season, Jean Béliveau, John Ferguson, and a few others had retired, leaving room for a new generation. Guy was stepping into the shoes of his childhood idol, receiving the famous torch that Béliveau passed on to him. He couldn't turn away from the idea of being the next great one. He knew he was—and had to be—the next one.

A new core was being built around Yvan Cournoyer and Jacques Lemaire. Frank Mahovlich was still there, along with Terry Harper, Jacques Laperrière, and Jean-Claude Tremblay. We had a strong foundation—a promising one. Our challenge was to build the future of the team.

And then came Guy. And Scotty Bowman, too. Even though Scotty had already enjoyed success in St. Louis, he was still a young coach who needed to prove himself in Montreal and across the NHL. Plus, he was a hometown guy, from Verdun—just ten minutes from the Montreal Forum.

What were your first impressions of him?

Guy arrived with all the background of a superstar, and I assumed he would quickly become one in the NHL. He performed well—but not at the level everyone expected. Our season started solidly, but that's all it was.

It was the year Richard Martin also entered the league as a rookie and scored goals by the handful for Buffalo. I don't remember many articles criticizing Guy as a disappointment; it was more about how spectacular Martin was.

That said, any other player would have been thrilled to score twenty-nine goals in their first season! But Guy always wanted more—to play more, score more, and achieve more.

Despite that strong start, it took until his fourth season for Guy to truly become the superstar everyone had been waiting for. Why the delay? Because the Montreal market is particularly tough. Even compared to Toronto, Montreal likely has the most intense media coverage—and with it, enormous pressure.

All Canadiens players, especially rookies, must adapt to the often unrealistic expectations of the fans. Guy understood that he bore a greater responsibility in Montreal than Gordie Howe in Detroit, Bobby Orr in Boston, and later on, Mario Lemieux or Wayne Gretzky did in their cities.

His 1976–77 season was probably his most dominant: He won the scoring title for the regular season, the Hart Trophy as MVP, and the Conn Smythe as playoff MVP—and our team won the Stanley Cup!

Could you describe him in a few words?

Guy was the thoroughbred horse of Thurso. He was tremendously creative with the puck. His work ethic was also remarkable.

He was an explosive skater—a player with exceptional talent, always approachable with fans, and a great teammate with a wonderful sense of humour that I loved.

I remember once, just before a game against Detroit, he came over, glancing around as if to share a state secret. "They're on fire," he whispered, knowing full well the Wings were having a terrible season. Then he laughed that big, hoarse laugh of his and went off to get ready.

When I look at photos of Guy in action, I notice two things: his hair flying in the wind, and the fans in the background, mesmerized by him. No one else in the NHL created that kind of electricity.

Tell us about the athlete.

Mornings at the Forum followed a familiar pattern: I'd arrive to find the guys chatting in the locker room, while employees painted, repaired, or polished things around the rink. And from the hallway leading to the ice, I could already hear pucks banging off the boards—I knew Flower was out there, training by himself before the full team practice. He needed that solitary time to skate and fire pucks at the net. When he was alone on the ice, he was being creative, he was happy. The Italians have a perfect expression for him: *Inventa la partita*, meaning "inventing the game."

Guy was the player who could fly. He skated like no one else and simply *did things* on the ice. He only wanted to play one way:

full speed, full attack. He didn't want to develop a more cautious or rounded style. His joy came from blasting down the ice, blasting the puck, and scoring goals—lots of them.

And nothing he did was left to chance. How the puck bounced after each shot mattered as much to him as the shot itself. Physiologists call it muscle memory—the ability for learned movements to happen automatically, without conscious thought. That kind of memory guides both musicians and athletes.

I was probably the goalie he practised against the most. Every second of our training mattered to him. I think about other teammates who would shoot loosely—pucks flying everywhere, sometimes dangerously. Equipment back then wasn't what it is today; our masks were thin, right against the face. Injuries were always a risk, and Guy understood that. He was dangerous—but never reckless.

His shot was powerful, but also precise and intentional. He often targeted my stick side—both the top corner and a few inches above the ice. The best example of that kind of shot is probably his famous tying goal against Boston during the 1979 Stanley Cup semifinals.

We sharpened each other—I wanted to stop him; he wanted to score on me. If I could stop him, I'd be ready for anyone else. If he could beat me, he knew he was ready to beat any goalie in the league.

What kind of teammates were you?

We were excellent teammates, doing everything we could to help the Canadiens win. But we weren't close friends outside the locker room. I visited his home only once, for a team party. He never visited mine. And on the road, a right winger didn't share a hotel room with a goalie anyway.

When you think of the three greats—Richard, Béliveau, and Lafleur—what connections do you make?

Their commitment to the Canadiens was identical—100 percent, every moment they played. But their playing styles, leadership styles, and relationships with the fans were very different.

The Rocket was pure energy and unstoppable force, bulldozing his way to the net. Jean Béliveau was tall, majestic, elegant—a dignified presence on the ice. Guy was sheer speed, lightning quick, his hair flowing behind him.

Everything Guy did depended on speed—and that kind of game doesn't age well. Jean Béliveau, by contrast, already had a more mature style when he was young, which allowed him to adapt as he grew older.

Even as ambassadors for the Canadiens, they were different: Béliveau was the wise father figure; Guy was more like a favourite friend. Different generations, different personalities.

Guy understood he had a responsibility to be gracious with the public—because they had always been gracious with him. He knew that as a Canadien, as part of the club's history, he had no right to be anything less. It wasn't always easy or natural for him. He valued his privacy. He liked being alone. But he understood what was expected of him.

In short, Guy never tried to become Rocket Richard or Jean Béliveau. He drew inspiration from them but stayed focused on being Guy Lafleur. And that was already a monumental task.

Do you still have a story to share?

I have one—and it's a good one!

In 1976, during the Stanley Cup Finals against the Philadelphia Flyers, the RCMP warned us that Guy and I were potential kidnap targets! Imagine that—two Canadian players kidnapped to help the Flyers' chances. We were told, but not allowed to tell anyone else. Still, Guy and I knew about each other. During the series, we would exchange these little knowing smiles—ones we didn't share with the rest of the team.

What was funniest was the way we were followed around by private detectives who couldn't have looked *more* like private detectives—guys hiding behind newspapers, parked awkwardly near our homes, appearing in rearview mirrors. We had them on our heels 24/7!

The most interesting thing? Neither Guy nor I ever really felt threatened. And we beat the Flyers in four straight games!

What do you remember about his two retirements and post-career life?

When Guy announced his first retirement, I was surprised—but not shocked. I knew he wanted to keep playing for a long time. His comeback four years later surprised me, too. Honestly, Guy often surprised me!

Once, I asked him why he kept playing so long and why he became such a tireless ambassador for the Canadiens, travelling constantly. My question caught him off guard. He said, "What else could I do? I played all my life. I didn't have time to learn or study anything else. After fifteen or twenty years of hockey, what else do I know?"

Later, he found another passion: flying helicopters. I never felt entirely comfortable imagining him as a pilot—and I certainly wouldn't have volunteered to be his passenger! But it gave him new purpose.

What is his greatest legacy?

Guy Lafleur will always be remembered as both an exceptional player and a vital public figure in the history of the Montreal Canadiens.

But beyond that, he was fundamentally a private man—always seeking, from childhood in Thurso until the end of his life, to balance who he was inside with what the public expected of him.

Viggo Mortensen

Born in 1958 in New York City, Viggo Mortensen grew up in both Argentina and the United States. A true polymath—actor, painter, poet, musician, photographer, and director—he's best known internationally for his acting. Before starring in *A History of Violence*, *Eastern Promises*, *The Road*, *Captain Fantastic*, and *Green Book*, he became iconic for playing Aragorn in *The Lord of the Rings* trilogy (2001–2003). In 2020, he directed, wrote, and co-produced *Falling*, followed by the acclaimed Western *The Dead Don't Hurt* in 2024. One of his lifelong passions? The Montreal Canadiens.

When and why did you become a Montreal Canadiens fan?

I was born in Manhattan, but when I was an infant, my father got a job in agriculture in Argentina, so we moved there. I spent most of my early childhood in South America. When I was eleven, my parents separated, and we returned to my mom's hometown in northern New York, close to the St. Lawrence River—across from Quebec and Ontario.

In the 1970s, it was a different world. Today, you can keep in touch with friends using phones or social media. Back then, we didn't even have cable TV. I was suddenly cut off from everything familiar—my Argentine culture, my friends, my beloved football. Nobody spoke Spanish where we moved.

We had only a few TV channels. I watched CBS, NBC—and also, CBC, out of Kingston, Ontario. That's how I discovered hockey. CBC/Radio-Canada often broadcast Canadiens games because they were a dominant team. Not every game, but enough to catch my attention. I'd sometimes even listen on the radio.

I started hearing names like Richard, Béliveau, and Lafleur. Maurice Richard had already retired, but I saw Jean Béliveau in his final season and Guy Lafleur rising as a new star. The games were broadcast in French out of Quebec on a radio station that covered the Canadiens more than any other station we could tune in, which made me want to learn the language. Gradually, aided to some degree by my knowledge of Spanish as well as French class in junior high school, I did.

The Canadiens jersey featured blue and red, the colours of San Lorenzo, my favourite football team in Argentina. But what really won me over was their fans. Their passion reminded me of the football fans back in Boedo, Buenos Aires.

I fell in love with hockey. It was like football but faster, with skates, sticks, and fights. The fights I was not crazy about, but the speed and skill of the players—none more so than Guy Lafleur—really impressed me. I wanted to learn everything about it. I didn't really play much myself, other than some pond hockey, but I was fascinated by the game.

The 1970s were a golden era for the Canadiens. I don't suppose any team in NHL history has had a more impressive run. I watched them and thought, "Who are these guys? They're incredible." My affection for the team has stayed with me ever since.

When possible, I carry or wear the CH logo hidden somewhere when I work as an actor or director. Especially when I work in Toronto. I respect and cherish the old rivalry between the Leafs and the Habs. Having the CH on me helps me feel calm—even on stressful sets. In acting, as in sports, when you're relaxed you perform better.

Where did your admiration for Guy Lafleur come from?

I first noticed Guy when he was a rookie. He didn't score much at first—which makes sense. Having been a tremendous goal scorer as a junior hockey player, he was expected to follow in the footsteps of Jean Béliveau and Maurice Richard in a city where hockey is religion. That's a lot of pressure for a young player. But he handled it patiently and gracefully. He had been in the spotlight since he was a kid, and now all eyes were on him in Montreal. That kind of fame isn't normal. And yet, he stayed composed.

Season after season, Guy became more essential to the Canadiens' success—especially during their run of four consecutive Stanley Cups. Watching him was electrifying. His blond hair flying as he skated at top speed—that was his trademark. It wasn't even particularly long, but it floated because he accelerated so quickly and skated so fast!

He was explosive. His acceleration was unreal. When he had the puck, the entire arena stood up. It was electric!

Back then, it seemed like NHL players were tougher, grittier. Road games in Boston, New York, or Philly were intense. You could feel the fear in some players—but not Guy. He wasn't reckless, but he wasn't scared, either.

He didn't follow a pattern. That made him hard to defend. He had a sixth sense on the ice, predicting plays before they happened, seeing the possibilities. That's what made him unique—like Gretzky or Lemieux, but with his own unique style.

He worked harder than most people probably gave him credit for. He had grace and vision, but also a great work ethic. That's why I compare him to Lionel Messi—the most complete and visionary football player I have ever seen. Both Lafleur and Messi have shown extraordinary playmaking ability. Lafleur wasn't just a scorer; he was a brilliant passer, too. For six seasons straight, he scored fifty-plus goals and one-hundred-plus points. That's extraordinary.

Also like Messi, Guy was humble. You saw that in his interviews. He was a global icon, not just in Montreal or in hockey, but he seemed affable and at ease speaking with anyone he met, whether they were famous or not.

He had a magnetic charisma. People loved him. But I suppose fame wasn't always easy for him. He couldn't walk down the street unnoticed. And yet, he never acted like a big-city celebrity. He stayed grounded—Thurso, Quebec, never left him.

What was your relationship with Guy?

My primary relationship to Guy Lafleur was as a lifelong fan—the same one so many fans have had. I only met him once—December 4, 2009, at the Canadiens' centennial celebration at the Bell Centre. It's a moment I'll never forget.

A few months earlier, the Canadiens, knowing I was an ardent fan of the team, reached out to invite me to the ceremony. Of course I said yes, not knowing exactly what I'd be doing. Later, they asked if I'd like to introduce a player—and if so, who? Without hesitation, I said, "Lafleur, of course," thinking that was everyone's answer and that this honour was already taken by someone else. To my surprise, they said, "Great, you'll introduce Guy Lafleur."

That night, wearing a replica of Guy's home red sweater, I stood on the ice and introduced him to a roaring crowd. I was more nervous than I've ever been on a film set. Guy walked out, dressed to play, looked me in the eye calmly, smiled as if to say "Relax!," and gave me a nice hug. Le Démon Blond, generous of spirit and elegant by nature.

We chatted after the ceremony. He was so easy to talk to. That was one of his gifts—making others feel at ease.

I left that night with a huge smile—and a signed Lafleur jersey! I also have some rare Lafleur player cards, but I didn't dare ask for more autographs. Just being there was enough.

Are there parallels between professional hockey and filmmaking?

Absolutely. In both worlds, it's better to show what you can do than to talk about it. That was Guy's approach, and it certainly resonated with me.

Also, none of us—actors or athletes—exist without the fans. Guy understood that deeply and always showed respect for the people who admired him. He was also an artist. Not a term I use lightly for athletes, but Guy had grace, flair, and instinct. His movements were like brushstrokes—inventive, bold, expressive.

To me, he was the Marlon Brando of hockey. He had presence and made instinctive choices—sometimes even seeming to surprise himself—which were almost always prescient and effective.

Were you surprised by his retirement—and comeback?

I remember how sad he was when he left the Canadiens and hockey in 1984. There were tensions with his former teammate who had become Montreal's coach and imposed a rigid system that didn't fit Guy's style. Guy, being such a big deal in Montreal, couldn't be traded by the team, as he had requested, because the fans and the media would have rioted, so Guy walked away from the game. Honourable and discreet as always.

When he came back with the Rangers after a few years, and later played for the Nordiques, he didn't have the same speed, but still had the same instincts and playmaking vision. Watching him read the game and make plays again was wonderful.

Do you have a personal story you'd like to share?

More of a minor tribute, really. In 2020, I directed *Falling*, which we shot in the Toronto area, though it was a story set in northern New York in the mid-'70s.

That part of the state, where I went to junior high school and high school, had lots of Rangers fans, and some people liked the Sabres and Bruins—but there were also plenty of Canadiens fans like me. Because a scene in *Falling* took place in a diner in 1974, I said, "We need a couple of Lafleur photos on the wall, please." The production designer agreed, but said we'd need permission—from the team, the league, and certainly from Guy.

I reached out and ended up speaking with his son and then Guy's agent, who were both incredibly kind. I explained what we wanted, and they immediately said yes. That's when I learned Guy was having health issues. . . .

How did you react to his passing?

I was in British Columbia scouting locations for my second film, *The Dead Don't Hurt*, when I heard the news. It made me very sad. He left us far too soon. I was subsequently invited to appear on Radio-Canada to honour him, which I did via iPhone. It was quite early on the West Coast, but I was up and ready. Across Canada, I'm sure many people of all ages wore number 10 that morning, like me, out of respect.

Once again, I was reminded of the great honour I'd had in 2009—introducing Guy Lafleur to a packed Bell Centre to fellow fans.

What legacy did he leave?

Guy's legacy, apart from his remarkable playmaking skill and goal-scoring prowess, may well be how deeply fans connected with him. Wherever he went, people approached him for autographs, photos, or just to say hi. And he looked them in the eye and gave them his best—always.

Acknowledgements

When we first embarked on the wild adventure of editing *Lafleur: The Legend*, Steven Finn and I asked ourselves, “What kinds of things would be worthwhile to reveal about him?” The answer to that question seemed obvious to us because, no matter all the coverage of “le Démon Blond” over the decades, there were still aspects of him and his life that weren’t well-known, and that could be shared.

The emotions that arose out of the death of Guy Lafleur on April 22, 2022, helped us to understand two fundamental realities that would guide us in producing the book you hold in your hands. First, the people who most often spoke about Guy Lafleur over the years hadn’t yet said everything: They had other revelations, context, and terrific anecdotes to share. And second, many key people who knew the Thurso prodigy had barely ever spoken publicly about him.

That’s why this gathering of forty-one people—some more well-known than others, but all important in Guy’s life—is unique. The book is full of friendship and love, commitment and passion, candour and emotion.

Steven and I dove into the special challenge of getting each person to talk about “their” Guy Lafleur. During our interviews, we had the privilege of witnessing a huge number of touching moments, as a great many men choked on their words, had tears in their eyes, or let those tears flow. The silences were heavy. They missed "their Guy" terribly, gone much too soon, after battling cancer to the very limit—as if it were the seventh game in the Stanley Cup playoffs.

Each one of them displayed great generosity in speaking so openly, and at a time when their grief was still fresh. We offer them our sincere thanks.

This book exists because many people contributed, in many ways, to achieve the same precise goal: to make the fans happy—which was Guy Lafleur's raison d'être.

From the outset, having the trust of Martin Lafleur and Réjean Houle was key: Without them, we would not have been able to assemble such a high-quality group of interviewees.

I must also recognize once more the trust of the entire team at Les Éditions de l'Homme, especially Judith Landry, Florence Bisch, Liette Mercier, and Catherine Bédard. Thanks also to their colleagues in publishing, distribution, and communications.

I would also like to thank my son, Étienne Goyer-Gince, as well as my friends Claude Lussier and Bruno Fortier for their ongoing support.

In closing, I want to acknowledge and thank my coauthor. Steven and I have known each other for a long time, from a former professional affiliation. I knew that in everything he did, he gave it his all. But would he have the time to go full-bore on such a project when the research and editing needed for a book were quite far out of his comfort zone?

He didn't have the time, but somehow, he found it. For him, it was essential that Guy Lafleur—an idol who became a teammate—should be honoured by the people he loved. Just as he did in the NHL, Finner worked energetically and with respect, and I sincerely hope that you have enjoyed our book.

—*Pierre Gince*

Photo Credits

Every effort has been made to locate and properly credit the source or rights holder of each photo.

Title page spread: Courtesy of Maurice Filion.

The following page numbers correspond to pages in the photo insert.

Page 1: (*all photos*) Courtesy of Suzanne Lafleur.

Page 2: (*top*) Photo Moderne, courtesy of Jocelyn Paquet; (*middle*) courtesy of Maurice Filion; (*bottom*) Pierre-Yvon Pelletier.

Page 3: (*from top to bottom*) Denis Brodeur/NHLI/Getty Images; Adrien Hubert/Bibliothèque et Archives nationales du Québec/06M_E6S7SS1P780678_004; courtesy of Suzanne Lafleur; Photo Charles Michaud/TopoLocal.

Page 4: (*top*) Doug Ball, The Canadian Press; (*centre*) Archives/MédiaQMI Inc.; (*bottom*) The Canadian Press.

Page 5: (*top*) Courtesy of Pierrette Lafleur; (*bottom left*) The Canadian Press; (*bottom right*) courtesy of the Lafleur family.

Page 6: (*top*) The Canadian Press; (*middle*) Lucien DeBlois; (*bottom*) courtesy of the Lafleur family.

Page 7: (*top*) Clément Allard/The Canadian Press; (*middle*) Rob MacDuff; (*bottom*) courtesy of the Lafleur family.

Page 8: (*top left*) Courtesy of Claude Meunier; (*top right*) Réjean Tremblay; (*middle*) courtesy of Réjean Houle; (*bottom*) Reuters/Alamy Stock Photo.